The Remaking of an American

The
Remaking
of an American

Elizabeth Banks

With an introduction by
Jane S. Gabin

University Press of Florida

Gainesville · Tallahassee · Tampa · Boca Raton
Pensacola · Orlando · Miami · Jacksonville

Copyright 1928 by Doubleday, Doran, & Company, Inc.
Introduction to paperback edition copyright 2000 by the Board of Regents of the State of Florida
Printed in the United States of America on acid-free paper

05 04 03 02 01 00   6 5 4 3 2 1

Library of Congress Cataloging-in-Publication Data
Banks, Elizabeth L., 1870-1938.
The remaking of an American / Elizabeth Banks; edited and with an introduction
by Jane S. Gabin.
p.   cm.
Originally published: Garden City, N.Y.: Doubleday, Doran & Co., 1928.
ISBN 0-8130-1776 (alk. paper)
1. Banks, Elizabeth L., 1870-1938. 2. Journalists—United States—Biography.
I. Gabin, Jane S., 1950- . II. Title.
PN4874.B3 A4   2000
070'.92—dc21 [B]   00-023532

The University Press of Florida is the scholarly publishing agency for the State University System
of Florida, comprising Florida A&M University, Florida Atlantic University, Florida International
University, Florida State University, University of Central Florida, University of Florida,
University of North Florida, University of South Florida, and University of West Florida.

University Press of Florida
15 Northwest 15th Street
Gainesville, FL 32611–2079
http://www.upf.com

To S——

Who has Waited Long and Patiently,
ever Prophesying my Final "Coming
of Age," I dedicate this story of
The Homing Time

CONTENTS

PART THREE

The American (1926–1927)

ACKNOWLEDGMENTS

Many individuals have assisted me over the years as I gleaned information from various collections and archives. They helped make my quest a treasure hunt. Thanks to: Gail Cameron of the Library of the Museum of London; Terry Charman of the Library of the Imperial War Museum, London; Jennie Davidson of the Society of Women Writers and Journalists, for sending information on the history of that organization; David Doughan of the Fawcett Library, National Library of Women, London Guildhall University; Timothy L. Ericson, director of Archives and Special Collections, Golda Meir Library, University of Wisconsin-Milwaukee; Mark LeFanu, general secretary of the Society of Authors; Rosemary Nunn of the Golders Green Crematorium in London, for kindly providing the details of the inscription of the memorial plaque to Mabel Spink and Elizabeth Banks; Peter Kenneth Sharpen of Australia, a descendant of W. T. Stead, for providing research leads; Dr. David C. Sutton of the University of Reading, U.K., director of the WATCH (Writers and Their Copyright Holders) Project; and the staffs of the Library of Congress, Washington, D.C.; Library of London; British Library Newspaper Library, Colindale, London; and Walter Royal Davis Library of the University of North Carolina at Chapel Hill.

Very special thanks go to the Independent Scholars' Association of the North Carolina Triangle, for a research grant that enabled me to travel to England to begin my work on literary expatriates; to Jane Ehrlich of London, for warm friendship and hospitality, and for introducing me to some of the special delights of her adopted city; and to my family for adapting to the obsessiveness that often accompanies an extended research project.

To Elizabeth L. Banks, my respect and my apologies: you wanted the story of your life hidden, and I am not letting you have your way.

Jane S. Gabin

CHRONOLOGY

Year	Her Life	Her World
1870 [1865?]	Elizabeth Banks born in New Jersey	
1883	Enters Wisconsin Female College, Fox Lake	
1886	Graduates from Milwaukee-Downer College	
1889	Works as society reporter in St. Paul, Minn.	
1890	Works at American ministry in Peru	
1891	Returns to U.S., works as society reporter in Baltimore	
1893	Arrives in London; "In Cap and Apron" published in *Weekly Sun;* joins Pioneer and Writers' Clubs	
1894	"The Almighty Dollar in London Society" published in *St. James's Gazette; Campaigns of Curiosity* published; Banks interviewed for *Young Woman* magazine	
1895	Works steadily as freelance writer in London	
1897	Returns to New York City, dabbles in "yellow journalism" while continuing to freelance for British and U.S. periodicals	
1898	Working in New York	Spanish-American War; trial of Oscar Wilde
1899		Boer War begins
1900	Returns to London	

Year	Her Life	Her World
1901	Listed in British *Who's Who;* living at 7 Harley Gardens, The Boltons, London	Death of Queen Victoria; accession of Edward VII
1902	Publishes *Autobiography of a "Newspaper Girl"*	Boer War ends
1903		Militant organization Women's Social and Political Union breaks away from the NUWSS
1904	Continues to write for several periodicals, including the *New York Times*	
1905	Though living in London, lists address as Box 238, Madison Square Post Office, New York City	
1908	Joins WWSL	Women Writers' Suffrage League organized
1909	Privately publishes *Mystery of Frances Farrington*	
1910	Serves as WWSL delegate to Anglo-American Arbitration meeting	Death of Edward VII; accession of George V
1911	Joins staff of *Referee,* creating character of "Enid"; also creates second pseudonym, Mary Mortimer Maxwell; moves to 5 Robert Street, The Adelphi, London	Increased militant suffrage actions, hunger strikes, imprisonment of suffragists
1912	Sails for New York in September, returns to London in December	Sinking of *Titanic;* Cat and Mouse Act; Woodrow Wilson becomes president of U.S.
1914	Organizes the Authors' Belgian Fund, writes *Dik* and other works to raise money for refugee assistance	Beginning of WWI; Belgian refugees arrive in London; martyrdom of Emily Wilding Davis for cause of suffrage
1915	Visits New York and Washington (November–December) to raise money for "Dik's Fund" and to protest lack of U.S. involvement in war	Sinking of *Lusitania;* epidemics in the trenches

Year	Her Life	Her World
1916	Resigns from *Referee*	Easter Rebellion in Ireland
1917		U.S. enters war; Russian Revolution
1918		End of WWI; suffrage granted to British women over age of 30
1920		Ratification of the 19th Amendment, granting U.S. women the right to vote
1922	Begins study of British educational system	
1924	Visits U.S. and Canada; publishes *School for John and Mary*	
1926	*School for John and Mary* has second printing	
1928	*Remaking of an American* published in U.S.	Suffrage granted to British women over age of 21; Amelia Earhart flies over the Atlantic; Stalin's first five-year plan; Hoover becomes U.S. president
1929	Now living at 104 Sumatra Road, West Hampstead; death of friend Mabel Spink	Stock market crash and beginning of Depression
1933	Living at 117 Broadhurst Gardens, London NW6; composes will	Hitler becomes chancellor of Germany; Nazis burn Reichstag and build first concentration camps; purges in USSR; FDR's New Deal
1938	Residence now at 10 Braden Street, London W9; dies on July 18 in Surrey County Hospital	Abdication of Edward VIII, coronation of George VI; Spanish Civil War

INTRODUCTION

Elizabeth Banks: An American on Fleet Street

Jane S. Gabin

The story of Elizabeth Banks (1870–1938) is the American "luck and pluck" saga with a transatlantic twist. Though her life is at present almost unknown to contemporary readers and scholars, it should be a life rediscovered. *The Remaking of an American* introduces a new generation of readers to a lively and thoughtful observer of a vibrant age. Banks is a compelling and direct writer and a good storyteller, offering an insider's view to many of the great events and issues of her day.

Personally, she is a bit of an enigma. As a young woman, writing about herself and her adventures as a journalist, she was outspoken, courageous, brash, and independent—and at times a bit self-important. As an older woman, though, she chose silence. She apparently published nothing during the last decade of her life, and requested that after her death all her personal items be sold or destroyed. In her will, she mentioned letters, papers, and photographs in particular—all to be destroyed.

What would a historian learn about you from one hour at your desk? There are clues to your life in the framed photographs, letters, invitations, concert programs, bills, and phone numbers on scraps of paper. Certainly there is evidence of your domestic habits, your cultural tastes, whether you are social or solitary, where or even if you like to shop, what projects demand your attention, what your handwriting is like. But from Elizabeth Banks we have nothing other than what was published—that, and her will. So I have had to reconstruct her life and cobble it together from the information she provides plus documentary print evidence.

We can begin by using her autobiographical works as guides, corroborated by other sources. Her name is recorded in newspaper articles, her college's alumnae records, directories and lists of writers, and rosters of English suffrage groups. We can also look at changes in self-reported information—for instance, in thirty-seven successive entries, each a mini-vita, in the annual

British *Who's Who*—to track the development of her career and personal interests. But the lack of a body of personal papers adds an element of mystery and sadness to her story.

The Remaking of an American, covering events in the years from 1912 to 1927, is a sensitive account of an expatriate journalist's experiences during a period of great conflict and social upheaval. Full of fascinating and often moving anecdotes, it covers major political events—World War I, the granting of female suffrage in both Britain and the United States, the effect upon the United States of the great wave of immigration. The segments on American expatriatism, the English educational system, Canada and the American Midwest, the British class system, and the fate of the British empire combine fact and opinionated analysis. And there is also the obligatory literary name-dropping that is so often a part of any writer's autobiography. However, it *is* a fact, for instance, that the renowned writers Banks mentions as neighbors—George Bernard Shaw, John Galsworthy, J. M. Barrie, and Thomas Hardy—were indeed all living close by in the Adelphi buildings near Charing Cross.

Elizabeth Banks was an American journalist who lived in London from 1893 until her death in 1938. Frustrated by the lack of opportunities for women at the Midwestern and Eastern newspapers where she first worked, she decided to try the challenges offered in England. She arrived there with no connections and very little money, yet through determination, brashness, and a compelling writing style soon had a recognized byline. Within a few years she had a large audience devoted to her regular columns in several well-known newspapers and magazines, including the *Referee, Strand, London Illustrated, Fortnightly, Pall Mall Gazette, Punch,* the *Daily News,* and *St. James's Gazette.* She may not have gotten the press of her flamboyant American contemporary, Nellie Bly, but she also had an outstanding career and made a significant impact upon her readers, particularly through her exposés of social iniquities.

Early Life and Career

Many of the small bits of personal data about Banks come from large directory publications in which much of the information is self-reported. Banks provided much the same information to the British *Who's Who* as to the *International Who's Who: Who's Who in the World,* published in New York. But in the former she never listed her parents' names or places of birth, and in the latter she stated that she was born in Taunton, New Jersey, in 1870 to John and Sarah Bristen Banks. In several of her writings, she mentions that her father was born in England, and her awareness of this contributed to her devotion to it as her adopted country. In a letter to W. E. Dowding of the National

Relief Fund dated March 3, 1915—while the United States was still resisting involvement in the World War—Banks stated her credentials: "I am an American citizen, but my father was born in England, and I have made my home here for many years. Needless to say, I am not 'Neutral!'"[1]

Orphaned at an early age, Banks was raised by an uncle and aunt on a Wisconsin farm. She discusses some of this background in her earlier autobiographical works. She worked her way through Milwaukee-Downer College, which, according to the school records on file at the University of Wisconsin-Milwaukee, was then called Wisconsin Female College. In the class rosters "Lizzie" Banks lists her hometown not as a rural Wisconsin community but as New York City. Perhaps even then she was yearning for the excitement of city life, and indeed, following her graduation, she moved to increasingly large urban centers. In college her studies were especially serious because she knew, from the family's finances, that her own support depended upon her education. Years later she mined these experiences in an article for *Nineteenth Century* titled "Self-Help among American College Girls." She remained concerned throughout her career with the link between social mobility and educational opportunity. And she always maintained a working-class perspective.

After completing college in 1886, Banks learned typing and stenography so that she might find a post as a reporter. In *Campaigns of Curiosity,* she describes her efforts to find work. She wrote to dozens of newspapers asking for a position, but not one editor replied. Her first break eventually came from a wholesale grocer, who offered her a clerical job. It was not ideal, but it got her to the city (she never, in her first autobiography, specifies which one), onto a payroll, and finally independent. It was a first step up and out into the wider world.

In *Ladies of the Press: The Story of Women in Journalism by an Insider,* Ishbel Ross describes the reluctance of nineteenth-century American newspapers to take women readers seriously and their greater reluctance to allow women writers into the newsroom. The first woman offered a writer's position on a major American paper was Margaret Fuller, who was asked in the 1840s to write for the *New York Tribune* by its editor, Horace Greeley. But both Greeley and Fuller were exceptions to any rules, and it was years before women writers and reporters were again offered the chance to write about the news—not "women's news" or news "from the woman's point of view," but unadorned current events. Between the 1850s and the 1890s, growing numbers of women writers worked on newspapers and magazines, usually covering the society, charity, fashion, and domestic beats. Often women "correspondents" were happy to have their observations and impressions appear in the columns of local papers, sometimes without pay.

Then in the 1890s the "stunt" era began, and women, following the example of the flamboyant Nellie Bly, began to outdo themselves in strategies for getting stories. In that age of yellow journalism, where increased circulation was what interested editors most, women had more free rein in going after their stories. They posed as factory workers, beggars, evangelists, servants, and women of the streets. Into their ranks stepped Elizabeth Banks from Wisconsin, who would first try the standard "girl reporter" assignments in the States, then go to London and create a sensation by recording her observations while disguised as a street sweeper, Covent Garden flower seller, servant, laundry worker, and American heiress.

We must rely upon Banks's own writings for information on her early years. Her first book, *Campaigns of Curiosity: Journalistic Adventures of an American Girl in London,* was published in 1894 by the firm of F. Tennyson Neely, Chicago and New York, publishers of "Neely's Library of Choice Literature." By 1902, when her *Autobiography of a "Newspaper Girl"* was published (by the better-known companies of Methuen in London, and Dodd, Mead in New York), she was well established in literary circles. The *Autobiography* gives us most of the information we have about her early life, her decision to go to England, and her rise to success in turn-of-the-century journalism.

The 1912 *International Who's Who* states that Banks began her career "As a stenographer in St. Paul, becoming in 1889 society reporter on Globe and Evening News."[2] Banks remained in the Midwest for a few more months, writing up fashion and society balls, and turning down a marriage proposal from a policeman who insisted upon walking her home when she returned from covering late-night events. According to her memoirs, Banks had a short stint as secretary to an American diplomat in Peru, and then worked for an unnamed inventor-astronomer in New York. But she maintained her search for a newspaper post.

Within a year Banks found a situation as society editor on a prominent southern newspaper. In *Campaigns of Curiosity* she does not name the paper or its city, but again the *International Who's Who* provides the specifics: "was society editor, 1891–93, Morning Herald, Baltimore." The managing editor, according to Banks, was an older man who had been a colonel in the Confederate army, and who had traditional and narrow views regarding women in journalism. But as a businessman he realized that someone would have to cover ladies' news, and he had to compete with the other paper in town, which already had a woman on its staff. The male reporters treated Elizabeth "chivalrously," fixing up a corner for her to work in and placing a curtain around it so that in the heat of summer she would not have to see them at work in their shirtsleeves. Dutifully, Banks covered women's meetings, society events, and church activities for the woman's page.

But again the time came when she felt a change was due. One day she went to see the colonel and simply announced, "I am going to London." After his initial surprise, he made a simple prediction: "You will starve in London" (*Autobiography of a "Newspaper Girl,"* 66).

That decided it. To be told she would fail was the extra incentive Banks needed. Her choice of London does not seem to have arisen out of any great dream or obsession to go there. She was aware of her family's English heritage, and in college had enjoyed the study of English literature; and surely she was aware of London as a hub of journalistic activity. A dramatically expanding literary market was starting to make it possible for women to earn their livings by writing. Scores of new publications were being established, particularly in London and New York, providing new material for a rapidly increasing reading public. By the end of the century, the "woman reporter" was no longer an anomaly, particularly in London, where assignments went far beyond the society page. So Elizabeth Banks decided to try to make her mark there, not in New York or Washington, and this decision was hastened by her editor's challenging pronouncement.

The London Banks Entered

It is 1890. If we were to ascend above Westminster in a hot-air balloon, the same kind used by artists in the late Victorian era to sketch panoramic cityscapes for London guidebooks, what would we see? Below us the neogothic towers of the Houses of Parliament rise in splendor, only in their third decade but already landmarks, and already acquiring their black patina of coaldust grime. Just beyond, the Victoria Embankment, part of the vast civic improvements of the late 1860s, stretches toward Somerset House and the City financial district. In the evening this wide promenade will be lit with new electric lights. To the left the government buildings in Whitehall dominate the eastern end of St. James Park, but the Admiralty Arch has not yet been built. To the right, the Thames curves toward Pimlico and Chelsea, passing a vast penitentiary where the Tate Gallery will soon be built. Across the river and over in the East End, scores of factory chimneys cough up columns of black smoke—to the Victorians, a sign of productivity and prosperity. The air is yellowish gray, the Thames runs brown, and in the streets, sweepers rush to push away the muck from before the feet of the gentry. Though many aspects of London are far from glamorous, to those who can afford its many pleasures and cultural attractions, it is a land of delight.

For the privileged, this London revolves around balls and galas, races, the opera and ballet, private clubs, and the comings and goings of royalty and the international set. Many elegant restaurants and fine hotels serve their pleasure—and several from that time are still in existence, such as the Charing Cross, Claridge's, and Brown's.

What place would an American find in this world? If we descend to street level and make our way across Trafalgar Square to the world of the Strand, Fleet Street, and Covent Garden—the center of publishing, journalism, and the theater—we will encounter an intellectual life where Americans have found a vigorous role. Among the four hundred newspapers published in and around London in the 1880s and 1890s are the *Anglo-American Times* and the *American Register*. In addition, the *New York Herald* and the *New York Tribune* have London offices. Here in the West End—"the quarter of London," says the 1885 Baedecker guide, "which spends money, makes laws, and regulates the fashions"—Americans have taken their place.

In the 1880s and 1890s, a substantial number of Americans lived and worked in London, many involved in diplomacy, banking, and commerce. Americans appeared often in key roles, at important events, with significant people, and, increasingly, in the world of the arts. Many actively sought to ally themselves with traditional British society through marriage; an example is the Jerome family of New York, whose daughter Jennie married Lord Randolph Churchill in one of the most famous of the Anglo-American matches. Other renowned marriages were between Consuelo Vanderbilt and the Duke of Marlborough, and Mary Leiter and Lord Curzon, who became Viceroy of India in 1899.

A number of Americans in London were prominently involved in literary activities. Henry James was one of the leading figures in London literary life during this period; his sister Alice had arrived from Boston even earlier and would keep her famous diary until her death in 1892. The American actress Elizabeth Robins was shaking the English theater world with her introduction of the plays of Ibsen. In 1894 an American publisher, Henry Harland, collaborated with a young Englishman named Aubrey Beardsley to produce the famous and controversial *Yellow Book*. In 1897 Stephen Crane arrived for a brief stay in London, then moved to Brede in the south of England, gathering about him a coterie of writers and artists. In 1899 the prominent English actress Mrs. Patrick Campbell came upon a twenty-one-year-old American woman dancing at night in a London square; and so Isadora Duncan was "discovered." Depending upon the source, one has the impression that this was a time of both serene elegance and exciting stimulation.

> There was an air of great repose in the London of the nineties. Men went late to business—and all wore silk hats. Nobody seemed to hurry. During the afternoon, and even morning, there were sauntering throngs in Piccadilly: men of leisure, who knew nought of business, save, per-

haps, to sit on some board of directors, and whose main interests were hunting, shooting, racing, sport of all kinds, the innumerable diversions of the world of fashion. . . . Even in the Strand there was little evidence of fret or rush. England was at peace with a peaceful world, and looked forward to centuries of dominance and prosperity. . . . No man or woman was admitted to a restaurant or to the stalls of a theatre unless in full evening dress. There were three or four balls every night, and during the afternoon all the world of fashion drove in Hyde Park, the women in their flowered hats and summer gowns, looking like immense sweetly scented bouquets. . . . It looked like the most carefree city in the world.[3]

Like much else written by those who lived in England during the Victorian era, this passage from the memoirs (published nearly forty years after the period described) of Gertrude Atherton, a Californian who first came to London in the 1870s, reflects only one aspect of the city. And that was the side of London in which she and most of the other Anglo-American women moved: the world of "fashion," of exclusive clubs, elegant teas, literary salons, and the right people. London could seem carefree to those who entered it with the correct credentials, important friends, money, and even talent. It is a fact that the overwhelming majority of Americans in the London of the nineties were financially secure and socially welcome; and of this group, a number turned to literary pursuits. A major change would occur over the next few years, however, and by the turn of the new century, the positions of the socialite-authors would be challenged by American women who did not come from the ranks of privilege.

By the 1890s other American women were being drawn to England—journalists, suffragists, and those pursuing the arts. In London particularly, women, both American and British, found an environment that was becoming increasingly receptive to their intellectual interests. London was also acceding more and more to women's demands for a fuller participation in city life. One example of this trend is the proliferation of clubs. While social clubs for men—bastions of gender and class solidarity, political power, and intellectual clout—had been fixtures in London for generations, those for women in London came into existence late, beginning in the 1870s. The Women's Club and Institute opened in 1869, and after that a succession of clubs was established. Many new clubs reflected, in their membership, the increasing diversity in the types of work in which members were engaged. In 1878 the Somerville Club required two qualifications: "personal respectability, and interest in social and political questions." The Green Park Club (1894) stressed an interest in theatrical and musical entertainment, and the Sesame (1895) was concerned with "the New Education and the rationale of learning." The Writers' Club was founded in 1892, requiring of its members that they "should be engaged in literary or journalistic work"; there were three hundred members in the 1890s.[4] In 1894 the Society of Women Journalists was founded, and it still flourishes, as does the American Women's Club, founded in 1899. The growing number of these affinity and professional groups tells us that by the 1890s large numbers of women were entering the work world and taking an active part in the educational, cultural, and political life of London.

The perspectives of women in London varied widely. Their reactions to the great issues of the day, for instance suffrage, ran the entire range from militant support to open hostility. And there could be a difference of opinion on the quality of daily life in general. Gertrude Atherton's image of a refined and serene London contrasts sharply with the experiences of others; her contemporary, Elizabeth Robins, reported being subjected daily to crude and vulgar harassment on the streets of London. While many authors confined themselves to their clubs and salons, others wrote of the realities of Victorian London—life was not gilded and carefree, but a constant struggle against sexism, professional exploitation, and nastiness.

Beyond the glittering exterior of the charming world of Victorian high society, as reported by those who had the benefit of enjoying its rewards, was the other London with which any student of the era is familiar. Past the gilded boundaries of Mayfair and Bayswater and Kensington and the sturdy middle-class neighborhoods lay a world of slums, sweatshops, poverty-induced disease, child labor, prostitution, and street crime—the 1888 "Jack the Ripper" murders were recent enough in memory to cause any woman walking alone to shudder. The class system, so much stricter than today's, divided people and limited opportunities, though a growing middle class had made substantial material and social gains. Half the population was still disenfranchised, and the suffrage movement was gaining momentum even as resistance to it became harsher.

The turn of the century was a crucial time for women in Britain. Once all the romance and fancy dress balls are put aside, it was a difficult time for them. Motherhood was extolled; birth control was virtually nonexistent. Wealth helped, for it allowed women to escape the prospect of the workhouse, the struggling farm, the "dark satanic mills" of the factory system that entrapped their poorer sisters. But rich or poor, what they had in common was their lack of political power. Women were glorified, idealized, set upon a pedestal; but if they demanded a vote, they were publicly ridiculed, chastised, even beaten. In "the most carefree city in the world," a petition for the Woman Suffrage Bill, signed by over a quarter of a million people, had been recently and quickly defeated in Parliament. But the suffrage movement, though thwarted, was growing in momentum and strength. Women were banding together for more than social events.

As London led England to the turn of a new century, it represented a world encompassing both a vibrant artistic and intellectual life and a simmering vat of social injustice. While many observers, British and American, of the age felt, with typical Victorian optimism, that the close of the nineteenth century promised a continuing progression of all good things, others were more pessimistic. This paradoxical nature of the Victorian Age and its transition into the modern age is reflected in many of the topics covered in *The Remaking of an American*—the treatment of women, the relationship of the classes, the place of the American in English life, and the reception accorded the woman writer. The 1890s were not easy times in London, though thousands of lives of ease were enjoyed there. American women were adding their own zest to London life with fresh infusions of ideas. The heiresses still provided money, but the new wave of journalists, writers, actresses, and other artists provided intellectual energy and fresh viewpoints.

Banks Arrives in London

This was the England that Elizabeth Banks found upon her arrival in 1893. Since the expense of the journey and maintaining oneself in a foreign country precluded travel by all but the most independent of spirit and pocketbook, simply arriving, with little money, no social connections, and no prospects of employment must have taken incredible gumption. But that was exactly what Elizabeth Banks possessed.

Banks arrived in London with four hundred dollars (a considerable, but not substantial, sum in the 1890s), her typewriter, and Judge, her beloved French poodle, for whom she had broken many regulations and bribed many staff members on shipboard. This behavior was typical, a continuation of the brashness she had displayed earlier. She does not seem to have been abrasive or unpleasantly aggressive, but she was assertive, persistent, and impossible to intimidate. She also had a strong sense of what she felt was right, which she displayed in a variety of ways, from offering practical Yankee advice on the way to do household chores to flag-waving in the cause of prodding the United States to step into the Great War.

Banks found a small flat, and did her best "to make it look as American as possible, using the Stars and Stripes for a couch cover, and hanging a picture of George Washington over my writing desk."[5] At this point, Banks was very consciously and blatantly an American, and made no attempt to become assimilated into English culture. Ironically, years later she would have difficulty convincing the English police of her American citizenship.

But in those early days, she was deeply Americentric. She seems to have done little research on British customs before her arrival. For instance, she was unaware of the meaning of Boxing Day and was embarrassed when several service people turned up at her flat on this day after Christmas asking for their traditional boxed gifts. Her lack of information extended into the world of journalism; actually, her first appearance in the British press came about as a result of this ignorance.

After reading each of the many London papers, Banks wrote a piece and sent it to the largest publication—literally, she chose the heaviest issue. She assumed this would be the most successful and prominent paper. The article appeared two days later, followed by a check. She later understood why she had had this amazingly rapid success: "I did not know then, as I know now [1902], that, in this editorial stronghold, the audacity of an American girl in daring to attack it had so amused the editors that they decided to let me in."[6] Her actions indicate a pattern that would work well for American writers in later years as well—that they could get away with behavior that might be condemned in British writers. Though within a few years Banks would be thought of as completely English by the English, she admitted that in the first year of her residence in London, "I had gained but little knowledge of English home-life, English customs, and English manners." She had also made no English friends, nor had she visited any of the many women's social clubs in London. The American Woman's Club was not founded until 1899, but even then Banks did not join. However, soon after her first articles were published, she did join professionally oriented organizations. In 1894 she wrote, "I have been impressed by the kindly feeling that the women journalists of London have shown towards me and the interest they have exhibited in my work. Especially is this true of the members of the Pioneer and Writers' Clubs."[7] Later she also joined the literary Lyceum Club and then the English-Speaking Union.

After her first London article was published, Banks was able to place several more, and she made a little money—but not enough to keep up with expenses. She mortgaged the furniture she had bought and began to eat irregularly. Finally, one morning she found that all the money she had was two and a half pence. But rather than feel depressed, she was defiant. She remembered the "half-pitying, half-threatening prophecy made by the Colonel," and fiercely determined not to starve in London. Moreover, she decided to make a symbolic gesture to announce this defiance.

With her purse and Judge, she set out along the Thames riverbank to Westminster Bridge, where she cast her remaining coins into the water. Then she and the small dog crossed into Camberwell, a working-class section of the city. Here, small children watched them with interest; to the children, Banks thought, she probably appeared "as a rich West End lady."

One little girl, entranced with Judge, persuaded Banks to take him to see her sister, who took in sewing, back at their lodgings. Several flights up, Banks saw a very different kind of poverty, one which made her own rather genteel situation seem absurd. When Banks suggested to the older girl that domestic service would draw a greater income than what she could possibly make by sewing, the girl flared up: "She would rather sew and have her liberty, she said, than be a servant and have none, and, as for caps and aprons, did I expect a self-respecting girl to put them on?"

Banks's "Idea" was born. She would do what she herself had suggested. She would become a housemaid and see if, indeed, that would mean giving up one's liberty. And then she would put her experiences in the papers, and see if her career would afford her anything more than genteel poverty. "London's got to give us a living," she said to Judge, "a decent, comfortable, satisfying one. It's got to give us three square meals a day and afternoon tea besides. . . . We're going to work for Old London, honestly and honorably, and Old London has got to pay us our Wages."[8]

She secured from one newspaper editor a promise of twenty pounds for articles resulting from her experiences as a servant—of course, he told her she couldn't possibly do it—and then put her idea into action. She placed a "situation wanted" ad in the August 23, 1893, edition of the *London Daily Telegraph,* and received over one hundred responses. The editor had been partially correct; because of her lack of character references from former employers, her "suspicious American accent," and her short stature, Banks was turned down by almost all of the prospective employers.

Finally, she found several short-term jobs in homes whose mistresses ranged from kind to stingy and overbearing. She also saw that some people were being taken advantage of by their employees. She noted that as a result of her experiment in living as a housemaid, "my sympathy for London mistresses equaled, if it did not exceed, that which I felt for the servants." Banks had not set out to be a muckraker, but what she described, so matter-of-factly, caused quite a stir when the paper, the *Weekly Sun,* published installments of "In Cap and Apron."

By November Banks's series on servant life was familiar to readers all over England as well as in the United States. While some newspapers called Banks a reformer concerned about "the domestic servant question," others accused her of being frivolous. Banks began to be inundated with letters from all over Britain, from servants who felt she was their champion as well as employers who accused her of "putting false notions of equality" into servants' minds. After another installment, in which she described incidents in which dishonest servants had misled their employers, she received angry letters from domestic workers who felt she was stirring up trouble. The "In Cap and

Apron" series was widely noted in other prominent periodicals, including *Punch,* the *Daily News,* and the *Lady's Pictorial.* Whatever their reactions, they had one thing in common—no one was indifferent to what Banks had written, and no one ignored it. Had Banks, as one observer suggested, "come to London to set up the servants against the mistresses"? Or was she out to discredit servants?

Banks's motive in doing the series was purely practical. She wanted to write something that would sell, and she succeeded. And while she said she wrote impartially, taking no sides, the topic was one about which readers were not at all impartial; it was controversial. Now Banks's name was becoming well known in London; she was recognized by editors and writers as she walked along Fleet Street and the Strand; and she was starting to sell more articles. She was interviewed by George R. Sims of the *Referee;*[9] another interview, this one by Marion Leslie, was published in the November 1894 issue of *Young Woman.*

Banks followed her "Cap and Apron" series with other articles that equally engrossed the public interest. Posing as a working-class girl (this time watching for Americanisms in her speech), she obtained a number of positions. She worked in a "sanitary" laundry that was filthy and where she lived in terror of being injured or killed by the machinery. She sold flowers, like Eliza Doolittle, in the Covent Garden area. And as a street sweeper, she found there was a great deal of territorial competition for a chance to push mud and dust out of the way of privileged feet. But while these experiences raised her sympathies for the working poor of London, the thing that aroused her wrath was what she exposed as the power of the "Almighty Dollar" in British society.

"The Almighty Dollar in London Society" was, in fact, the title of her next series, appearing in the *St. James's Gazette.* The negative comments aroused by "In Cap and Apron" were mild compared with the reactions to these new articles. Having spotted a number of classified advertisements in the London papers which suggested that enough money could purchase social favors in Britain, and seen notices from businesses that specialized in "researching" genealogy and especially in accommodating Americans with no "family background" but plenty of money, Banks was inspired. "It's astonishing," she wrote, "that Americans can go to certain people who will manufacture certain pedigrees for them, and then, you know, American heiresses buy their way to Court and kiss the Queen's hand. American money can do anything in England." To expose a sham, Banks decided to engage in one herself. She posed as an American heiress to see how far into society her "fortune" could take her.

Banks placed the following advertisement in the personal columns of a "prominent" London paper:

A YOUNG AMERICAN LADY of means wishes to meet with a Chaperon of Highest Social Position, who will introduce her into the Best English Society. Liberal Terms. Address, "Heiress,————."[10]

Within two days she had eighty-seven responses from every fashionable London neighborhood—Park Lane, Grosvenor Square, South Kensington. Nearly all the letters were marked "personal" and "confidential," and they were signed with the correspondents' full names and titles. "The confidence they exhibited in the 'honour' of a total stranger was rather remarkable," wrote Banks. And although she set out to expose the status-for-hire routine, and did quote from the letters sent to her, she was gracious in never revealing the identities of anyone who wrote.

In general, the people who answered her ad did not seem to care what kind of family "background" Banks had—as long as she had money. One letter came from an aristocratic dowager who told Banks honestly that she was simply in need of funds, and had never before tried to profit from her social status; but for about a thousand pounds she could probably arrange for a court introduction and a husband. Ladies and countesses and other women of rank all offered their services—and their rates. These terms, wrote Banks "were touched upon in a gentle, lady-like way. Prices ranged from £500 to £10,000."

The *St. James's Gazette,* in which "The Almighty Dollar" was first published, was a very popular conservative evening newspaper.

As the morning Post went into the homes of the "best people" every morning, so the *St. James's Gazette* went into their homes in the evening, and those who had answered the advertisement in the Post read the series of articles in the Gazette, giving no names or addresses, but quoting their letters in part or in whole, with pointed remarks by the American girl. . . . And now all over England town houses and country houses trembled upon their very foundations. Everybody in society suspected everybody else of being in the "chaperonage" business. . . . Ladies out shopping in Bond Street suspected one another of being able to patronize that select and expensive district because of "easy money" obtained from American aspirants to social recognition.

Not only did the series get a great deal of attention in the press, it had political repercussions as well. Banks describes another outraged reader: "In one of the largest mansions of England, a little old lady had the *St. James's*

Gazette serial read aloud to her every evening as the separate parts appeared, and as she listened she grew very ashamed and angry. She was ashamed for her country and angry at the women who were offering for money to introduce this unknown and unvouched-for American 'heiress' not only into society but to their Queen."[11] This reader was Queen Victoria herself, and that was the end of the "chaperonage" business.

Women Journalists in England

Elizabeth Banks had come to England at an opportune time for women journalists. Other women had already broken down some of the barriers, and at the same time the newspaper industry was expanding and needed more writers to help them reach a wider market. Women in England and Ireland had written in and produced newspapers since the late seventeenth century; more women writers and "women's pages" began to appear in the nineteenth century. While British and American newspapers acknowledged the necessity of having women write about fashion and other "feminine" topics, their editorial boards did not suddenly become liberalized. But they did realize that to be successful they had to cater to the growing number of women readers. So most of this first group of women journalists were assigned to a new section of the paper called the "women's page," which featured articles on fashion, family, and society activities; this was the kind of work Elizabeth Banks had done in the States. Some exceptional individuals became well known, such as Eliza Lynn Linton, who, writing for the *Morning Chronicle,* was the first salaried woman to write for a London daily,[12] and a Mrs. Emily Crawford, who was sent by the *London Daily News* as a correspondent to Paris to cover the Commune riots in 1898. But on most papers that employed women, these writers were relegated to the woman's page and, not surprisingly, paid a lower wage than men.

Fleet Street was a man's domain, and not until the end of the nineteenth century did women begin to be employed as regular staff members on English and American newspapers. The situation began to improve dramatically in the 1890s, which from some accounts sounds like an incredibly exciting time to have been a woman journalist just setting out on her career. In an extended essay published in 1894 in the *Fortnightly Review* (July-December), Evelyn March-Phillipps lists twenty women's journals that had been established since 1861, citing in this statistic alone the fact that the modern woman was asserting her place, "and perhaps the multiplication and development of newspapers devoted to her special interests, is not the least significant token of her vitality." Unfortunately, she continues, much of what is included in women's pages or women's magazines is superficial and unimportant, such as society balls: "what can be more unmeaning and monotonous than a long array of pictures of distorted dolls, decked in trains and plumes?" What is needed, writes March-Phillipps, are articles on how a women may travel safely, how she may find employment, columns on legal and health matters, and intellectual topics; even articles on traditional "women's" subjects like fashion should be well written. The result would be periodicals "truly valuable to every woman of sense and understanding."

And the situation was indeed improving. Newspaper work provided exciting possibilities in a field becoming increasingly accessible to women. Enough women had entered the profession by 1894 to form the Society of Women Journalists.[13] Articles extolling the opportunities for women of a writing career appeared in numerous magazines. Examples include "Journalism for Women" by Mrs. D. M. Leslie in the *Monthly Packet* (October 1894), "Women As Journalists" by Miss Catherine Dew in the *Englishwomen's Review* (October 1894), and "Editorship as a Career for Women" by Margaret E. Sangster in the December 1895 *Forum*. Apparently, by 1898, sufficient legions of women writers had descended upon the London press that Arnold Bennett—not yet famous as a novelist, but a seasoned veteran of five years in journalism—felt the necessity to produce a special book for them. His *Journalism for Women: A Practical Guide* was published by John Lane (publisher also of the *Yellow Book* and Jennie Jerome Churchill's *Anglo-Saxon Review*), and it is full of "sensible," paternalistic, and fairly patronizing advice.

London was then, as now, the hub of a vast publishing industry and home to hundreds of regular publications. In England there were so many newspapers and magazines for all tastes and interests that no one could possibly read all of them. For the overloaded reader who needed to keep abreast of events, there was even a special journal, *The Review of Reviews*, which summarized and provided excerpts from all the major publications. (For many years its editor was the crusading journalist and reformer W. T. Stead, who would befriend Banks.) There were the daily newspapers—the *Globe*, the *Evening Standard*, the *Daily Mail*, and many others of varying quality. Popular weeklies provided another outlet. Among this group were the *Pall Mall Gazette* and *St. James's Gazette*, which serialized Elizabeth Banks's works. The *Illustrated London News*, *Black and White*, *Cassell's Saturday Journal*, *Success*, *Pearson's Weekly*, and *Tit-Bits* were other popular journals. The most famous comic weekly was the renowned *Punch*—but there was also *Judy*, edited by a woman. The daily, weekly, and monthly newspapers and magazines—including many targeted solely at women—provided a formidable mountain of print for the ever-growing reading public. And while several journals had women on their editorial boards, or even working as editors, these were not the most powerful publications. Still, progress was steady; a 1903 article by Rudolph de Cordova in *Cassell's* lists the accomplishments of ten successful London women editors of the day.[14] And in 1911, *The Woman's Book,* a practical handbook for the aspiring woman professional, declared: "London is essentially the Mecca of the Woman Journalist."[15]

A number of women had regular salaried positions, but the vast majority of women journalists were freelance correspondents, also called "special writers" or "outside contributors." They were constantly preparing articles on the topics of latest interest, and trying to convince editors to accept their work. Once she had steady work and established a name for herself, the woman writer was on a more secure plateau. *The Woman's Book* notes that this is "by far the most lucrative journalistic employment for the woman who is not actually a member of the staff of any newspaper or periodical. . . . she may receive a retaining fee from as many as half-a-dozen papers for a weekly, fortnightly, or even a monthly contribution, and she can command £2,2s to £3,3s per column for her work."[16] This was good money, and the arrangement seems to describe Banks's situation, as she wrote for many different magazines during the same period. But freelancing was also very stressful and competitive, an arena where few journalists could afford to slacken their pace.

Banks Finds Her Niche

By the turn of the century, Elizabeth Banks had made herself well known through her freelance articles, and she worked hard to keep her name in front of both the British and American publics by contributing to many different periodicals. Her autobiographical *Campaigns of Curiosity* was a reprise for American readers of "In Cap and Apron" and "The Almighty Dollar," coupled with her account of arriving in London and trying various ways of earning a living. In 1902 her *Autobiography of a "Newspaper Girl"* was published in New York by Dodd, Mead. Here she related her life leading up to her decision to go to London, her initial work for English periodicals, a brief stint in New York featuring a foray into "yellow journalism," and her return to London, where she resolves to give both American and British editors what they want so she can continue to live independently. Some of the most interesting anecdotes in this volume involve prominent individuals she interviewed during her first years in London. One was Eliza Lynn Linton, a prominent English writer and journalist whose preconceived ideas of what an American woman was like were soon dispelled by Banks. Another was Sir Thomas Lipton, who offered Banks a cup of his tea while she interviewed him before his boat entered the America's Cup yacht race. The first interview she did in London—but after she wrote the "In Cap and Apron" series—was with the writer Walter Besant, who befriended her and soon after published a poem in the magazine *Queen* called "The Lady Housemaid":

> The house and all about it, within it and without it,
>   Its manners and its residents, we know;
> Lines of houses, miles and miles — from the ground floor to the tiles:
>   How they live and carry on their show.
> But the mysteries begin, — deep and dark and black as sin,
>   When you ask about the Cap and Apron ranks;
> How they spend their busy days, what they think of Fashion's ways —
>   "Let me clear this mystery up!" said Miss Banks.

It was a humorous poem, and it gave Banks more publicity, for which she was grateful. "Was there ever a kindlier thing," she wrote in *Autobiography of a "Newspaper Girl,"* "done by a busy author for the sake of encouraging a struggling young woman just entering on her career?" (294).

The *Autobiography* was reviewed in, among other journals, *The Nation* (United States), which found Banks's memoirs a bit naive and containing "frank egotism." But the reviewer admired her straightforward writing. "The future historian of nineteenth-century journalism will obtain more light from the story of Miss Banks's career than from many more pretentious volumes, especially through the contrasts it presents between the pursuit of the profession in London and New York."[17]

Elizabeth Banks was successful because she wrote well, she was spurred on by idealism, and because she had assessed her market and wrote for it. She wrote what she knew and she learned how to give periodicals what they wanted. When she arrived in England in 1893, what were her areas of expertise? Being American, working her way through college, her first jobs, and coming to England. These subjects provided the grist for many articles. In 1895, for instance, she published an article in *Cassell's Family Magazine* titled "Some Differences between English and American Homes," and to *Nineteenth Century* she sold "Some American 'Comparisons' and 'Impressions.'" *Cassell's* liked her work; it published several other of her pieces including a two-part article on "Paying Occupations for Gentlewomen."

Around 1897 Banks returned briefly to the States, probably trying to further her career with freelance work in New York; she maintained her contacts with the magazines in London, giving her English readers glimpses into life in the States.[18] The Cassell firm in London also published a journal called *Quiver,* an "Illustrated Magazine for Sunday and General Reading." *Quiver* featured articles on religion, missionary work, moral tales, and favorite hymns. So Banks gave them articles on American religious traditions:

"American Country Parsons and Their Wives" and "The Story of Thanksgiving Day in the United States." She also contributed an article to *Nineteenth Century* on "The American Negro and His Place," basically a study of racism in the States.

The trend of "yellow" journalism, then at its height in New York, had little appeal for her, but she had to write for some of these papers in order to support herself.[19] Additionally, the work provided her with the opportunity to sell a disapproving article on "American 'Yellow Journalism'" to *Nineteenth Century* and another a month later to a Boston magazine, *Living Age.* The only good thing she could say about yellow journalism was "its tendency to recognise the equality of the sexes so far as the matter of pay is concerned."[20] The work was disheartening and disillusioning. And the pull of London was stronger. Banks felt she was actually better known there than in her native country. In 1900 she sailed back to resume her career in London.

By 1901 Banks was prominent enough to rate a listing in the British *Who's Who.* She had a flat at 7 Harley Gardens, in a quiet neighborhood called The Boltons, between King's Road in Chelsea and the Old Brompton Road in South Kensington. Her building, a tall white Regency terrace house, faced the gardens of the houses in the next street. The neighborhood, then as now, was quiet and gracious. The singer Jenny Lind had lived nearby; and during the years that Banks was in the neighborhood, Beatrix Potter was living two blocks away.

She continued her freelance career, contributing articles to *Quiver, Nineteenth Century, Longman's, Fortnightly, Temple Bar,* and *Women's Home.* She maintained some of her New York contacts as well. In 1904 she published a review in the *New York Times* of Frances A. Kellor's book *Out of Work,*[21] and the next year had an article in the *Times* opposing the practice of tipping as "un-American."[22] She also sold articles to American magazines whose readers were interested in her English experiences. For instance, she published "Maid-Servant in England and America" in a Chicago magazine, *World To-Day,* and "Window Boxes of London" in *Good Housekeeping* (the latter under the byline Mary Mortimer Maxwell, one of her two pseudonyms).

Elizabeth Banks was a versatile writer, producing short stories as well as articles on a variety of subjects. Although many of her articles were written as straight observation, most contained some element of social criticism. For the *London Illustrated Magazine* she contributed a first-person account of flower-selling to a series called "How the Other Half Lives."[23] Her subjects were often working-class or middle-class people, both English and American. Probably one of the reasons Banks could look at America critically, and at the British status quo critically, is that she was not a typical expatriate, and she kept herself at a distance from the moneyed Americans in England, writers or otherwise."[24] A number of the wealthy and prominent American women writers living in London during Banks's day (for example, Pearl Craigie, Jennie Jerome Churchill, Louise Chandler Moulton) mention each other in their writings; but among all the names they mention Banks's does not appear. Nor does she mention them.

Elizabeth Banks was a working woman from a working-class family. Though she sometimes moved among the monied elite, she never lost her detachment from them. "I am not the sort of person," she wrote, "that rich Americans who live abroad generally 'take to,' nor do I seem particularly to 'take to' them. Most of my friends on this side are British" (*Remaking,* 33). Because we do not have a body of correspondence to and from Banks, we really cannot know who these friends were. But occasionally there is a clue to her hidden personal life that illuminates like a brief beacon. Such is the case with a reference in the biography of the renowned crusading journalist and editor, W. T. Stead. Stead had worked on the *Pall Mall Gazette* since 1880 and was its editor from 1883 to 1890, before Banks's arrival in London. He changed the *Gazette* from a rather conservative journal to one that used daring tactics to bring social injustice to the attention of readers."[25] From 1890 Stead had been the editor of the *Review of Reviews* and was a well-known figure in journalistic and reform circles.

In *The Life of W. T. Stead,* Frederic Whyte describes the hospitality Stead offered at his vacation house at Hayling Island, about seventy miles south of London, just off the the coast near Brighton:

There was an almost unceasing procession to [his home] of London workers—journalists, novelists, artists, typists, all sorts and conditions of men and women needing change and rest. Miss Elizabeth L. Banks, the talented American writer, whose first book, *In Cap and Apron* [actually never published as a book], had won Stead's favor, was one of the many. Her experience was typical of all. "One day I went to Mr. Stead's office," Miss Banks writes me. "I was breaking down under a very great mental strain and passing through a tragedy. I was hard up, too, as my worries had prevented my sleeping and working, but nobody in London knew that. Mr. Stead noticed how I looked at once and he said, without asking what was the matter, 'American girl, you go home and pack your bag and meet me at the station at six o'clock. I'm going to send you off to my place at Hayling to stay a week or so. You're going to be ill.' I did what he told me—it was no good refusing—and at the station I was surprised to find that he had decided to accompany me. He took me to Hayling and left me there with his people, returning back to his work in London at once. He had actually taken that trip with me because he thought I was too ill to go to a strange place alone."[26]

This brief letter, which Banks probably sent to Whyte when he was collecting reminiscences to include in his biography of Stead, tells us that all was not cheerful in her life, although everything she published about her adventures sounds chipper and feisty. The visit to Hayling Island took place after 1895, for that is when the Steads bought their cottage."[27] From the context it seems that although Banks was starting to make her reputation as a writer, she was not yet making a comfortable living. So this visit may have occurred between 1895 and 1897, when she returned to New York. What caused the "very great mental strain"? Perhaps writing several articles simultaneously, for several different papers and magazines, was taking its toll. And what was the tragedy? Banks was unwilling to reveal more. This incident reveals not only Banks's vulnerability but Stead's great compassion and calming influence. Banks admired him tremendously. Toward the end of *The Remaking of an American* she writes of Stead that she "had the honor of counting him as one of my best and most helpful friends. I look upon him as the greatest journalist who ever lived, and I believe that he will so be recorded in history."

In 1911 Banks's career reached a pivotal point as she was offered a regular staff position on a weekly paper called the *Referee,* where she remained for five years. This paper was an unusual but highly regarded weekly published in London every Sunday from 1877 to 1928. It billed itself as "The Paper that makes you think," and consisted mainly of articles on politics, sport, and the theater. That it was financially well supported is evident from the large number of advertisements it was able to solicit (including a very sizable one featuring George Bernard Shaw touting Formamint lozenges). In addition to a regular letter-to-the-editor column, the *Referee* had a special column in which staff writers replied to questions from readers ("W. F. Harding: Vanoc thanks you for your interesting letter; Anxious: You can book for Boxing Night at Drury Lane at the theatre's box-office. But you had better hurry up."). The paper addressed its public as the "Refereaders," and there seemed to be a strong rapport between them. An unusual feature of the paper was that all its writers had pen names taken from stories of the knights of the Round Table, presumably as a way of indicating that they saws theirs as a mission for truth, chivalry, and patriotic valor. The editor was "Pendragon," and regular columnists were "Vanoc," "Percival," "Tristram," "Lancelot," "Gareth," "Boris," "Launvel," "Balin," and "Dagonet." The identity of the last gentleman was well known, however; he was George R. Sims, a prominent writer of drama, ballads, sentimental stories, and muckraking articles and books on the condition of London's poor.

When she joined the paper in the spring of 1911, Banks, the lone woman on the staff, became "Enid," and she originated a series called "The Lady at the Round Table." Each author, it seems, had a set place in the *Referee;* the paper was always fourteen pages long, and Enid's column appeared, with few exceptions, on page seven. Very soon she was receiving as much correspondence as the older, more established columnists.

Banks noted that until about 1910 the *Referee* was known as a "man's paper" and a conservative one. An examination of numerous issues of the paper reveals an assortment of attitudes—male supremacist, jingoistic ("England for the English"), anti-Semitic, xenophobic—that characterized the "traditional" educated Englishman. But the paper also supported good causes, such as a children's home, and eventually its politics even veered to the liberal. Banks knew she was hired because the editor realized the practical need for a "woman's column." But this suited Banks for, as she said, "I was looking for a Sunday pulpit from which I could preach the Gospel [of women's suffrage] to every creature" (*Remaking,* 10).

The editor warned her that the paper was "dead against Votes for Women. . . . You don't happen to have turned suffragette, do you?" (11). Actually, Banks did belong to a group called the Constitutional Suffragists; so she could, in all truth, say she was not a suffrag*ette.* She also promised not to mention the word "vote" without the editor's instructions. This pleased the editor mightily and posed a creative challenge for the new writer.

Banks found that gentle but pointed commentaries in her column had results. She did not exactly preach herself; she mentioned in one article how fashionable suffrage rallies were in America, and how everyone there was so matter-of-fact about the issue. American men were not at all worried about the prospect of women voting; and Banks's implication was that British men should be equally fearless. Never strident or angry, Banks introduced the idea of suffrage as a completely natural development, at the same time criticizing the most violent and destructive of the militant suffragists. Banks was a voice of calm, but she was a constant voice. She was so effective that at one point a member of Christabel Pankhurst's branch of the suffrage movement called her to say she was going to write a letter to the *Referee* thanking it for its change of stance. Banks begged her to refrain, for the paper had no idea that it had a pro-suffrage writer on its staff.

Banks did her share of "sandwich"-sign duty for the cause, wearing boards to advertise meetings, but she did so far away from the premises of the *Referee.* Banks wrote for suffrage, advertised meetings, and helped sell copies of the newspaper *Votes for Women.* The *Referee's* prohibition against her using the word "suffragette" did not apply, of course, to what she might write for other publications under a pen name. Therefore, "Mary Mortimer Maxwell" could publish "In Jail with the Suffragettes" in *Harper's Weekly* in 1912, at the same time she served on the *Referee* staff. This article describes the conditions in prison for her friend Henrietta Marston, who also appears in the first chapter of *Remaking of an American.*

In fact, during the time Banks was writing for the *Referee,* she traveled to Budapest for an International Women's Congress. She was also a member of the London-based Women Writers' Suffrage League and was its delegate in 1912 to the Anglo-American Arbitration Treaty Meeting. Over the years "Enid" gently kept the suffrage issue alive in her column, tucked into other stories and observations. By July 20, 1915, her column urged Londoners to greet suffrage marchers in Hyde Park and support them by buying their paper, *Common Cause.* The evolution of the *Referee* from an anti-suffragist newspaper to one sympathetic with the women's rights movement has to be due in large part to the efforts of Elizabeth Banks.

During her tenure at the *Referee* she again moved, this time to a building with historic and literary significance. Her new address was 5 Robert Street, The Adelphi WC 1. Two blocks east of Charing Cross Station and just off the Strand, the Adelphi was only a few minutes' walk from Fleet Street and the theaters. The Embankment Gardens, where Cleopatra's Needle had been set up in 1878, was only a few steps away. In the eighteenth century, when the buildings were new, J.M.W. Turner used to come to the Adelphi Terrace to paint views of the Thames. These terraced houses built by the Adam brothers were, from all accounts, a desirable and fascinating neighborhood; and residency there symbolized for Banks the fact that she had "arrived" as a writer in England.

Among her neighbors were George Bernard Shaw (Banks called him the "Dean of the Adelphi"), John Galsworthy, Thomas Hardy, and J. M. Barrie. Several suffrage groups and other "anti" organizations—the Freedom League, the Actresses' Franchise League, the Tax Resistance League—had their headquarters on the street, and Banks recalled that, to learn the latest news, she had only to lean out of her window to read the new placards in the opposite windows. And when there were "meetings, processions, or smashings, our quiet street becomes something of a 'show-place' and ceases to be secluded and 'select'" (*Remaking,* 9–10).

Banks noted that her street was also a favorite haunt of tourists, particularly Americans, who would come looking for Shaw's door. This behavior is corroborated by Sir James Barrie, who lived nearby at 3 Adelphi Terrace House; in a letter to a friend he confessed that he sometimes gave 2 Robert Street as his address, or listed an incorrect address in *Who's Who,* to throw off unwanted visitors.[28] Only a few of these houses still survive, most having been replaced in 1938—the year of Elizabeth Banks's death—by a large block of Art Deco offices. Some of the buildings in John Adam Street, however, retain the elegance of their origins, including No. 8, currently the home of the Royal Society of Arts.

Banks was more upwardly mobile now, and she enjoyed being in a prestigious neighborhood close to the excitement of Fleet Street, the Strand, and the West End theaters. But her literary focus remained strongly attuned to social justice. It was not wealth she detested but complacency and apathy about crucial social issues. She saw a rigid class system as something that hindered the progress of a society because it always doomed certain people to limited options. Her own joys in London life were diminished by her awareness of poverty just around the corner.

The Adelphi years seem to have been the golden ones of Elizabeth Banks's career. She was now a well-known figure in newspaper and other literary circles. Even if she herself were not recognized on the street, almost every English reader knew "Enid" or Banks's other persona, "Mary Mortimer Maxwell." One time during the war, Banks traveled to Devon—an area off-limits to aliens—for a break. She had unluckily traveled without her identity papers, and was detained by the police. When she convinced the officer of her identity and that she was "Mary," he was astounded, so certain was he that "Mary" was thoroughly English. She was released.

Between Banks's very engaging early works, written in her twenties about her first experiences as a journalist, and *The Remaking of an American*, which she wrote in her late fifties, there are a dozen titles of varying purpose. Her one attempt at novel writing, *The Mystery of Frances Farrington* (1909), appears to have gone unnoticed. It had one printing, on cheap paper with a plain paper cover, without any publisher's imprint. Very likely it was a "vanity" production.

The War Years

When the Great War broke out, Banks had another reason to dissociate herself from her wealthy compatriots. She was sympathetic with tourists caught overseas by the war. But she was angry with those Americans who had lived in England so long that their only remaining American aspect was their legal citizenship, and who were now invoking that citizenship to get out of the country quickly: "England at peace they loved. England at war they forsook" (*Remaking*, 77).

Banks's love of both America and England shaped her writing and activities during the war years. Although she could have left Britain, she stayed to do her part as a journalist and keep morale high. She organized a highly successful fund-raising campaign on behalf of Belgian relief. This was the "Authors' Christmas Belgian Fund," and for it she enlisted the aid of every writer she knew, asking them to autograph copies of their works, to be sold for the cause. First she recruited her neighbors, the Adelphi authors, then others whom she knew, and soon her kitchen was crowded with famous authors, including H. G. Wells and Sir Arthur Conan Doyle, and stacks of their books. Other writers who obligingly sent signed copies of their books for Banks to sell for the cause included Hardy, Galsworthy, Kipling, Masefield, Alfred Noyes, and Arnold Bennett.

One of the most popular sellers during this campaign was Banks's own *Dik: A Dog of Belgium*, the story of a heroic dog at the front. Banks wrote *Dik, On the Boat That Uncle Sam Built*, and some other short works especially for her campaign in support of the Allied war effort. She refers to these as books, but they are actually pamphlets (and designed purposely to be small and inexpensive so they could be bought in quantities and would be affordable for children).

This charitable effort seems to have been one of the highlights of Elizabeth Banks's life. Every year after 1914 she included in her *Who's Who* entry: "Originator, Hon. Organiser and Hon. Secretary of the Authors' Belgian Fund and Dik's Fund for the Allies." Banks seems to have gone about the mobilization of this effort in a highly organized way. She realized that having some illustrious names as patrons of the project would attract attention. And she capitalized on the popularity of "Enid" as well, signing her announcement of the book sale:

Elizabeth Banks, ("Enid" of the Referee)

Organiser and Hon. Secretary

Ultimately she obtained autographed books from over seventy authors, including many of the best-known writers of the day. She obtained donated sales space at the office of Canada's Great Trunk Railway. Banks wrote that the management of the railway "were most kind in allowing me the use of their offices, the counter, large desks and a very large show-window, which was decorated in Belgian colours with always a large number of books opened out at the title page showing the autographs."[29]

Although, for Banks, a certain amount of self-promotion was inevitably involved in the Authors' Belgian Fund, her motives were altruistic and she was careful to demonstrate that the project was run in a businesslike way. The funds were managed by a chartered accountant who served as "Honorary Auditor"—probably meaning he did the bookkeeping work pro bono. Proceeds were kept at Harrods Bank, and then sent to Belgian relief organizations, primarily to aid children. According to papers in the Imperial War Museum, about three hundred pounds were raised in 1914 and a similar sum in 1915. The *Referee* publicized the sale, but so did other publications. A notice in the *Morning Post* of December 28, 1914, read:

The sale of autographed and inscribed books by famous living authors will continue during the coming week at the Canadian Grand Trunk Railway offices, 19, Cockspur-street. These books were collected by Miss Elizabeth Banks in connection with the Authors' Belgian Christmas Fund, the object of which is to make a gift to the King of the Belgians for his people. Seekers after valuable autographs should visit the shop and note the various treasures. Miss Banks's little penny story of a Red Cross dog, "Dik, a Dog of Belgium," has had a large sale as a Christmas card, and can be used as a New Year's card as well.

Banks reported that the author with the most books sold for the fund was Sir Arthur Conan Doyle, with sixty-four volumes. "The next largest number autographed and inscribed were by myself. The next largest in number were by Mr. Kipling and Mr. H. G. Wells".[30] The concerted efforts of all involved in the fund resulted in a demonstration of both patriotism and solidarity with a national ally, and a not-inconsiderable sum donated to the children of Belgium. But for Banks it must have been much more than that. Chapter 9 of *The Remaking of an American* practically glows with the excitement of having literary celebrities come to her flat with their offerings for the fund. She describes Sir Arthur Conan Doyle, "come to autograph and inscribe six dozen big and little books. . . . When he had finished what he laughingly called his 'stint,' he, too, looked about the kitchen and declared himself to be in glorious company. . . . [C]elebrated authors climb to my kitchen, writing their names in the books I have gathered there ready for the Authors' Belgian Christmas Fund" (100–101).

Some curious ironies come out of this. Banks's writings convey the impression that she was at the center of a lively writers' village, enjoying the comradeship of other authors and marshaling them into pleasurable patriotic activity. Yet the writers whom she knew as a neighbor or as a contributing member of the Authors' Fund do not mention her in their own letters or reminiscences. Neither does George R. Sims, the *Referee*'s "Dagonet," in his 1917 autobiography, although he worked with Banks from 1911 to 1916. Clearly these men did not value Banks's work and friendship as much as she valued theirs. Perhaps Banks's perspective on the Authors' Fund made the project sound grander than it was. At the least, it was more important to her than it was to participating authors. Having Sir Arthur Conan Doyle autograph books in the kitchen of her flat was a major event for Banks; but to Sir Arthur it was a relatively minor occasion.

Banks must have been on cordial terms with her literary neighbors at the Adelphi, or she would have not have mentioned them so warmly in her autobiography. But why did they not mention her at all? In a letter of October 26, 1917, Barrie describes an evening of German air raids against London and searchlights sweeping the skies for invading airplanes. Thomas Hardy was visiting that night, and "he and Wells and Shaw and Arnold Bennett and I sat up one night watching the strange spectacle."[31] Was the American woman from around the corner ever invited to a vigil such as this? Or to any social gatherings among the literati in the neighborhood? Probably not—for if she had been, this surely would have been mentioned in *The Remaking of an American*. So why was she absent? Not because she was a woman, or an American—Barrie was a great friend of the American actress Mary Anderson de Navarro, and used to visit her home in the Cotswolds regularly for parties and cricket matches. Shaw and Wells also enjoyed wide social circles. Perhaps Elizabeth Banks just wasn't notable enough; perhaps her status as a journalist rather than a writer of belles lettres excluded her from the inner circles of literary groups.

Another possibility is that, although she enjoyed a certain readership in London, first as "the American girl" and then as "Enid" and "Mary," she may not have been a very social person. She was a member of several London clubs, and she was active in suffrage efforts—but did she have any close friends? Aside from Henrietta Marston, whom she mentions in writing about suffrage—assuming Henrietta is a real person, not an invented character—Banks does not mention specific close friends. Perhaps she was a rather solitary person who lived a full life professionally but a quiet one personally. In her *Who's Who* entries she usually listed as her recreations "playing with children, dogs, and kittens." Whose children? Did she have friends with families, who invited her to dinner on the weekends? Did she work with children after she retired from journalism? Without the evidence of any journals, diaries, address book, or letters we can never know about this aspect of her life.

The first part of the Great War was a time that greatly tested Banks's patriotism. She was impatient for America to enter the conflict and could not understand its stance of neutrality. In 1915 she returned to the States for a couple of months; during this period she was interviewed by the *New York Times* about her efforts to raise money for Belgian relief through "Dik's Fund." She went to Washington, D.C., then on to Canada and the American Midwest, listening to people's feelings about the war in an attempt to understand why freedom-loving Americans were taking so long to become involved. During this trip she revisited her family's home in Wisconsin, but her uncle and aunt had passed away many years earlier, and only a couple of people remembered the red-headed girl who had once lived at their farm. This section of her reminiscences she called "The Alien," for while she was considered politically an alien in England, she now felt emotionally alien in America.

Banks was back in London when America did decide to enter the war. She saw her duty as a journalist as maintaining the morale of her readers while keeping quiet enough about certain details to protect England. In *The Remaking of an American,* she relates the story of a Royal Air Force flyer who wrote to his favorite columnist, "Enid," because, he said, she was listened to and had the power to sway opinion. Risking court-martial for violating the rules of military secrecy, he begged her to ask journalists at home not to give details of the results of German bombing raids against English targets. When specific descriptions of areas hit were reported, and what sorts of targets were destroyed, he explained, the German command knew that their bombing pattern had been successful and would know how to gauge their next raids. Banks writes that she relayed this request to the press, while protecting the soldier's anonymity, and within a few days only the most generalized descriptions of bombing damage were allowed in the papers. Was this true? Did Banks actually change the way bombing damage was reported in the papers?

In *The Press in War-Time,* published just after the war, Sir Edward Cook wrote that initially there were no restrictions about reporting air raids:

> This period was short. "Copy" about raids was especially good from a newspaper point of view, and it was found that papers, especially in the raided areas, published a great deal of information likely to be useful to the enemy. The raiders had definite objectives, but they might not know, and often could not know, unless they were told, how far they had succeeded in reaching them. Enterprising newspapers told. Even charts were published of the actual route taken. This was clearly intolerable. . . . [T]he matter ended in a compromise. The Press were told that nothing was to be published until an official *communiqué* had been issued. The newspapers were to be free to write up the raids in their own way, but they were requested to submit their reports to censorship.[32]

It is not noted in this book, and there seem to be no records anywhere, whether the restrictions on reporting air raids resulted from the efforts of any specific journalists. But even if Banks's efforts did not directly change the way war news was reported, it is doubtless that her uplifting stories such as "The Blinds of Hope" offered solace to a worried and often dispirited readership.

Her "Reconversion" Begins

Banks's postwar transatlantic attitude was paradoxical. She remained devoted to England, but became increasingly critical of it, disillusioned especially by its rigid and persistent class system. And while she asserted the superiority of the American way, she ultimately chose to remain a resident of England.

In the mid-1920s, Banks traveled again to the United States, this time to examine the phenomenon of the "new Americans." After traveling thoughout the country to meet the newest Americans, immigrants and the children of immigrants, she observed: "My native land became a land of delight and a place of enchantment. So much was new to me, the returned native" (*Remaking*, 219). This was the beginning of Banks's "re-Americanization."

She had heard terrible reports of conditions at Ellis Island, and was pleasantly surprised when she went there to discover a warm and positive atmosphere in which people of many nations were made to feel comfortable and welcome. She shared the Ellis Island food, finding it wholesome and substantial. But when she wrote articles about the true conditions at the immigration center, she could not get them published in England. One London editor told Banks that if he ran her "'glowing description of the American Reception Palace,' all the best British workmen will be getting themselves and their families into line for the Quota immediately" (*Remaking*, 221).

A symbolic experience in New York's Madison Square seems to have confirmed Banks's new appreciation of the American democratic ideal. A new and hygienic fountain had been installed, where all could drink pure water; she compared it with the fountain in the Embankment Gardens, where everyone had to share a common cup, which was therefore a health risk. The upper classes would not even use the cup. But in New York she watched a washerwoman, a shoeshine boy, and a businessman all drinking from the fountain. They all shared benches in the park and did not seem to care who was next to them or who had occupied the seats earlier. Although Banks was aware that the United States was not a paragon of social equality, the free and easy access to the park and the unself-conscious way in which people seemed to move among one another impressed her as she had not been impressed in England. There, so much had been lovely, but so much had been separate—and she had always been put off by the "upstairs-downstairs" physical separation of the classes.

This separation was emphasized by the educational system, whereas she saw the system in America as bringing people together. Banks was inspired to begin, in 1922, a study of what she called "The Trail of the Serpent of Caste"—how the English educational system conspired to keep classes separate and prevent poorer children from attaining a better position in life. The famous "public" schools, she contended, which had originally been founded to give poor and needy boys a chance, "were gradually filched from those for whom they were intended by chicanery and sharp practice." The playing fields of Harrow, Eton, and Rugby, she asserted, were stolen.

After completing her study of the British school system, she published *School for John and Mary: A Story of Caste in England.*[33] The first part of the title suggests a tale of sweet and simple innocence; but there is indictment in the subtitle. In the story, an English family returns to London after having lived in Canada for several years. The children, John and Mary, had attended good "state schools" in Canada and their parents assume they will have similar educational opportunities in the mother country. But the school systems in England fail them, largely because of their emphasis on class. Ultimately, in order to succeed in school and life, John and Mary must return to Canada.

This book briefly attracted a good bit of attention and elicited overwhelmingly positive reactions in the United States. The *New Republic,* for instance, called the book an "arraignment of England's abominable caste system in education . . . [which] ought to prove needed ammunition to the Labor Party."[34]

Publication of *The Remaking of an American*

Banks's final work is *The Remaking of An American,* originally published in 1928 by Doubleday, Doran. It was published only in the United States. The text of the present volume is a facsimile reprint of the original publication; therefore the typographical errors in the original have been reproduced here.

In contrast to her two earlier autobiographical books, *The Remaking of an American* presents the maturer woman's perspectives on change, not only in herself but in the two countries to which she is most closely bound. The book is not a straight narrative but rather a compilation of reflections and anecdotes from three periods in her life. Throughout, she mentions well-known people and places, and events with clear historical context.

But there are some mysteries as well. The volume is dedicated "To S——— — Who has Waited Long and Patiently, ever Prophesying my Final 'Coming of Age.'" Who is "S"? An American? A literary colleague? A distant relative? Without Banks's letters or any publisher's records we cannot know. In some chapters Banks quotes from letters from a friend whom she refers to as "The Democrat," and who seems to be an American politician. Or he may simply be a persona created by Banks; she may have felt that including the viewpoint of an American male might broaden the readership for her book.

What makes this book particularly interesting is its perspective of being simultaneously inside and outside the circle. Banks can write about the British class system, for instance, while living within it. Likewise, when she returns to the United States for a visit, after an absence of many years, she is both at home and a foreign tourist.

The Remaking of an American is written, like Banks's earlier works, in an engaging and personable style, one of the reasons it received many favorable reviews when it was first published. The New York *Herald Tribune* called it "a document in contemporary international relations and interesting to those who would rather tackle the study of Anglo-American relations in personal narrative than in economic or political analysis."[35] And the *Educational Review* called Banks "the most untiresome recorder of her own experiences and views you can find in a multitude of autobiographers. You'll like Elizabeth on every page."[36] Indeed, the image of "Elizabeth," a friendly though opinionated guide to British life, remains constant throughout the book. It is factual, and the facts are often hard-hitting, but the reader cannot help but feel affinity for the writer. She is still the brave and headstrong woman she was in her earlier years of muckraking journalism, but with more experience and literary acquaintance to expand her views.

In only one area does she remain dogmatic, and that is in the recounting of her "reconversion" to American ideals. Weighing British and American values in the years following the Great War, she finds the latter substantially superior. In the *New York World,* reviewer Marie Luhrs noted, "Her argument for the superiority of America is not developed in a connected narration or in ordered arguments, neither is it developed with violence. She rambles about among brief paragraphs, letters, disjointed notations. Few of her chapters have firm and jointed structure. In such a method she is very clever. A flaming, thunderous argumentation of her own would invite challenge and contradiction. Instead, she presents her material with little comment—the reader draws conclusions. 'Here is England that I love, here is America that I love,' she seems to say, 'What do you make of them?'"[37]

The Silent Years

While Banks seems to have enjoyed the brash, bold activities and writing adventures of her youth, she also seems to have become rather reclusive and self-effacing in her later life. After *The Remaking of an American* appeared in 1928, she published nothing else. She suffered from arthritis, and that may have kept her from writing. She seems to have retreated almost totally from public life. By the 1920s she had moved from central London to the "suburb" of Hampstead, where she lived first at 104 Sumatra Road and later a few blocks away in Broadhurst Gardens, a street of comfortable red-brick homes, some of which were multiple dwellings. A 1934 post office directory in the London Library lists the Broadhurst Gardens address as a boarding house.[38]

Banks was independent but she was never affluent. Indeed, in her last years she may have had financial difficulties. As she published nothing—indicated by the complete lack of evidence in any periodical index or book search—she would have had no earnings. How did she manage? The Probate Registry listed the value of her estate at the time of her death as just a little more than ninety-seven pounds. In the London of 1938, that would have been enough for about a year's rental of a small flat, so it was not a negligible amount; but neither was it a comfortable financial cushion, and Elizabeth Banks must have had to live very frugally during the last years of her life.

Around this time Banks became a close friend of a young Englishwoman, Mabel Spink, a great lover of small animals, as was Banks. Mabel Spink was briefly well known as the designer of a poster for the Royal Society for the Prevention of Cruelty to Animals (RSPCA) titled "The Crime of the Cage!" Its purpose was to make people stop the cruel practice of capturing wild birds and placing them in cages, either to keep or to sell as pets. The October 1922 journal of the RSPCA noted that "The artist, Miss Mabel Spink, bought the bird at a shop not long after it was caught. The bird had broken its tail feathers in beating against the bars of its cage. Miss Spink kept the bird in her studio long enough to make the drawing, and then released it in the Embankment Gardens at Charing Cross in the presence of some boys, upon whom she impressed the lesson of her act." The poster depicts a chaffinch in opposing conditions, "Happy and Free," flying over the fields, and "A Miserable Prisoner" locked in a tiny cage.

Sometime in the mid- to late 1920s Spink became terminally ill, and it was Elizabeth Banks who initially took care of her, until the last months, when Spink entered a nursing home on Priory Road in West Hampstead. But Banks apparently continued to visit and care for her friend faithfully. In her last will, which she wrote while in the nursing home, Spink stated: "I leave all I possess real and personal to my dearly beloved friend Elizabeth Banks of 104 Sumatra Road N.W. 6 absolutely and make her my sole EXECU-TRIX in love and gratitude for what she has done for me having given up in order to care for me in my illness her literary career and even her return to her own country." This moving testimonial is the only hint we have that Banks was considering a return to the States. As for the nature of the relationship between the older woman and the younger, we know only that they were obviously devoted to each other, the emotion discernible in just the few sentences of each woman's last will and testament.

Elizabeth and Mabel were neighbors in West Hampstead, and they shared an interest in small animals. Banks had always loved dogs, and had gone to extraordinary trouble to bring her French poodle, Judge, to England in 1893. The pamphlets she sold to benefit the Belgian war relief were all dog stories. In every entry in *Who's Who* she mentioned her interest in dogs and kittens. And then in 1922 there was a subtle change in her annual entry. Earlier entries had noted that "Dik's Fund," established during the war years, was "now merged in Dik's Dog-Tale Fund to help children and animals and protect birds." Perhaps Elizabeth's interest in bird protection came as a result of her friendship with Mabel. Or perhaps Elizabeth and Mabel met through their mutual interests. For six consecutive yearly entries in *Who's Who*, Banks listed her interest in bird protection. But from the 1928 volume—with the entry written in 1929, when Mabel Spink was already critically ill—Banks never again mentions birds.

Mabel Spink died on September 13, 1929, at the age of thirty-eight. She was cremated at the Golders Green Crematorium, where a bronze memorial plaque was installed in the west Cloisters. The plaque is decorated with copies of the pictures of the flying and caged birds, and beneath them is inscribed:

MABEL SPINK

Artist—Writer—Teacher

Dear Friend of Elizabeth Banks, by whom this tablet is erected, assisted by children of the British Empire and The United States of America, in remembrance of her work for our kindred of the wild. She who freed many captives was herself set free on September 13th 1929.

Although she never gave up her American citizenship, Banks also never gave up living in London. And while she always proudly proclaimed herself an American, socially she did not identify with her compatriots. Her friends and associates were, for the most part, British. She had not joined American organizations, such as the American Women's Club, which had been founded just a few years after her arrival in London. The only organization of which she remained a member for many years was the English-Speaking Union; in fact, for the last eight years of her life, she listed her address in care of the ESU headquarters in Charles Street, near Berkeley Square. Her last residence was in Braden Street in Maida Vale, a quiet neighborhood not far from the Regent's Canal. The street took a direct hit during the Blitz, and modern blocks of flats now stand on the site.

Elizabeth Banks's most active professional years were those early in her career, from her arrival in London in her twenties through her wartime activities in her forties. When she died in the Surrey County Hospital on July 18, 1938, the Associated Press obituary, wired from London to the *New York Times,* concentrated in its six paragraphs on her early journalistic experiences and the Authors' Belgian Fund.[39]

It is ironic that Banks's death was listed in the leading American newspaper but seems to have gone unnoticed in the British press. Although Banks had lived in London for forty years, her passing seemed to be ignored there. But actually it was just eclipsed by other events. The day of her death, an eloquent plea appeared in the *London Times,* written by a number of Christians who were alarmed by reports of what was happening to the Jews of Vienna. This letter, so chilling in retrospect, was relegated to a small inside column. The paper much preferred to concentrate its attention upon the King's upcoming visit to Paris, and almost every page of the paper was devoted to French history, art, cuisine, landmarks, fashion, and hotels. Francophilia bubbled from the pages like a happy vintage.

These were modern times, and the news of an earlier day—what life was like belowstairs in 1894, how Americans used to be able to buy presentations at Court during Victoria's day—was irrelevant. But perhaps the readers of 1938 would have found interesting Elizabeth Banks's account of her travels in the United States in 1915, in which she anxiously probed the psyche of a nation that was trying, desperately, to stay out of war.

In January 1933 Banks had composed her last will, which attests to her strong identity as an American, her devotion to her lost friend, and a desire for posthumous obscurity. "I, Elizabeth Banks, writer, AMERICAN CITIZEN . . . direct that my body shall be CREMATED, that there shall be no religious ceremony, other than silent prayer, that the plain gold ring I wear on the third finger of my left hand shall not be removed, that my ashes shall be scattered, and my name and the date of my death only (nothing else) shall be engraved at the bottom of the Tablet which, with some help from some British and American children, I have had erected to the memory of my dear gifted English friend, Mabel Spink."

And to frustrate any future biographers, she also wrote: "I earnestly request my Executors to remove all inscriptions from my jewelry and to destroy all private papers and photographs." Her executors were Jemima Steevens and Denys Kilham Roberts. The latter was a writer and editor and served as secretary of the Incorporated Society of Authors, Playwrights and Composers, a predecessor of the Society of Authors. We can assume that her executors carried out their instructions faithfully, for there are no original Banks papers in any library or archive, and we have no photographs of her other than those appearing in her early books.

How ironic that a woman who had been so independent, bold, and adventurous had become self-negating to such a final degree. Someone who, over the course of thirty-four years, published three autobiographies had to have a very strong sense of self. Therefore her wish to erase herself—her possessions, her pictures, even her ashes—is beyond the analysis of this essay. What happened? We can speculate, but we cannot know. It is profoundly sad.

Perhaps Elizabeth Banks wanted anyone who might remember her, or who might learn about her, to focus on the earlier and probably happier woman. In 1902 she thanked "the fate that endowed me with a certain kind of reasoning power that helped me to distinguish between what I could and could not do, as a 'yellow journalist,' and still retain my womanhood and self-respect, and I can especially thank the fate that endowed me at my birth with a particularly prominent self-assertive and combative disposition that enabled me to recognize my rights and then to fight to the death, if necessary, to maintain them."[40] And so she remains for us—the young woman with serious eyes, who set out with her typewriter to survive in London.

NOTES

1. Original letter in the archives of the Imperial War Museum, file BEL 8, London. While Banks is often quite specific about the people, places, and events in her life subsequent to her arrival in England, she is consistently vague about her early life. In her autobiographies, she never gives her date or place of birth. However, 1870 is the year appearing in all *Who's Who* entries, and this information was usually supplied to the *Who's Who* editors by the individuals listed.

A search of the New Jersey State Archives revealed no records of Banks living in Taunton, though there are several references for the state capital, Trenton, in Mercer County. (Taunton might have been the result of a misreading by an editor.) According to the 1865 census, John Banks, a thirty-nine-year-old painter born in England, lived in Trenton with his wife, Sarah, thirty-seven, and their five children (none of whom was named Elizabeth). The eldest, a boy of fifteen, worked in a wool mill; the youngest child was an infant. Subsequent birth records for the city of Trenton indicate that John Banks, painter, and his wife, Sarah, had a daughter, Elizabeth, born on May 2, 1865. The Banks family was not listed at all in the 1870 Mercer County Census Index.

There are two arguments for the probability of the Banks family in these records being our Elizabeth's family, but they are both circumstantial. Registration records from Milwaukee-Downer College indicate that Elizabeth Banks was a senior in 1886. Her college graduation in 1886 at the age of twenty-one (having been born in 1865) seems more likely than at sixteen (having been born in 1870). And she mentions in several writings that she was orphaned as a child. The disappearance of the Banks family from the Trenton census records within five years of Elizabeth's birth indicates a major change in the family's condition. It could be as simple a matter as their having moved away. Or a disaster could have befallen them, leaving the children orphans. But this also raises more questions than it resolves. What happened to the other children? Several of them would have been old enough to work by 1870, but what of the younger ones? Who exactly were the unnamed uncle and aunt in Wisconsin? And why doesn't Elizabeth Banks ever mention what happened to her parents, or mention older siblings?

What incentive or motive would Elizabeth Banks have had to shave five years off her age? She seemed to get a lot of mileage out of her "American girl" persona. The relative youth of their author may have given her articles more appeal for readers, who would see the fresh insights of an ingenue writer. The longer Banks could keep herself under thirty, the longer she could maintain this image.

2. Or at least *International Who's Who* repeats the information that Banks herself provided.

3. Atherton, *Adventures of a Novelist*, 231–32.

4. Eva Anstruther, "Ladies' Clubs," *Nineteenth Century*, April 1899, 598–611.

5. *The Autobiography of a "Newspaper Girl,"* 57.

6. Ibid., 63.

7. *Campaigns of Curiosity*, xvi.

8. *Autobiography*, 79, 70, 71–72.

9. *Campaigns of Curiosity*, xv. Banks would later work with Sims on this paper from 1911 to 1916.

10. Ibid., 98.

11. *The Remaking of an American*, 41. Hereafter cited in text.

12. This is the same Mrs. Lynn Linton who, as a much older woman, was interviewed by Elizabeth Banks in 1893 or 1894.

13. Only a few papers from the early years of the Society of Women Writers and Journalists remain in the group's archives. Pearl Craigie, the American novelist, was one of its first officers, but Elizabeth Banks does not seem to have been a member.

14. Cited in the *Review of Reviews* 27 (January–June 1903), 485.

15. *The Woman's Book: Contains Everything a Woman Ought to Know*, ed. Florence B. Jack and Rita Strauss (London: T. C. and E. C. Jack, 1911), 626.

16. Ibid., 627.

17. *The Nation*, December 25, 1902, 501.

18. The annual periodical indices published by the *Review of Reviews* are helpful but not exhaustive. They do not include every article from major publications of the day, as I have found by sheer chance several Banks articles, unlisted in any index.

19. "I at first took up journalism in New York after my four years' stay in England" (*Autobiography*, 196). She does not name the papers for which she freelanced or the "yellow" journals to which she contributed when she was financially desperate.

20. "American 'Yellow Journalism,'" *Nineteenth Century*, August 1898, 333. Notice that Banks had adopted British spelling style.

21. December 10, 1904. The full title of Kellor's work (1904 edition) was *Out of Work: A Study of Employment Agencies, the Treatment of the Unemployed, and Their Influence upon Home and Business*. It was published in both London and New York by Putnam.

22. "Tips versus Social Equality and Self-Respect," June 11, 1905, sec. 3, p. 7, col. 1.

23. The series was published in 1894, so the title must have been inspired by Jacob Riis's work of the same name, published in 1888.

24. For many years Banks was a member of the English-Speaking Union, whose members were predominantly well-educated, affluent, and sophisticated. But there

are no written records that can give us any clues about the relationship between Banks and other ESU members.

25. One of Stead's most famous campaigns was against the child abduction and prostitution that plagued Victorian society. His 1883 article "The Maiden Tribute of Modern Babylon" shocked readers with his account of literally being able to buy a thirteen-year-old girl for five pounds. For actually doing this, he was sentenced to three months in London's Holloway Prison; but the result of his exposure of the problem was Parliament's raising of the "age of consent" to sixteen in order to protect young girls. Stead was known for many acts of kindness and fairness; he gave the same pay to men and women doing the same work on his publications, and he offered the use of his paper's offices to groups needing a meeting place at night. In 1886 he wrote an article strongly criticizing British maritime regulations for allowing ships to embark without adequate safety features such as sufficient lifeboats; he predicted a terrible disaster if improvements were not made soon. In 1912 W. T. Stead went down with the *Titanic.*

26. Frederic Whyte, *The Life of W. T. Stead,* 2 vols. (London: Jonathan Cape; New York and Boston: Houghton Mifflin, 1925), 2:70–71.

27. Ibid., 2:68.

28. *Letters of J. M. Barrie,* ed. Viola Meynall (London: Peter Davies, 1942), 65.

29. Letter of March 3, 1915, to W. E. Dowding of the National Relief Fund. Original in the library of the Imperial War Museum, London.

30. Ibid.

31. Meynall, *Letters of J. M. Barrie,* 65.

32. Cook, *The Press in War-Time* (London: Macmillan, 1920), 129–30. Cook was a scholar and journalist who worked with W. T. Stead on the *Pall Mall Gazette* and later edited the *Westminster Gazette* and the *Daily News.* During World War I he worked as press censor. Sir Edward Cook died in 1920.

33. New York and London: Putnam, 1924. There was a second edition in 1926. The book was, understandably, more positively reviewed in the United States than in England.

34. *New Republic,* July 1, 1925.

35. New York *Herald Tribune,* May 20, 1928, 4.

36. *Educational Review* (New York) 76 (September 1928): 78.

37. *New York World,* May 20, 1928, 9.

38. Many of the surnames of the people listed as residing at Nos. 114 and 116 Broadhurst Gardens seem to be European rather English, reflecting the influx of refugees in the years before the outbreak of World War II.

39. The *New York Times* obituary mentions that Elizabeth Banks had suffered from arthritis in her later years. The death certificate, completed on July 20, 1938, two days after her death, lists the primary cause as "cerebral arteriosclerosis" and the second condition as "senility." Here then is a clue to the reason for the silence of her latter years.

Sixty years ago (and even more recently), medical practitioners did not know as much as they do now about the various forms of elderly dementia, and much was misunderstood and mislabeled. "Hardening of the arteries of the brain"—cerebral arteriosclerosis—was often given as a cause of decline and death. Medical practitioners now know that a series of small strokes can cause "multi-infarct dementia," in which areas of the brain are damaged, with results including memory loss, mobility problems, and difficulties in speech. Cumulative damage from these small strokes can lead to dementia, which in the past was broadly labeled as "senility." Or Banks may have suffered from a dementia of the Alzheimer's type. Senile dementia is less common, though not unknown, in people in their sixties than in their seventies. If earlier in her life Banks had indeed misrepresented her age by five years (as speculated above), she would actually have been seventy-three years old at the time of her death rather than sixty-eight (although sixty-eight is the age on her death certificate), and a somewhat more likely candidate for such an illness.

In 1933, when Banks wrote her will, she was of sound mind. Five years later, she was dead. The usual progression of Alzheimer's is longer from onset to decease. Perhaps Banks had had some warning of the dangers that lay ahead—one of those small strokes, perhaps—and in 1933 was getting her affairs in order. We cannot assess the degree of her mental and physical disability, but we know that she never needed institutionalization and lived in her own flat at 10 Braden Street until her final hospitalization. A sudden series of strokes of increasing severity might be a more likely explanation for Banks's apparently rapid decline and death.

Jemima Steevens was a loyal friend to Banks. She was one of the two executors named in her will, and it is she who is listed on the death certificate as "causing the body to be buried"—she made funeral arrangements according to Banks's wishes (cremation rather than burial). As Elizabeth Banks helped to provide compassionate care for her friend Mabel Spink in the previous decade, it is likely that Mrs. Steevens provided much-needed assistance to Elizabeth Banks as her condition declined.

40. *Autobiography,* 211–12.

BIBLIOGRAPHY

Anstruther, Eva. "Ladies Clubs." *Nineteenth Century* (April 1899): 598–611.

Atherton, Gertrude. *Adventures of a Novelist.* New York: Blue Ribbon Books, 1932.

Baedecker, K. *London and Its Environs.* London: Dulau and Company, 1885.

Banks, Elizabeth. "American 'Yellow Journalism.'" *Nineteenth Century* 27 (August 1898): 328.

———. *The Autobiography of a "Newspaper Girl."* New York: Dodd, Mead, 1902.

———. *Campaigns of Curiosity: The Journalistic Adventures of an American Girl in London.* Chicago and New York: F. Tennyson Neely, 1894.

———. *Dik: A Dog of Belgium and His Allies.* New York: James Kempster Printing, 1916.

———[writing as Mary Mortimer Maxwell]. "In Jail with the Suffragettes." *Harper's Weekly* 56 (August 3, 1912): 9–10

———. "The Lady at the Round Table" columns. *The Referee,* 1911–1916.

———. Letter to W. E. Dowding, March 3, 1915. Original in the Library of the Imperial War Museum, file BEL. London.

———. *The Remaking of an American.* New York: Doubleday, Doran, 1928.

———. *School for John and Mary: A Story of Caste in England.* London and New York: G. P. Putnam's Sons, 1924.

———. "Tips versus Social Equality and Self-Respect." *New York Times,* June 11, 1905, sec. 3, p. 7, col. 1.

Bennett, Arnold. *Journalism for Women: A Practical Guide.* London: John Lane, 1898.

Cook, Sir Edward. *The Press in War-Time.* London: Macmillan, 1920.

"Dog Story Fund to Aid the Allies." *New York Times,* November 21, 1915, sec. 3, p. 7, col. 1.

"How Titled Foreigners Catch American Heiresses." *New York Journal,* October 24, 1909.

Jack, Florence B., and Rita Strauss, eds. *The Woman's Book: Contains Everything a Woman Ought to Know.* London: T. C. and E. C. Jack, 1911.

Linton, David, and Ray Boston, eds. *The Newspaper Press in Britain: An Annotated Bibliography.* New York: Mansell, 1987.

"London Editors Who Are Women." *Review of Reviews* 27 (January–June 1903): 485.

March-Phillipps, Evelyn. "Women's Newspapers." *Fortnightly Review* 56 (July–December 1894): 661–67.

Marzolf, Marion. *Up from the Footnote.* New York: Hastings House, 1977.

Meynall, Viola, ed. *Letters of J. M. Barrie.* London: Peter Davies, 1942.

Motter, H. L., ed. *International Who's Who: Who's Who in the World.* New York: International Who's Who Publishing, 1912.

Review of *The Autobiography of a "Newspaper Girl." The Nation,* December 25, 1902, 501.

Ross, Ishbel. *Ladies of the Press: The Story of Women in Journalism by an Insider.* New York and London: Harper Brothers, 1936.

Rubinstein, David. *Before the Suffragettes.* Brighton, England: Harvester Press, 1986.

Sims, George R. *My Life: Sixty Years' Recollections of Bohemian London.* London: Eveleigh Nash, 1917.

The Suffrage Annual and Women's Who's Who, ed. A.J.R. London: Stanley Paul, 1913.

Who's Who. London: Adam Black, 1901–38.

Whyte, Frederic. *The Life of W. T. Stead.* 2 vols. London: Jonathan Cape, 1925.

PART ONE

The Expatriate (1912–1914)
From Notes, Letters, Diaries.

THE REMAKING OF AN AMERICAN

CHAPTER I

''HOME''

"**S**OMETIMES I wonder if you are always going to live over there, or whether, one of these days, you will come home again to stay."

The American mail is in, and with it this letter from very far away, farther than New York, much farther even than the Mid-West village of its postmark—far, far away.

I try to be interested in the news it brings. "Jennie Cranbourn's daughter was married the day after her graduation from the High School." Now, who is Jennie Cranbourn, to say nothing of her daughter? Cranbourn? I don't know the name at all. It seems as if there had once been a Jennie Turner. At least, I think it was Turner. We were about the same age, and at school we were one another's "best friend," locking arms and walking about the playground telling our "great secrets." I was backward in Arithmetic and Jennie was a brilliant little mathematician and would help me with my sums during recess. Yes, I'm sure now her name was Jennie Turner.

Did she marry? I don't remember. Years ago when I first came to England, every once in a while there would come, from out West, cards announcing weddings and births and deaths. Perhaps in those olden, or rather those youngen, days, I received a card announcing that Jennie Turner, in the parlor of the Turners' farm house, had married a Mr. Cranbourn and, in that case, it would be her daughter who got married the day after her graduation.

3

"The Englewoods have a fine new car. It cost two thousand dollars. You wouldn't know their place now. Remember how they were the first people around here to get one of those new coal stoves that would keep the fire in all night? Well, they've got the best heating furnace now in the whole neighborhood. And their bathroom! It's like those you see in Milwaukee, and the tub sets right out in the middle of the room, so you can get all around it to clean it, and no breaking your back bending over. You remember Sam Englewood, of course. He was two years older than you, and so tall and gawky, and he used to draw you on his red sled. Sam's son, Martin, has gone to the University at Chicago."

I can't remember Sam or the red sled, but I do remember that once I had a sled of my own. It was home-made of a deal box, unpainted, and it had the rusty hoops off a wooden pail for runners. I remember that we were horribly poor that winter, and the only thing we seemed to have been able to raise on the farm that year was a mortgage. There was enough to eat, but it was plain and monotonous. Nearly always for our breakfast we would have fried potatoes and johnny-cake. Because Uncle John, in asking the blessing, always began with, "Oh God, we thank thee for these thine earthly bounties," the hired man used to call potatoes "earthly bounties." "Come, Lizzie," he would say, "you pick up the earthly bounties while I dig 'em." He used to work for us in the spring and summer and fall and go to the State University at Madison in the winter.

Along with the American mail is the London post, which brings news of things that are near and of people not far away. There is a notice from the club, a letter from Devon and an invitation to an Authors' Society dinner. There is a batch of press cuttings about my work: "This latest exploit of our best known lady journalist (We seem to have known her from her youth up, so we think she will now allow us to claim her!)——"

That means that the writer of the review remembers how I used to be called "the American girl in London," waving my flag and getting "impressions" and making all sorts of "comparisons" between my native land and this. It means that I have ceased to be considered as an "outsider" and an on-looker, and have fallen in with English ways, and so I have. I have become what might be called more "human," taking things for granted and not continually "noticing" things from the point of view of a critic, even a friendly one. To be sure, there are some things, born and bred in the bone, which I suppose will always make me just a little different from the genuinely English people who are my friends, but even those things I have learned to take as a matter of course.

There's Briggs, for instance, and her "plain cooking," which I cannot abide, and her determination always to wait on me, whereas I rather like to be let alone and to wait on myself. The other day I said to Briggs, "If only you would simmer the vegetables, as Augustine simmers Mrs. Pennell's across the way, instead of galloping them like a race-horse, I wouldn't have to go over to Soho every other day for luncheon."

"Madam," replied Briggs, respectfully, *"I never have simmered."*

I know that means she never will simmer, just as I have learned that other things Briggs never has done, will never be done by her for me nor for any other mistress. She is uncompromisingly conservative, and she is training me to fall in with her ways instead of learning to fall in with mine. It may be that I am becoming morally lazy. At any rate, I am learning to take the path of least resistance, except in the most important matters. I suppose there is little in the way of house work and cookery that I don't know, yet boldly to air my knowledge would mean a month's notice from Briggs. Now, I am too engaged with other things to be able to afford to take notice from Briggs, so I eat peas that have no flavor, because they have been galloped for fifteen minutes and the water thrown down the sink. I eat cabbage to-day and cauliflower to-morrow and watery vegetable marrow the next day, and turn around about and begin on the same *régime* over again, and accept the boiled fish with the never-varying white sauce, and have given up coffee for breakfast, because Briggs cannot make it, though she makes excellent tea. In so far as Briggs is concerned, I am like Miss Flemming's model young lady:

Always I am wondrous calm,
And never say a single damn.

Perhaps the time will come when I, with my back to the wall, must fight Briggs and either conquer her or send her on, with an excellent "character" to another mistress who must be, as Briggs puts it, "one lady living alone"; but the time is not yet. More and more I am realizing the importance of the great days in which I live, and by that importance I measure the need of concentrating rather than dissipating my energy. I happen to live in a neighborhood where I have but to look from my window to see some of the world's greatest workers at their tasks, and I am determined to keep up with the procession.

Here in the Adelphi, beautiful, quiet, secluded, we may at first sight give to the stranger and the tourist, who is ever penetrating into our fastnesses, an impression of being "shut-ins," cut off from the stress of London life. We are but a minute from the Strand and Charing Cross on the right and another minute from the Thames Embankment on the left. We are really neither "select" nor protected, but are up to our necks in busy-ness and are foremost in promoting fights for all good causes to which we give our hearts, some of us willing to offer up even our lives.

Last night troublous thoughts and restlessness drove me out on the Thames Embankment at midnight. I could not sleep, so I got out of bed and dressed myself and took the turning through Villiers street toward the River. The policemen nodded as I passed them, for the "bobbies" of the neighborhood know me well in many guises which I don when I am copy-hunting. All the seats along the Embankment were crowded with men and women of dull, sodden countenances. I wished that I could mark rebellion in their eyes; that I might even hear curses as I passed, for in cursing there is virility and while there is virility there is still hope. But on the faces of these hundreds of the most wretched of my fellow creatures in London, I could see only the look that denotes that worst enemy of human progress, resignation. Men and women of all ages were huddled together on the benches, hungry and chilled, some sitting indecently close for warmth.

Sometimes I wish I did not live so near the Embankment. There is something about the Embankment at night which fills me with a terror I cannot explain, a sort of foreboding concerning England's future. Last night this feeling became even more haunting than usual. Up and down I walked and looked first at the benches, then across at what we call the "ugly side," south east London, and I found no hope, no cure, no solution of the terrible problem of London's homeless poor, rain-soaked, beer-soaked, sleeping fitfully on the benches of the Thames Embankment, a minute from my Adelphi flat.

To-day I brought up this subject of the sleepers on the Embankment when Henrietta Marston called. In all London I have no other such woman friend as Henrietta, nor one more full of sympathy and understanding.

"What is the remedy, Henrietta?" I asked.

"Votes for Women!" she answered promptly.

There was a time when she would have discussed the Embankment problem with me, would have offered to accompany me another night, to look and to ponder and discuss ways and means; but now she has this one way of disposing of all problems in a bunch. She is hewing, she says, straight toward the one Big Thing, without which, she feels convinced, all other work that we women attempt to do will be useless.

"What's the use of patching, patching, when a garment is entirely worn out?" asks Henrietta.

"But if you can't get a new one?" I object.

"Well, then, I think it's more decent to go naked!" she retorts.

Not that Henrietta would ever pass a beggar without diving into her purse. In these days she gives generously, quickly, and then passes on to what she calls her "job," working for the Vote.

To-day when she told me that the first thing I knew she would be in prison, I reminded her of her husband's need of her and tried to dissuade her from going on the next window-smashing raid.

"That's all right," said Henrietta. "I've brought Jim round to the idea of my going to prison on the promise that I'll take my food like a perfect lady, so it won't be necessary for them to forcibly feed me. Besides, I want to keep my health for the years to come. When I get 'sent up,' Jim will shut the house and take lodgings for a while. What I want to know is if you'll take on Daniel?"

At the sound of his name, the short-legged Highland terrier trotted over and looked up at me, his head cocked fascinatingly on one side, as if to say, "Will you have me?"

Wouldn't I just! "Of course, I'll take him on," I said, stroking his stiff hair, and then I added,

"Henrietta, you ought to have a baby to play with Daniel."

"No," said Henrietta, "not till we get the Vote. Jim quite understands that. Rather a good way to make him keen for the Cause, if he gets into the House of Commons, don't you think? You know he's nursing a constituency. No Vote, no Baby in our house. If all the women would go on strike in that respect, we'd get the Vote in no time."

"Like Lysistrata and her women," I said, mindful of Lawrence Housman's play, which we had both seen round the corner at the Little Theatre.

"Yes," said Henrietta, "only I suppose there'd be black-legs who'd spoil everything."

"Mrs. Havie is in favor of a general strike of women on every conceivable matter of work and love," I said, referring to Havelock Ellis' wife by her pet name to all those of us who love her. "At the Lyceum the other day she had a ring of us around her trying to help her plan it out, but in the end we gave it up, because we didn't see how it could be done."

"Couldn't!" said Henrietta. "Mrs. Havie's a dear old thing, but she's not always practicable. Her idea is that on a certain day at a certain minute of a certain hour, all women should stop whatever they're doing and sit still and not do anything again till the men give them the Vote. Doesn't it stand to reason that the men would say, 'Sit still and starve and be damned! We won't wait on you!'

"As far as I'm concerned, at any rate, I'm practicable, and

other women could take the same course if they would. Jim knows I want a baby, but I don't intend to bring a girl into the world to be treated as if she were created just for some man's pleasure."

"Might be a boy," I said.

"And I don't intend to bring a man-child into the world to lord it over the women-children, so that's that!"

Henrietta's face was tragic. In her eyes I seemed to see un-conceived children clamoring to be born. Quickly she turned her face away and pointed across the street, saying, "Look here!"

At one of the windows of the Women's Freedom League offices opposite, stood Mrs. Despard with her white hair glisten-ing beneath the black lace mantilla which she always wears in-stead of a hat. She was helping one of her followers to hang out a colored poster. The picture showed two well dressed little English girls in a fine nursery. They were digging their fists into their eyes, crying, while a fat baby bully on the floor was playing with half a dozen toys one could see he had snatched from his sisters. In the distance was a smart-looking nurse. Underneath the picture were the words,

"Nurse says we had better get used to the Baby Brother taking our things, because when we grow up, we shan't have anything. HE WILL TAKE IT ALL!"

I depend upon the posters of the opposite windows to keep me always up to date in Suffrage matters. Every week a new poster from the League's newspaper, The Vote, is hung out, and I have only to go to my window to learn the latest news. This particular street is what the "Antis" call a "hotbed of rebellion." Several of the Suffrage societies and their news-papers are located here. In the same house with the Freedom League is the Actresses' Franchise League, with Janet Steer and Eva Moore in the foreground, and on the same floor Maude Royden edits the Common Cause, organ of Mrs. Faw-cett's non-militant society. Then there is a Militant Church as-sociation and a Tax-Resistance League, so when there are suf-frage doings in the way of meetings, processions or smashings, our quiet street becomes something of a "show-place" and ceases to be secluded and "select."

Last week, when I volunteered to be a "sandwich" to advertise a meeting, I had a painful time with my boards, because they were intended for a tall woman, and at every step I took my knees got banged and they are still black-and-blue. They are making a special pair of boards for me now, so I shall soon be fixed up for the summer campaign. It is understood, however, that I shall not be given a "beat" anywhere near Fleet Street, where I might run the risk of meeting other members of the staff of the Referee, which newspaper, though now among the most valued and helpful advocates of Votes for Women, is blissfully ignorant of that distinction. The story of this journalistic transformation from "anti" to "pro," is unique in the annals of Fleet Street.

Up to two years ago, it was known as a "man's paper," and when the editor of the then entirely man-made Referee sent for me and told me he had decided they needed a column written about women, for women by a woman, and that he believed I was the woman for the job, I was very much astonished. At that particular time I was looking for a Sunday pulpit from which I could preach the Gospel to every creature, for I felt that in these troublous times of the suffrage agitation, I had a message to deliver. But "about women, for women" was not the thing I had in mind. Yet I took on that weekly column, trusting to my wit to make it the means of reaching my goal.

The Referee was founded as a sort of Round Table at which gathers each Sunday a company of the Knights of King Arthur for the discussion of subjects interesting to men, and every member of the staff must write over the name of one of the old-time knights. I was told I must have the name of a woman who had been associated with the Arthurian legend, but that we must hit on a woman who was of reputation such as that of Cæsar's celebrated wife. It was not entirely easy to comply with this condition. The name of Melissa, the Prophetess, was at first suggested by the editor, a name which I declared sounded "sweet and sissy." Great was my joy, when after close investigation of Melissa's character it seemed to be established beyond a doubt that her connection with the knight, Merlin, in the cave, had been something more than platonic. Then the name of "Enid" was chosen, and I took my place as "The Lady at the Round Table."

"I want to warn you," said the editor, "that we are dead against Votes for Women (As if every woman didn't know that!) and don't want to pay any attention to this suffrage agitation. You don't happen to have turned suffragette, do you?"

Now, the particular society to which I belong is made up of "gists" and not "gettes." We are Constitutional Suffragists and keep within the law, while having a sort of fellow feeling for those women in other societies who don't seem to be able to keep within bounds. So, quite truthfully I said, "No, I'm not a *suffragette* and, furthermore, I promise you that I'll never so much as mention the word 'vote' without your express instructions."

"Right!" he said, and our bargain was struck.

I have never, so far, used the word "vote" or referred to the suffrage agitation, but there is nothing that women need and are determined to get by the Vote that I haven't tactfully advocated, either in my lines or between them. But, knowing that women cannot get the Vote, without the consent of men, I have so written my articles that they would appeal to men, indeed, written them *for* men, and now, in less than two years, it is said that "Enid" alone, of all London preachers, has an audience composed of more men than women, the proportions being seven-tenths men and three-tenths women. Wives suggest to their husbands that they read "Enid," but more often men suggest to their wives and other women that they go to "Enid," consider her ways and be wise. And there are women who, following this advice, become very "wise" indeed, and, smiling to themselves, keep their own counsel.

I have always liked men and had many good friends among them, and in recent years I have come to feel sorry for them, knowing that they are living in a Fool's Paradise, blind to the fact that their scepter of supremacy is bending even to the breaking point. It is my sympathetic desire and intention to drive them from their Eden and keep them from returning, if needs be, with a flaming sword. I wish to see a common scepter held securely by the intertwined hands of man and woman, and until that scepter is so held I know there can be neither justice nor common sense in world affairs.

But to say this outright from my pulpit every Sunday to the seven-tenths men of my congregation is not included in my policy. For centuries men have been declaring that women are past masters in the art of lying and deceit. Well, they have given us no choice but to gain some of our ends by subtlety, trickery and "managing." If we have been apt scholars at learning, who is to blame? Always we have rebelled, against putting the lessons we have learned into practice, but have felt that needs must when the devil has driven. In the matter of my own case in my Sunday pulpit, I confess that I knew from the beginning that I must do a considerable amount of "manipulation" and "managing" in my determination to do my part in getting rid of the necessity for eternal tricking and deceiving. I went to work on the "suffer it to be so now" plan. Jesuitical? Doing evil that good may come? Well, I am convinced that I am not doing evil, and my seven-tenths men would certainly resent any imputation of evil-doing on my part. Some of them are sick, almost unto death, and I administer sugar-coated pills which they find pleasant in the taking. That the pills are stirring up their little insides, they at present have no suspicion. Some of my women friends who are in the secret of "Enid's" identity (They are few), warn me that when the men learn that they have been "duped," their pride of sex will be so hurt that they will become my enemies and demand my scalp. Nothing of the sort. They will remain my friends and declare that they knew all along what I was doing, but didn't want me to know they knew!

My letter-bag is very heavy. I am told there can be no woman in all Europe who has so many men correspondents. Good letters, bad letters, humorous letters, tragic letters—here and there threatening and abusive letters—come daily to me from every quarter of the world. Over some I laugh, over others I cry. Some of the simple, confidential, self-revealing letters must have very private replies indeed from her whom so many call their "sister confessor." Some letters I keep, many I burn, carrying their secrets only in my heart.

Just now the violently anti-suffrage men of England are taking their last stand in the last ditch, fighting against what any true sort of logic on their part ought to tell them is bound to come. Among these is Sir Almroth Wright, with his letters in the Times, exposing the weaknesses and idiosyncrasies of women, the while he declares that man must not "tattle" on woman, because "the woman that God gave him is not his to give away!" With all the lack of logic of which many great men are capable, Sir Almroth, whose professional career has brought him almost exclusively into contact with neurotic and nerve-racked women, makes it most clearly understood in his important communication to the Times that women are continuously in a state of menstruation, pregnancy or change of life, during which times they are merely irresponsible fools and should be treated as such—kindly and considerately, of course. Therefore, according to Sir Almroth, they must not be given the Vote.

I considered long as to the advisability of advertising these amazing views by any exhortation from my pulpit, but I finally decided that Sir Almroth would make a good text. I gathered my seven-tenths men around me and left the three-tenths women to look after themselves. I explained to the men that a renowned man of science had insulted them, calling their well-known perspicacity and good sense into question. Merely and incidentally reminding them that they had all been born of mothers, though they had not been able to choose *them,* I put it to them whether they were so unobservant and such "bad pickers" as to choose the kind of women described by Sir Almroth for wives. Was what Sir Almroth said true of *their* womenkind, whatever might be the case of other men's womenkind?

Thus appealing most eloquently to their *amour propre,* I pronounced my benediction upon my beloved brethren and felt I could very well leave Sir Almroth Wright to them.

The secret of the identity of "Enid" is being well kept, but once in a while I am obliged to take some too-enthusiastic soul into my confidence in order that the Referee may not become acquainted with the good work it is doing to advance the "cause" of which it does not approve. One day this week a delightfully soft and musical voice called to me on the telephone, giving the name of a highly-placed member of Christabel Pankhurst's branch of the suffrage movement. She not only wanted to thank me for the great work I was doing but said she had just written a letter to thank the one-time "anti" Referee for having seen the error of its ways and having the courage publicly to change its mind.

"Have you posted the letter?" I gasped.

"Just going to post it," she replied.

"Don't post it," I said, "unless you want to queer my pitch."

"Oh Enid!" she said. Then there was a chuckle, and the telephone wires fairly rippled with her laughter.

Yes, we women understand one another. We may disagree as to methods, but our solidarity is unquestioned.

From my Sunday pulpit there is never the faintest trace of an "American accent" and the use of "Americanisms" is strictly taboo.

Only a few trusted confidantes whom I know intimately, like Henrietta, have the faintest suspicion that "Enid" is not an Englishwoman, born and bred, but she is supposed to have traveled a lot.

.   .   .   .

Summer is here and these are lonely times, with so many of my friends in prison, but Daniel's companionship is a great comfort to me. He and I go every day for our walks in Embankment Gardens, his short legs trotting rhythmically with mine, I having learned to adapt myself to his gait. Henrietta's time is not up yet, for she smashed an extraordinary lot of valuable plate glass before a "bobby" caught her. It was the most gigantic of all the suffragette raids and they do say that the London glaziers are in full sympathy with the *agitation,* while hoping it will be long in gaining its ends. In court Henrietta gleefully owned up to all the damage she had done and refused to engage herself to keep the peace if she were let off by a fine instead of imprisonment. Henrietta belongs to a very great family, connected with no end of belted earls, and it was plain that the judge was inclined to make it easy for her if she would only meet him half way. The night she was out on bail from Bow Street she spent at my flat on the comfortable box-spring divan which I have put in the study for the purpose of accommodating over night any particular bailed-out friend before she goes up for trial.

When Henrietta was tried, she told the judge that she intended to have children later on, which was why she had broken the windows, whereupon the judge ordered the medical experts to examine into her mental state, because it didn't seem to him that was a sane reason for a woman to go out and break windows. The doctors reported her perfectly sane, and the poor kindly old judge is still puzzling over Henrietta's reason for window-smashing. Really, it seems to me that a good many otherwise intelligent men are showing a good deal of thick-headedness over the suffragette question. But once in a while a gleam of humor bursts forth amid the general dullness, as for example the placard in the window of a great shipping company whose principal boats go to Australia. The day after the raid, in their windows was this placard:

"WE TAKE PEOPLE TO A LAND WHERE WOMEN
HAVE THE VOTE. AVENGING ANGELS,
PLEASE PASS OVER!"

And the suffragettes appreciate a sense of humor, too. On either side of the steamship office the broken windows were boarded up awaiting repair, but the windows wherein hung the placard sparkled brilliantly, without so much as a scratch.

I hear from Henrietta frequently through a chaplain go-between. In prison she is learning a lot of things. She comes into contact with all sorts of other women not of her own class, women who are there for other reasons than trying to get the Vote. To-day I got a message in which she said she wished it had been possible for me to have gone with her, because I might, on release, have been able to use my pen to help solve the problem of the sleepers on the Embankment. And then she added that, of course, *I* mustn't do any law-breaking, even to the mild business of tax-resistance because, as she explained, "Not being British, legally, the Home Office would jolly well deport you and send you back to your own sweet native, which would be really sport-spoiling. As things are now, you are very useful to the Cause!"

Yesterday was Briggs' afternoon out, and when the bell rang I opened the door to a girl stranger with bright brown eyes, dark hair and a trembling, mobile mouth. She was smartly dressed, and as she stepped in at my invitation, she didn't seem to walk, but to dance with a springy step. I knew her for an American before she spoke with her quaint though not unpleasant accent.

After she had made sure of my own identity, she announced that she was my cousin, Mary Elizabeth Atkins, from North Dakota.

"My dear girl," I said, "I haven't any cousins in North Dakota. You must be mistaking me for somebody else of the same name, but as you have introduced yourself so properly, I am going to ask you to stay and have tea and a talk with me," and I pushed her gently into a chair.

"Oh, but I am really and truly your cousin!" she said. "Not a first, but a second. My mother is your first cousin, and that makes us seconds. Oh, I hope you don't mind that I hunted you up. I came over on a Cook's tour for my summer vacation, and for years and years I've wanted to know my literary cousin. I found a book you wrote in our public library at home. And see! I've brought proof. Mother didn't know I packed it in my trunk when she was out of the room. She'd be angry if she knew, because she says it's all we've got about her family."

Her fingers were trembling with excitement as quickly she untied a parcel and placed a large old-fashioned family Bible in my lap.

I examined the purple-scrolled pages of BIRTHS, DEATHS and MARRIAGES. Yes! She had certainly brought her credentials. I could not remember much of her mother. As children we had lived in separate States, and, when we were grown, she had married and I had come to England. Now I remembered there had been invitations to visit the Atkins home, letters telling of the birth of children.

Mary Elizabeth, looking at me with her large brown eyes half filled with tears of joy at having found me, was rather enticing. She told me she was seventeen and I tried not to show any surprise that a girl of that age should come abroad without her people. I am accustomed to English girls now, and I don't know one of seventeen who would be allowed to do such a thing. I just put my arm around Mary Elizabeth and pointed to an old-fashioned looking portrait hanging on the study wall. "Yes, we are cousins," I said. "That is my grandmother and your great grandmother." Then as the girl went over and looked intently at the picture of the old lady in the traditional cap of her times, I saw a certain subtle resemblance. There was certainly no doubt that Mary Elizabeth had descended from her.

Then I asked how she found out where I lived. "Well, that was a bother," she said, laughing happily, "because you see Mother said you hadn't written for years and years, not since long before I was born, and when I told Mother about the book I found in the library, she said, 'Well, let her alone. If she doesn't want us, we don't want her'; but when Father and Mother said I could take the Tour to study the English Cathedrals I didn't say anything more about you, but I just made up my mind I'd find you."

Now her eyes were joyously glad and she squeezed my hand. "I was in the British Museum with 'the party' this morning, and it seemed such a wonderful place that I thought they ought to know everything there, and I went off by myself into the big reading room and I saw such a nice old man with lovely manners, and I wrote your name on a slip of paper and told him you had written a book and asked did he know how authors could be found. He went away and came back with a big red book called 'Who's Who,' and told me to look among the B's and that I'd find your address there, and sure enough, there you were, and oh, I didn't know you'd written more than one book!"

Certainly Mary Elizabeth was very appealing, not to say compelling. There were proofs waiting to be corrected, a half finished article in my typewriting machine—so much to do; but I let Mary Elizabeth "disturb" me. When we had finished tea, I took her for a walk, and, as luck would have it, James Barrie, smoking his pipe, came out of his house just as we were at the corner, and Mary Elizabeth fairly squealed her delight. "To think I can tell the girls at the High School that I've seen the man who wrote Peter Pan as plain as this!" Then she looked embarrassed. "I mean plain*ly!*" she corrected. "We do have very good training in grammar at our school, but sometimes I forget an adverb." Then I comforted her by telling her that even Browning had quite intentionally forgotten that same adverb when he wrote,

> "Ah, did you once see Shelley plain,
> And did he stop and speak to you?
> And did you speak to him again?
> How strange it seems, and new!"

I showed her all around the Adelphi, pointing out the houses where live present day celebrities, and told her of the dead who once made this part their home. Then we went into the Gardens and along the Embankment. It was too early for the sleepers to have gathered there, and I was glad. I didn't want Mary Elizabeth, in all her youth and brightness, to see anything so sad as that just yet. I took her to dinner at the Lyceum and pointed out to her various noteworthy women writers and artists, and I went to the Bloomsbury boarding house with her and helped her to pack her trunk, carefully placing the precious family Bible where it would be quite safe.

To-day I started with the intention of going only to the boat-train to see Mary Elizabeth off, but I decided to stay on and go to Southampton with her, so that when the boat sailed, she would have somebody "belonging" to her, as she expressed it, to wave her away.

Now I look at the delightful photograph which she has left me, and am so glad I put one of myself in the parcel of my autographed books which I left in her stateroom along with the flowers and a box of sweets for the voyage.

Mary Elizabeth has asked me to "correspond" with her, and I have promised. She will be at the High School another year, she told me, and then she is going to a university. Mary Elizabeth did not tell me much about her parents' circumstances, but by this I judge they must be fairly well-to-do, and are giving her every educational advantage. It makes me think with sadness of my little English friend, Angela Thompson, just the age of Mary Elizabeth, whose people are so poor and denying themselves almost everything in order to keep her at school.

And to-night in my London home, I can imagine Mary Elizabeth going joyfully through her parcels on the boat that is carrying her toward her home in North Dakota, which seems to me so very far away.

CHAPTER II

FOG

LONDON is enveloped in a pea-soup fog which penetrates through window cracks and keyholes. No London house is fog-proof, not even these solid old Adam-built houses erected a century and a half ago. Up in the sky a round yellow pumpkin seems to be suspended in a field of hazy smoke, the winter sun of London.

My next door neighbor, George Bernard Shaw, has just passed under the bird-table formed of my kitchen window sill, railed in. The pigeons and sparrows from Embankment Gardens are eating their breakfast of buttered crumbs. Almost I have regretted the butter this morning. Two sparrows, fighting for one bit, though the table is bountifully spread, have dropped it on the shoulder of the Dean of the Adelphi. Small wonder if that ruddy face should show a frown, but no! He looks up smiling, waves his hand, and passes on to his club for his daily tub.

He is wearing his dark gray suit, the sort of suit he always wears in winter. Though I had lost my almanac and calendar, by the color of Shaw's costume I would always know the season of the year.

When the fogs of winter have gone and the spring days come, behold his bright navy blue suit, toning with the blue sky, strolling jauntily through our street. When summer comes, white flannels take the place of blue, and, later on, matching the Dean's beard, as well as the falling leaves, a reddish brown suit reminds me that autumn is here. Through all the changes that the seasons ring, his face is always full of cheer and the Irish blue eyes twinkle under the shaggy brows. Some have compared his enigmatic smile to that of Mona Lisa, and swear that none on earth will ever guess its meaning. To

20

me, it seems a smile of expansive bland contentment, the outer symbol of a clear conscience in a naturally shy and withdrawing man.

Shaw passes on, and the fog thickens, or is it that the street is only more lonely for the want of other courageous pedestrians? From the corner of "Of Alley" there comes the sound of a street organ. It dare not come nearer, for, greatly to my sorrow, the Adelphi itself is protected by a large sign warning off musicians and hucksters. Not for us the melancholy song of

> "Who'll buy my lavendar, sweet lavendar?
> Buy, lady, buy!"

Not for us the cheery bell of the muffin-man, or the quaint call of the cat's-meat-man with his string of adoring feline followers. Having been made "select," we are cut off from the Cries of London.

Yet, a barrel organ, if it will but take the route from the Strand through "Of Alley" to the corner of Duke Street, cannot help but make itself heard, even though unseen from my window. I have but to stand on my balcony and, taking good aim, speed a copper with resounding effect upon the cobbly paving of Duke Street to bring the wandering minstrel to the corner, hat in hand and bowing thanks.

Now, though I cannot see the organ nor its grinder, I know what is happening in "Of Alley." The man is playing near the public house, at which are gathered dozens of little boys and girls, waiting for their fathers and mothers to drink their "elevenses" beer and come out. There are small girls, putting the babies they have been minding down upon the ground, then, lifting their skirts with little red hands, and little boys with hands on hips or in ragged pockets. They are circling and dancing around the barrel organ as only London's little children of the poor can dance.

"Aw! Maike it fawster, Mister, maike it fawster!" they cry. There is a tightening and a straining and a hurrying of the grinding:

> "When we are married we'll 'ave sausages for tea,
> Sausages for you and kisses for me!"

while the children fairly whirl till they are dizzy, with the babies on the stones in their tears and their dirt erstwhile forgotten, till a drunken mother comes from the public house, wiping her lips and smacking a dancing child, shouting,

"That's 'ow ye minds yer baiby brother, is it?" and the organ grinder wanders on and the children scatter.

I close my window against the fog, and in the silence that only the Adelphi can know, my mind goes back over the past few months, which I spent in New York and Washington, returning a week ago. I went over as political correspondent for the Daily Chronicle to "do" the Presidential Election from the point of view of an Englishwoman, writing under the name of "Mary Mortimer Maxwell," my old New York Times nom-de-plume when I so successfully posed as "An Englishwoman in New York."

It was several years since I had been over, and certainly I found myself able to write as an outsider, a looker-on from England. I interviewed various politicians, saw Taft, Roosevelt and Wilson. I wanted the opinion of the Governor of New Jersey on a very important point for the paper I represented, and when I was introduced by a common friend, I looked for something needing to be cabled rather than a little thing that might wait for the slower mails. From the affable ex-President of Princeton University I received a delightful disarming smile, and a friendly letter which at first I thought was just what I wanted, but which, upon a re-reading, I found to mean just nothing at all. I don't envy Wilson's opponents or his own party leaders when he takes office next March. That smile! Yes! But, oh that jaw!

Now I, the third member of what has become known in Fleet Street circles as "the Trinity," try to separate myself from "Enid" and "Mary" and to think things over clearly, forgetting my triple personality.

I remember arriving at the dock, and the argument with the customs inspector. Was I an American citizen? Yes. Had I bought more than one hundred dollars worth of clothing and knick-knacks since I left America? Great heavens! I am an economical woman. I haven't much money to spend, but there is a limit to the clothing and "knick-knacks" that a hundred dollars will buy in quite a number of years. Politely and smilingly I explained this to the inspector.

"How many years?" he asked. I counted them on my fingers and told him. He scratched his chin, started to go to the head office and thought better of it, spread my clothing nicely in the till of my trunk, banged the lid, handed me my keys, and put the "passed" chalk-mark on my bags and boxes. It was fortunate that the examination took place late in the evening when the inspector was tired. In one way I had nothing dutiable, in another way everything was dutiable, for all I had was bought outside and away from my native land.

They welcomed me at the little New York hotel where I had stopped years ago, though, of course, all the servants had been changed times without number since last I was there. Pearl, the coal-black chambermaid was friendly and familiar, very unlike the stodgy but proper Briggs, whom I had left in charge of my London flat.

I happened to have a white woman to do my laundry, and I remember the little daughter of that laundress better than any one else I met in New York. There was a knock at my door one morning, and when I opened it, I found a huge oblong parcel suspended, apparently, in mid-air. Finally I noticed two small hands on the side of the parcel that faced me, hands that did not meet, but clutched the paper covering, so I asked the parcel to walk in, loosened it from the little hands that held it and discovered what had been behind it, a girl aged twelve or thirteen with shining brown eyes, nicely combed hair topped by a fetching hat, a figure clad in a becoming scrim frock.

"Good morning, little girl!" I said.

"Good morning!" she answered. "I'm Millie Lucca, and them's—I mean *those* are the clothes!"

"So you are studying grammar?" I said, noting the quick correction in her speech.

"Yes, so I got Mother to let me bring the clothes this time so I could ask you."

"Ask me what, my dear?" I said, pushing her into a chair.

"Whether it's 'politics is' or 'politics are' " she said. "My father can't read English very well, and my mother doesn't know grammar, but the elevator boy told her you were a writing lady, so she said you'd know."

She paused breathless, but without confusion or embarrassment. Her absolute lack of self-consciousness was something I had not seen in a child for many years. She did not need encouragement, but I smiled and said, "Yes, Millie."

"You see I want to know before I go to school, because we're going to have a lesson about collective nouns to-day. It seems to me that 'politics' are plural—more than one, but then it may be multiple like 'crowd' or 'party,' and then it would be 'is.' "

I explained to her that though the matter was sometimes muddling for older and wiser heads than hers, according to the best authorities I had consulted, one could most properly say that "politics is," whereupon she drew an exercise book from her school-bag and wrote,

"Politics is an interesting study at the present time, because we are having an election."

It was a curious and novel experience to me, this discussion of the intricacies of grammatical construction with a washerwoman's daughter. I learned that her father was an Italian day laborer, and as she was the only child, her mother was able to employ some of her time in laundry-work. The father was naturalized, and the child, having been born in New York, was a native American citizen. She fascinated me, and I asked her to come again, and the next week she brought me a "composition" to read. She spoke quite confidently of what she would do when she had "graduated" from high school. She was going to be a teacher, she said, a teacher of "things about plants and bugs and stones," and one Saturday morning I took a vacation from politics and went with her to the Natural History Museum.

And now in London, in the fog, I keep thinking about that little girl, daughter of my American laundress who "doesn't know grammar" and the one-time Italian and newly-made American who "doesn't read English very well."

Briggs is very restful to me these days. When she first came to me she took offence because I didn't call her to get my hat and coat and gloves whenever I was going out. She informed me that when she lived with "one lady alone" she always "maided" her. I began to protest that I was accustomed to waiting on myself, but she said, "Yes, Madam, but I always 'ave maided one lady alone," so I submit to being "maided." Briggs has a little niece, about the age of Millie Lucca, who sometimes comes to see her. She was here yesterday and I tried to get acquainted with her by asking about her school and her studies. The child was almost tongue-tied, though I understand from Briggs that she is very bright. She is, so Briggs tells me, to go to school till she is fourteen and then is to go as a kitchen-maid in some titled family where her mother and grandmother worked before her.

"Will you like that?" I asked the child.

"Yes, Ma'am," she said.

New York was in the midst of the notorious Becker Trial when I was there. New York seems so often to have a police scandal on hand that one can hardly keep track of the number. The official guillotine was vigorously at work and heads were falling one after another. To one of the good citizens I said,

"New York is very ugly, morally, these days, isn't it?" and he replied, "Does your house in London look nice and pretty in the middle of a general house-cleaning time? We're doing some fall-cleaning just now in New York, and the dust is flying—some!"

"It seems to get in one's eyes and mouth and nostrils," I said. "In London, I don't seem to remember ever hearing of such scandalous doings."

"No," he said, looking me sharply in the face, "over there, you are not so apt to *hear* of them! When we suspect dirt here, we search till we find its hiding place, and then we sweep it right out into the very center till it shows and stinks to heaven in the sight and nostrils of all good citizens, who then have a hell of a cleaning-up. In England they sweep dirt into the corners and make believe it isn't there."

After my trip, where so many things seemed new and

strange, I suppose it is natural that my mind should revert to recent experiences in New York and Washington, but the little things, rather than the big things I saw or experienced seem to remain more in my memory. One day in a large New York store I was carrying a library book under my arm. A girl was serving me with peanut butter.

"Can I see your book?" she asked.

Automatically I handed it over to her, without at once thinking how extraordinary her question was. She looked at the title and glanced through two or three pages.

"Is it a good book?" was her next question.

"I think so," I answered, "though I haven't read it yet." I did not tell her that I knew the author, and that he always wrote good books.

"I'll just jot down the title and get it at the library," she remarked, using her shop pencil. "I should think you'd know good books. When I see customers carrying books, I always take notice."

She handed the book back to me with a smile and a polite "Thank you."

To-day my mind seems to be full of the memories of little incidents like these. The little daughter of the laundress and the girl who sold me the peanut butter seem to have become a sort of panorama unfolding before my eyes. They are not as though they were new, but as though they were old, belonging to the past. They are like memories of bits of old songs running through the mind when at night, sleep will not come and the silence is full of music, once familiar, but long since forgotten.

On the whole, though New York and Washington interested me, they worried me, tired me. In the mad scramble of a presidential campaign, this is not to be wondered at. I was busy all the time earning my living, for it has always been with me that if I do not work, neither may I eat. I was glad to be busy, for if one is to be an onlooker, one should have something to do with one's onlookings. I turned mine over to British newspaper readers, who read and are still reading them, and that will be the end of what I did in New York and Washington. It will not live, it was but a skimming of the surface of things, superficiality. That is how I reckon up the work of the past four months, and yet I know I am not a superficial person. I like to dig down deep into the heart of things. I know I didn't do this. If there was a heart to them, I did not find it. I could not, for the life of me, discover any particular meaning in the election.

I think I felt more interest in Taft than in the other two candidates, because his position had elements of pathos in it— fat, jolly, fighting a battle which he and all his followers knew he could not win. His making public of the letters which passed between him and Roosevelt worked him irrevocable harm, though I heard it hinted that British imperialists ought to be exceedingly grateful for the quarrel that took place between these two men. The latest mail brings me a letter from Washington which seems to confirm this idea:

"We are all greatly interested here in Canada's offer to spend thirty five million dollars for three dreadnoughts, but there is a difference of opinion as to why it was made. Something of the sort was to be expected after Taft publicly opened the box o' tricks in the matter of reciprocity when he spoke of regarding Canada as an 'adjunct' to the United States. It may be that the dreadnought idea comes in certain sequence.

"In any event, those Canadians who had no objection to the 'adjunct' business were the first to be furious that Taft had given the show away, and who can blame them? It was bound to be followed by protests of loyalty to the British Crown. More than he had any thought of doing, Taft has probably succeeded in changing the whole course of the history of the British Empire. . . ."

Then he whom I always call "The Democrat," because his keenest desire is to be a real democrat in the broad and not in the party sense, proceeds in a more personal manner:

"You say that during your recent visit to New York and Washington (It appeals to my sense of humor that you should refer to your native land as a place to 'visit'!) you could not see that American institutions were more democratic than British institutions; that our elective machinery is not more democratic, and that there is not as much real liberty here as in England. This particular subject I cannot take up in this letter. I can only say that the peculiar kind of work you have done for the past many years in England seems not to have opened your eyes.

I remember you told me that you could not help noticing that while the Englishmen you met had 'manner,' the majority of Americans seemed only to have *manners*. You mentioned the lack of polish the average American shows as compared with the Englishmen whom you know. I will just remind you that there is a process of polishing that makes the surface very hard, very clear, but very thin, so thin that a discerning woman ought to be able to see through it. . . ."

I seem to have taken into my system the Microbe of Restlessness while I was in America, and I cannot get rid of it. The weeks have gone by since my return to London and now it is February, 1913. As the events of my visit recede somewhat in the distance, I find that my clearest recollection is of a Land of Discontent, where nobody was satisfied and where everybody I met seemed to be climbing a ladder. Some were on the lower rungs, some on the middle ones, others near the top. If those on the higher rungs made mis-steps and were flung back toward the lower, they began climbing again almost before they stopped to take breath.

I could not find any of my old friends living where I had left them years ago. They seemed to have been moving from house to house and flat to flat. When I asked them if they hadn't any real sense of home as an abiding place, they would reply that their present homes were so much better than their former ones, and that they'd rather have the trouble and turmoil of moving and settling them than to stay still and not progress.

Well, back here in London, I don't want to move in so far as my home is concerned, but I seem to want to keep *on* the move, trying new kinds of work, not content to just write. I want to dig, dig into things more than I ever did even in my earliest days of journalism, and then when I find out things by investigation I don't write the result of my investigations, but go on to something else.

Henrietta came out of prison before I went to America, and, of course, she took Daniel home. Briggs is no companion at all. I tried to interest her in some of the new time-saving and step-saving inventions that I found in American houses, and I couldn't get a rise out of her. "Yes, Madam, I suppose it *is* different from 'ere at 'ome," was all she would say. I brought her a convenient whisk brush, sharpened to a point for getting into corners, but I can't make her use it because she never *has* used that kind of a brush. I was on the verge of flying into an unholy rage with her two weeks ago because she wouldn't use a new American polishing cloth I had brought over, one that does away with the necessity for any powder. She folded the cloth neatly away in a drawer, got out her plate powder and had it all over the kitchen, though I will say she is as neat and careful as anybody can be with it.

Then one day I said, "Briggs, pack my box. I'm going to the Provinces."

"Yes Madam. 'Ow many changes shall I put in?" she asked, and late in the afternoon she handed me into a taxi and I took train for Birmingham. I went over several of the factories and became friends with the makers of buttons, hooks-and-eyes, needles, hair-pins and safety-pins. I went to Sheffield and watched the shining manufacture of knives.

Sometimes I labored among men and women as one of themselves, and was glad that I had not lost my old-time skill at dissembling and pretending to be an ordinary English working woman. As nearly as I could I spoke their dialect, and if to them I seemed "different," they put it down to my being a London woman. In this way I got invited to their homes, played with their children, offered to mind their babies while mothers rested their work-worn bodies or got a little pleasure from going to "the pictures." I went down to the mines of Lancashire and watched miners risking their lives for twenty shillings a week, and I cried over the miseries of the poor blind pit-ponies. This was too awful, so I went to Manchester among the weavers of cotton and the spinners of silk.

I found many married women operatives in the mills there, married early, old at thirty, breeding like rabbits. There was one who had borne seven children in as many years, buried five of them and was back at work two weeks after the birth of the eighth, born dead. A "district visitor" sought her out, and in the kind but never-understanding way of her class, said,

"Mary, what is the use of having children, just for them to die? And if they lived, you know you and your husband could not support them. There is such a thing as self-control, a restraining of passion—"

"Oh Gawd!" interrupted the woman, *"yer* can talk so, with yer belly full, but many a night *that's* all *we* 'ave for supper!"

I am back in the Adelphi. The fog still hangs black and heavy over London. Will it never lift?

CHAPTER III

DISCORD

IT is now more than a year since I returned from America, and the Microbe of Unrest has departed.

The spring of 1914 has chased away the fogs of winter, and London is full of sunshine and new paint. Happily now I tend my little garden of daisies and geraniums in my balcony window-boxes. Daily I walk in Embankment Gardens, often accompanied by Daniel, who is "lent" to me by Henrietta while she goes flying all over the country alone in her car, never so much as inviting me to go for a single trip.

"No, my dear," she said the other day, when I invited myself to go along. "I'm visiting lots of quaint little churches, and listening carefully to sermons and things. I say my prayers, too, so you see I must go alone."

"Henrietta the Heretic," as she is known in her family, visiting "quaint little churches" and listening to "sermons and lessons and things"! Henrietta saying her prayers! This is a new kind of Henrietta, one that many people would not be able to connect up with the old. I notice that she always carries a little silver-trimmed book and pencil and that sometimes she stops in the middle of a conversation to do a bit of scribbling. Yesterday when we were discussing the atrocities of hobble skirts and the sensibleness of trouser-skirts, out came her little note-book, and down went a jotting.

"What have I said that's so smart you must write it down?" I asked. "Nothing!" said Henrietta. "I happened to think of a little Bible verse, that's all."

Jim is now nursing another constituency, his former one having refused to "wean," and gracefully Henrietta gives up the car to him when he needs it. She will then take a train for some out-of-the-way place where a little church may be found, noted for its historical associations, its font or its stained glass. Then back to town again, secretive but jolly. That's Henrietta these days.

That is the reason I had Daniel with me to-day in the Gardens when I walked past the Arthur Sullivan memorial. He stopped respectfully at the railing while I read the inscription:

> "Is life a boon?
> If so, it must befall,
> That Death, when'er he call,
> Must call too soon."

The Gardens are gay now with flowers and shrubs, with large people and small people, and babies and dogs. Yes, life is a boon, and London is all-glorious these spring days. This is the London that James Russell Lowell loved, although he loved it in other seasons, too. Once he declared to an Englishman that he loved London in all its phases.

"Perhaps you have something kind to say about our fogs!" jested the Englishman.

"I have!" retorted Lowell. "I've found them beneficial to my asthma!"

In my adoration of London, I do not go as far as that. I live through the winter in the hope of spring, the spring that now is here.

.   .   .   .

The spring and the London "Season" have come together, and with them both, this year, has come Mrs. de Plays Bingham. Also Miss de Plays Bingham, for that, I find, is the way their card reads. Yes, "their" card, for although the daughter is of an age quite sufficient to have a card of her own, her name still appears beneath her mother's. Mrs. de Plays Bingham understands that over here an individual card for an unmarried daughter is one of the things that "are not done." In that, she shows herself not thoroughly up to date with many young Englishwomen. As far as certain aspects of life in England are concerned, Mrs. de Plays Bingham is twenty years behind the times.

I first met Mrs. de Plays Bingham in France two years ago.

We stopped at the same hotel. That was because a newspaper was paying my hotel bill. When I go on my own, I stop at a little pension on the fringe of the quarter. Mr. de Plays Bingham was not with her. He is the sort of American man who, while his wife travels abroad, stays at home and works, and keeps a mistress. After I got to know Mrs. de Plays Bingham, I felt that Mr. Bingham (without the "de Plays," which she says is a family name of her own) ought not to be blamed if he kept a harem.

Ill health and the need of that "repose," which she says cannot be found in her native land, are the reasons Mrs. de Plays Bingham gives for spending so much of her time abroad. Italy, Sicily, the Riviera, Greece, Austria-Hungary and Egypt have all been homes away from home for Mrs. de Plays Bingham. She has visited England, of course, but this morning when she called, she told me she had never, till now, been able to spend "the Season" in London.

When she walked in on me in the midst of my work, I could not believe that she had hunted me up out of pure affection. I am not the sort of person that rich Americans who live abroad generally "take to," nor do I seem particularly to "take to" them. Most of my friends on this side are British.

Mrs. de Plays Bingham and her daughter, Adele, were, she told me, living in Mayfair. She had taken a furnished house in one of those humble-looking streets, which have little more than a narrow hall in the named street, with a much larger part fronting, or, as I always persist in saying, "backing" on the park. Many Americans have come to understand the value of living in these streets. They give an "air."

"That is to say," continued Mrs. de Plays Bingham, when she had told me of the furnished house, "I pay for the house, but it is in Lady Emmeline's name," whereupon she began to explain to me just who was Lady Emmeline, and who were her ancestors. Had I heard of Lady Emmeline? Oh yes! I had heard of Lady Emmeline.

Lady Emmeline, it seemed, was supposed to be having Mrs. de Plays Bingham and Adele, two distant kinswomen, stopping with her for the Season. There was an arrangement that Lady

Emmeline was to "get" Mrs. de Plays Bingham and Adele "into society."

"And did she 'get' you in?" I asked, remembering that Lady Emmeline has the reputation of being one of the cleverest "getters" in London. She "gets" old prayer rugs from shopkeepers and sells them on a high commission from the very floor of her drawing room when rich Americans admire them. She "gets" a Burne-Jones or a Leighton or a Frith from a dealer, hangs it on her walls and sells it to a millionairess right down from the moulding—"seeing it's you, dear!" If any woman in London society could "get" Mrs. de Plays Bingham within the charmed circle, that woman is certainly Lady Emmeline.

"Well, she did and she didn't," replied Mrs. de Plays Bingham to my inquiry. "She's had nearly everybody worth knowing at the house to meet us, and she's taken Adele and me about a great deal, but yesterday she told me an astonishing thing. I expected to be presented at the first June court—Adele, also, of course. I told her that in the beginning, and it was quite well understood. Of course, you know we couldn't have a regular contract, stamped at Somerset House, about a thing like that."

"Yes, I understand," I said, turning my head and stroking Daniel.

"We had," went on Mrs. de Plays Bingham, "what men call a 'gentlemen's agreement.' In this case it would be a 'gentlewomen's agreement,' wouldn't it?"

"Would it?" I murmured.

"She's done everything according to the agreement, except this, which is the really important thing, what one would call the 'essence' of the agreement. She says she can't present us at court, although we would be presented from 'her' house, and she's attending court herself this year; that she'll give the 'presentation tea,' everything, except the actual presentation. She says that must be done through the American Embassy by the Ambassador's wife."

"Yes," I said, "that is the mode of procedure for American citizens. I can assure you there can be no doubt that Lady Emmeline is right."

"I can't believe it, though I don't want to contradict you," replied my visitor. "I think Lady Emmeline has some other reason. She may be playing for another three thousand."

"Dollars?" I asked.

"Pounds—I mean *guineas!*" said Mrs. de Plays Bingham, with rising voice. "She always puts everything in guineas!"

"Well, guineas are generally 'the thing' in the fashionable world. In fact, they are 'the thing' in the business world. Personally, I don't care for editors who say 'pounds' to me."

I smiled and tried to induce Mrs. de Plays Bingham to smile. She wouldn't.

"What I started to say," she continued, "is that I don't believe Lady Emmeline, and think you yourself must be mistaken, because I've known dozens, yes scores, of Americans who have been presented by titled people of the very greatest families—dowager countesses, and even duchesses. I know them personally."

"What! You know the dowager countesses and duchesses personally! Then why didn't you—"

"No!" interrupted Mrs. de Plays Bingham. "I know personally the Americans who were presented by them, and I know the American Embassy had nothing to do with it."

"When were they presented?" I asked. "They can't be young Americans."

"Well, what difference does it make whether they were young or middle-aged? But some were young, yes."

She named half a dozen American girls, that is, American women who had been girls in the early nineties. She confessed she did not know any who had been presented in that way since 1895.

"It can't be done now," I said.

"But Lady Emmeline advertised only six months ago, I answered her advertisement. Look at this!"

She handed me a newspaper slip by which I saw that Lady Emmeline, under cover, discreet as always, offered her social services and protection to wealthy American matrons and girls.

"She doesn't say she will present at court. If she had, you could sue her for obtaining money under false pretences."

Again I stroked Daniel, looking deep into his honest doggy eyes.

"Sue! You can't sue on a thing like this! I tell you that the presentation was taken for granted, was actually mentioned by me as an understood thing!"

Almost there were tears in my visitor's eyes. Certainly there were tears in her voice. For the life of me I couldn't think why Mrs. de Plays Bingham should have come to me in her trouble. We were only the merest acquaintances. I wanted to get back to my interrupted work.

"I can't help you," I said. "I can only again assure you that neither Lady Emmeline nor anyone else, except the Ambassador's wife, can present an American citizen at the English court. I know this. Why don't you go to the Ambassador's and present your credentials, though I should think it's rather late, even now?"

Then I looked meaningly toward my typewriter with its half finished page of a story.

"I'm just a working journalist, you know," I added.

"That's it!" exclaimed Mrs. de Plays Bingham. "That's why I came to you. I came to ask you to expose Lady Emmeline. You're smart enough to do it without mentioning names. You can turn suspicion on her without giving her name, and, of course, my name mustn't go in. You just write the thing in such a way as to show this Englishwoman up. She's probably duped many another American," and from what I know of Lady Emmeline, I rather fancy she has.

"And this is why you called on me?" I asked. "Lady Emmeline did convince you, then, that, at least, she was honest in telling you she couldn't present you?"

"No, I wasn't convinced, but I thought if you confirmed what she said, then I'd get you to expose her, because she led me to believe from the first that the presentation was in her hands."

Again I was on the point of mentioning the Embassy, which is within ten minutes by taxi, when it occurred to me that Mrs. de Plays Bingham must know why she preferred the roundabout way rather than the easy and plain one, if she were a legitimate candidate for the honor to which so many of my countrywomen seem to aspire.

"I'm sure you could get a big price from an American paper for the exposure," went on Mrs. de Plays Bingham, looking at me very meaningly, "but if not, you can depend upon me—"

I didn't know whether to laugh or to swear at her. In the end, I did neither. I took her hand and said. "Now, I must get to my work, but I'll give you the very best advice without charge— Go back and make it up with Lady Emmeline. Why, you two women ought to be as thick as thieves!"

Then I was alone. The sun still shone, the daisies and geraniums still glistened brightly in the window-boxes; a pigeon from Embankment Gardens perched himself on the balcony railing and said as plainly as possible, "Any buttered crumbs at this time o' day? Plenty of *un*buttered ones over in the Gardens!" I offered him a piece of thin bread and butter which he ate from my hand, then flew away. From across the street, proceeding through the open windows of the flat above Barrie's, came a droning sound, the noise of the shiftings of Joseph Pennell's printing press, and I wondered what new beauty of old London he might now be transferring to paper.

From the Adam doorway of Number One, four flights beneath the printing press, I saw John Galsworthy, with his earnest face and the Christ-likeness in his eyes, come out and look toward the River, with that sad smile of his which seems to say, "I have sounded the depths of woe that I might proclaim to you the world's miseries. Man and beast suffer always. How shall one be glad?"

Around the corner from the Terrace came Temple Thurston, looking keenly, stepping lightly. A good day for Temple Thurston, who has now forsaken the paths of his youthful genius which led him to the great heights of "Sallie Bishop" and "Traffic." Perhaps on this wonderful day he will find right out in the Strand by Charing Cross another "City of Beautiful Nonsense"—who knows?

As I sit at the window, Daniel's small self is curled up at my feet. He is asleep and dreaming. I know there is beauty all about, but now I cannot see it. The visit of Mrs. de Plays

Bingham has spoiled the spring for me. The sound of her voice lingers with me like a harsh strident note breaking into the music of a heavenly choir. Discord, discord everywhere.

What strange co-incidence sent Mrs. de Plays Bingham to me to-day to ask me to "expose" the misunderstanding that had been brought about because, long ago, another "exposure" by an American girl had been the sensation of two continents!

Times flies backward, and the years become as though they had not been. An American girl came over to London for just a few months to find the whereabouts of some English relations, paying her way by writing "pieces" for the American papers. She never found the relations, but she found England interesting and enticing, and she stayed longer than she had expected to stay.

London seemed to be full of Americans, some very, very rich. Many of them had great houses, town houses and country houses. Others came but for a time, remaining during what the American girl learned was known as "the Season." Some of these Americans she knew by name and reputation. They had tried to make their way into New York's "Four Hundred," at the portal of which stood Ward MacAlister barring their way. But over in London the American girl heard of their going about with what were called the "best People" and being presented at Court.

In the London newspapers the American girl found such advertisements as these:

"A LADY OF TITLE wishes to borrow £2000. Would act as chaperon to young American lady."

"TO WEALTHY AMERICANS—A lady of good position, speaking several languages, will chaperon ladies on the Continent during the winter, and receive them into her London home for the Season. Introductions. Address in strict confidence——"

Then an idea came to the American girl. The idea seemed to hold great possibilities in the way of copy, and she went to the office of the newspaper which she was told was read by all the "best families," the Morning Post, and inserted the following advertisement:

"Young American Lady of MEANS wishes to meet with a chaperon of highest social position who will introduce her into the best society. Liberal terms. Address 'Heiress'——"

Then, to the number of eighty-seven, came answers, written on the choicest note-paper, topped by coats-of-arms. Great titled ladies, many of them dowagers, wrote in the kindliest and most charming way, offering to take the young American lady of means into their homes and under their wings. Names, names, names, of women of rank and men of rank, till the American girl's head fairly whirled at the propositions made by the owners of the names, and at the thought of her own great social prospects, if only she had possessed those "means" she had falsely declared were hers. No references were asked of her, except those of bankers and solicitors—she had to hunt up the meaning of the word "solicitors" and found they were the same as lawyers.

Great ladies were willing to take her completely in charge, pretend she was a kinswoman from America, give her the finest suites of rooms in their town and country houses, introduce her to their highly placed friends and acquaintances and present her at court. There were men of title who said they wrote for their widowed mothers or sisters. Others poo-pooed the idea of the young American lady of means bothering with feminine chaperonage. They advised marriage, when there would be nothing extra to pay for going to Court, since the young American lady, having become a member of a great English family, would be "presented on her marriage."

Appointments were made for meetings, and the American girl was considerably "put to" in the matter of dressing herself expensively enough to carry out the "heiress" idea, but by dint of borrowing both finery and jewelery, she managed to give the correct impression of wealth. Her manners and general bearing, also, seemed to please, one dowager telling her that she had not nearly so much "accent" as she had feared. "You are," said she, "what I should call just 'nicely American.'"

"Terms," of course, were touched upon in a gentle, lady-like way. Prices ranged from £500 to £10,000, according to the rank of the chaperon, locality in which she resided, and the opportunities afforded for meeting marriageable men. All the terms included Court presentation.

Then the American girl, greatly to the surprise and chagrin of those with whom she had begun negotiations, seemed to disappear, and nothing more was heard of her till that fine old Tory evening newspaper, the St. James's Gazette, began publishing a series of articles entitled "The Almighty Dollar in London Society." As the Morning Post went into the homes of the "best people" every morning, so the St. James's Gazette went into their homes in the evening, and those who had answered the advertisement in the Post read the series of articles in the Gazette, giving no names nor addresses, but quoting their letters in part or in whole, with pointed remarks by the American girl.

Aristocrats now wrote frantic letters to the girl, begging for the return of their own letters, and received answers assuring them that all the original letters had been burnt. Close upon the newspaper publication came the gathering of the chapters together into the American girl's first book. Then reviewers rejoiced that they had something in the way of real "liveliness" to report. At the office of the Pall Mall Gazette the editor passed the book over to a rising member of his staff who was known to have "views" of a Fabian nature on the subject of "our old nobility."

"You might give it a spread," said the editor, and that is how it happened that the book got a full column review by George Bernard Shaw.

And now all over England town houses and country houses trembled upon their very foundations. Everybody in society suspected everybody else of being in the "chaperonage" business and of being the writers of the letters the American girl quoted. Ladies out shopping in Bond Street suspected one another of being able to patronize that select and expensive district because of "easy money" obtained from American aspirants to social recognition. Lady B. seeing Lady C. would say to herself, "I really believe she was as great a fool as I was in replying," while Lady C. would laugh within herself and think, "Ah, my dear! I'm pretty sure you were duped, too!" Aristocratic young and middle-aged men without "means" would meet at their clubs and discuss the latest social sensation, and damn themselves for having been such fools as to use the club note-paper for their correspondence.

In one of the largest mansions of England, a little old lady had the St. James's Gazette serial read aloud to her every evening as the separate parts appeared, and as she listened she grew very ashamed and angry. She was ashamed for her country and angry at the women who were offering for money to introduce this unknown and unvouched-for American "heiress" not only into society but to their Queen.

One evening the reading of the sensational exposure of the power of the Almight Dollar in England's high places was interrupted by the fierce tapping of the little old lady's stick upon the floor, while she exclaimed,

"It must be stopped! A new rule!"

The little old lady was Queen Victoria.

CHAPTER IV

SOME LETTERS FROM "THE DEMOCRAT"

I AM receiving some very interesting letters from the Democrat, who is taking a holiday from American politics and is making a leisurely tour of the England that is outside London. What he has to say of the effects of Oxford on American boys is giving me something to think about:

Oxford, April—, 1914.

. . . I fear that Cecil Rhodes did us a very bad turn when he provided those Oxford scholarships for American boys. I never was enthusiastic over this part of the will of the great Empire Builder, and now that I have spent a couple of weeks here, I am convinced that the sending of American boys to the old English universities is a mistake.

Rhodes' intentions were all directed toward bringing about harmony and understanding between the two countries, an important thing for the good of the world and the peace of the world. His virile mind and keen judgment did not often lead him astray, but had he understood a little more of American institutions and habits of thought, I feel sure he would have bound up his scheme with more conditions.

It is, as you know, fifteen years since I was last at Oxford. I am glad that this year, instead of making merely a hurried visit to London only, I am able to renew acquaintance with the smaller towns, villages and country parts of England, and I left London last month with your very urgent warning in mind—to look about me for the very conspicuous signs of England's progress toward democracy. I must tell you that up to date, I have come across very few signs pointing that way.

To be sure, here in Oxford, I have made the acquaintance of

a number of earnest men, young and middle-aged, who are looking things pretty squarely in the face, and I have renewed some old friendships with men whom I find to be in the path of Progress; but, on the whole, I find that Oxford is as Oxford was. I am struck with it as a place given over largely to the worship of the God of Sport and the spoiling of the English language, hide-bound, caste-ridden, and governed by the dead hand of Tradition. After hearing the modern Oxford pronunciation, accent and intonation, I am no longer quite so ashamed of the "slanguage" of our American college boys and girls.

I have made a point of getting acquainted with some of the American boys here, sons of our wealthy men, as well as the Rhodes scholars. The Oxford atmosphere, far from fitting them to take their places in American life, is filling their heads with ideas and tendencies unAmerican and undemocratic. One of the American boys has just been telling me that Oxford is "too damned democratic, don't you know, what with niggers from India and Ruskin College for workingmen." I pointed out to him that Ruskin College, which is not a part of the University, is a standing witness to the world of the English caste system, that where democracy is, there is no need for special and separate colleges for "workingmen." As to the "niggers from India," as he calls them, they seem to be sons of Oriental potentates under British rule. I asked this boy to introduce me to the son of any little green-grocer or laboring man who was "working his way." Another American boy called my attention to the fact that the most "popular" undergraduates wore the raggedest gowns, but as I knew something of the extent of the credit given by Oxford tailors to these same "popular" young men for their ordinary garments, I refused to accept ragged gowns as a proof of Oxford's democracy.

Perhaps it is of little consequence, one way or another, what a few rich American men, living at home or expatriated abroad, do in this matter of their sons. Such boys rapidly become de-Americanized and will probably end by giving up their nationality; but the boys picked out for the Rhodes scholarships make an altogether different case. In the end, they are likely to return to their native land, unprepared for taking up useful work there, while even if they wished to remain in England, I doubt if they will find a place here. I do not undervalue a certain amount of time spent in the old English Universities (although personally I should prefer one of the Scottish ones) by mature Americans, after they have their groundwork in our own public schools, high schools and State universities, if they then have time and opportunity to take a post-graduate course. The mellowing influence of Oxford or Cambridge should do them good, would not denationalize them, and they should bring us back something worth while.

County Durham, April—, 1914.

. . . Since I have been visiting the smaller English towns, I am reminded of a paragraph in Kipling's Curse of America. I think it was never published in the British or American newspapers. I happened to see it in an old copy of the Pioneer Mail, of India, somewhere about the year 1889. After various other unpleasantnesses he wished for us, he did his damnedest with this:

"You shall be cursed State by State, territory by territory, with a provincialism *beyond the provincialism of an English country town.*"

Well, I am finding that Kipling, in his youth, knew his English country towns quite as well as he seems to have realized certain of our American deficiencies. It was in 1899 that I last saw any of the English country towns. I presume they were then the same as when Kipling wished them onto us in 1889, and now they seem to be about the same as I knew them fifteen years ago. I am meeting a good many people, though in a different social circle, who reminded me of your quaintly conservative Briggs! I find little inclination for the newer and better ways of doing things, and I see little difference in the relations between employer and employed, except such as the trades unions have made necessary with threats and strikes. Even so, the increase in wages is so little that it is hardly worth consideration, although I am told that an increase of a shilling a week in a workman's wage sometimes represents a big conquest. The patience and endurance of the English "working class" is beyond my comprehension, but it cannot last forever. Surely there must come a time when the last forelock will have been touched in servility, the last groveling "thank you kindly sir" have been spoken and the last straw of humiliation and insult borne by the workman's back. Then, if there has not arisen a British Henry Ford (and his sort does not seem to grow in English soil), I should think there must come revolution. There is, of course, the Labor Party, which may fill the breach. The existence of the Labor Party, by the way, impresses me like Ruskin College, a witness to the world of an undemocratic Britain. The Conservative Party we know, with its what-I-have-I-hold principles, but that the Liberal Party ever allowed it to be necessary for a Labor Party to be formed, passes my political understanding. It looks to me like a case of Liberal suicide, a slow, long drawn-out suicide, of course, but death, nevertheless.

I have always been an admirer of what is great in British statesmanship, and surely in the past it has shown more than mere moments of greatness. But the present *impasse* in Ireland and the lamentable situation in regard to women's suffrage cannot certainly be the result of true statesmanship but of political intrigue and self-seeking. I say all this not as an international intermeddler, however. You asked me to give you some of the impressions I received of British politics and social questions, and I hand them on to you. My chief impression is that of the absence of any truly big leadership over here, and I think the whole nation might very readily be praying:

> "O God, for a man, with head, heart, brain,
> Like one of the simple great ones
> Gone for ever and ever by;
> One still strong voice in this blatant land—
> Whatever they call him, what care I?
> Aristocrat, Autocrat, Democrat,
> One who can rule, and dare not lie."

May—, 1914.

I am experiencing the same unbounded and delightful hospitality in these small towns that so many of our countrypeople have experienced over here. It is all quiet and restful, and the Englishman knows how to let his guests alone if they want peace, which many an American host forgets to do. . . .

One notes the maturity and ripeness of the English country town as contrasted with the rawness and crudeness of the small American town, but in those raw towns of ours there is no deadening self-satisfaction as there is in the English small towns. We have, in all conscience, sufficient self-esteem, but that is not the same as self-satisfaction. Our "Boosters" fling out their banners of "Welcome! Watch us Grow!" and that makes for health and progress. When I see the ripeness of the English small town, I wonder what will come next. Ripeness is not an enduring state. It is pleasant while it lasts, but it must naturally be followed by decay, sometimes even to senility. These country towns, these Cathedral cities that I am visiting, what next for them? . . . Let us hope that it may really not be ripeness after all, but only a case of arrested growth and development, which is not always incurable. . . .

May—, 1914.

. . . You certainly seem to have been most successful in disguising your nationality in your writings during these later years of your career. I often hear your name mentioned and your work praised or criticized, but people make no mention of the fact that you are an American woman living in England. In the library to-day I found my host reading something of yours, and he passed it on to me with a recommendation! In some of your work I search for signs of your nationality, but never find them. This does not mean that all writing must show nationality any more than that all writing must proclaim the sex of the writer. There is literature that is non-national and non-sexual. It is the same with many of our thoughts. We do not always think nationally or sexually, but just humanly, and you have done some of that sort of thinking and have put your thoughts into writing. But there are kinds of work in which both sex and nationality should come to the front for the sake of justice as well as for the sake of art. There is a healthy sex-bias and a healthy national bias. I am convinced that there are times when you purposely suppress the national bias in your writing, and in so far as you purposely suppress it, you weaken it.

You see, I refuse to regard you as having really lost your nationality and love and preference for your own country, its ways and its people. You are my countrywoman, lost in a maze, wandering round and round, trying, even though perhaps unknown to yourself, to find your way out. Of course, I know some of the reasons why you may be happier, at times, living in a foreign land—for it *is* a foreign land, however much you may laugh at the notion of being a "foreigner" in England. If you are absolutely sure that your reasons for spending so much of your life here is good, then, in God's name, live as an American, not as an Englishwoman, and write as an American when the opportunity offers. There is much that you, as an American, might tell the British people that will be good for their souls. You have a deep love for children, but I ask you what have you done really to help the children of England? Yet, what could you not do, if you would write as an American, and dare to proclaim your views as an American. I have seen you stand watching little children shivering and crying outside the London public houses. I have seen you give them pennies, I have heard you speak gently to them, I have seen the tears in your eyes—and that was all. It is not enough. If you are going to live over here for the rest of your days, *do something*. Leave your mark on England.

May—, 1914.

. . . In London I grew rather tired of hearing so much about the comparative thickness of blood and water as referring to men like myself. When will the British learn that England is no longer the Motherland of the United States? You and I are of pure British descent and, in a way, England is our Motherland, but when I think of the many Americans I know, even those who are my closest friends, I do not find that anything like the majority of them are of British descent. If they think with affection of a Fatherland or a Motherland, they cer-

tainly do not think of the British Isles. I remember once
being with Roosevelt when this subject came up. He had been
accused of being anti-British in his feelings, (It was after he
had been instructing Britain what to do in Egypt) and he was
counting off on his fingers the different kinds of blood he
had in him. I have forgotten how many different races he
declared had gone to his making, and he is one of our finest
and most representative Americans. It was that same evening
when he said, "People accuse me of being impulsive, but I
just want to tell you that most of my 'impulses' are pretty well
thought out beforehand!"

There is too much sentimental talk about the language of
Shakespeare uniting our two countries. We had better take
heed that it does not eternally divide us to our mutual and
infinite harm, for language is the medium used for deceiving
and making misunderstandings.

My host here speaks very pleasantly of our "common language," ideals and purposes, while exhibiting the grossest ignorance of American institutions, and still greater ignorance
of the customs and institutions of the British Dominions.
Finding that I know Canada well he ventured to ask me what
chance there was over there for a nephew he seems to have
on his hands and wants to get rid of. "Just down from the
Varsity," he said, "and at a loose end just now—ought to be
doing something. What about a Canadian civil service job
for him?"

I tried to explain to him the scarcity of civil service jobs
for Englishmen in Canada, and the need for farmers. "Yes,"
he said, "but even with taking up government land, he'd need
money for machinery and agricultural laborers. I don't know
about the gentleman-farmer idea!" It was all I could do to
keep from saying, "Damn it, man, who said anything about
'gentlemen farmers'? If your nephew is strong and has common sense, let him take off his coat and put his hands to a
Canadian plow and tractor!" Well, he went on to say that
"we English" educated "our boys" at a pretty high cost, and
it seemed to him that "our colonies" ought to find places for
them, and then he came out with this;

"There ought to be good openings for English public school men over there—got no public schools there, I understand. Too bad! He might start a good public school there, or a chain of them, I should think—get some other fellows to join him— What do you say?"

At first I looked at his whiskey glass to see how far down it had got, but he hadn't drunk a thimbleful as yet. No public schools in Canada! A call for Englishmen to go over and start them! Then just in time I remembered how the language of Shakespeare made for cleavage not only between England and the United States, but between England and Canada. He was referring to the Etons and Harrows and Rugbys and Winchesters—those exclusive and expensive schools called "public"—for what reason no American or Canadian can ever understand. I tried to explain to this average Englishman, of the "county families" class, the educational system of Canada, precisely like the educational system across the border, but I gave up trying to penetrate through his density. . . . And one of these days I expect to hear of a Canadian knocking an Englishman down for having applied the term "colony" to the Canadian's country!

This conversation reminded me of the reason I had been disappointed in not finding the kind of English family life which I had anticipated during these visits. I like boys and girls of school age, and I told one of my hostesses I was looking forward to seeing her young sons.

"Ah! You have just missed the holidays," she said.

The other day I met the wife of one of the curates here. She excused herself for a tear-stained face, explaining that it was because she had parted from her boy who had been sent away to a preparatory school. When she happened to mention his age—eight—my heart went out in pity to the poor little chap and I felt that his parents ought to be had up for cruelty to children. Later, when I learned that the curate was in receipt of less than fifteen hundred dollars a year all told and saw the state of poverty in which he and his family (three other children) lived, I did some strong thinking on the subject of English customs and English family life. . . .

May—, 1914.

. . . . Luck has just come my way in the matter of meeting a most refreshing specimen of English girlhood. The young lady of the house where I am now staying has been brought home from a girls' college under circumstances that, to me, at least, are absolutely unique. Before she arrived her father explained to me that they had withdrawn her from —— Hall because of the pernicious teaching she was receiving from "godless women" who declined to read certain of the Anglican Church lessons at chapel because they taught the subjection of women. The whole teaching staff, it seems, is made up of suffragists who, though taking no part in militancy during term time, yet teach the girls that militancy is the only way to force the government to give women the vote.

This young lady and I have struck up a friendship that promises to be truly invigorating and illuminative to us both. She seems to be about eighteen or nineteen, and is almost distractingly pretty with that English complexion of which we hear so much. She has a way with her that is truly disarming.

"Do you believe in votes for women?" she asked, as she was showing me the greenhouses on the afternoon of her arrival home.

I told her that, being a democrat, I held to the first principle of democracy, which was equal and universal suffrage.

"I suppose your American women don't have to do what we do to get the vote," was her next remark. I explained the American situation to her, told her the number of States which had already given women the suffrage, and went thoroughly into the difficulty of amending our federal constitution, in order to enfranchise the women of the nation at one stroke. I found her a most appreciative listener and with a much better understanding and open mind than many of her elders. Yesterday she said to me,

"Dad's an old 'woman's-place-is-the-home' Tory, Mother's a constitutionalist and a 'votes-for-ladies' woman, Peter Paul is a silly anti ass, and I'm a suffragette."

I ventured to inquire as to the identity of Peter Paul, of whom I did not seem to have heard.

"That's my half brother," she said. "I call him Peter Paul because he looks like a Rubens madonna. He's over twenty-one, and when an old relation of ours dies, Peter Paul will sit in the House of Lords and make laws. He's got a vote now, because he's male. Brains and sense don't count in voting, you know. It doesn't matter that he never passed an exam. in his life till Dad hired a 'crammer' for him, oh no! He's got no mind, but they'll let him vote now, and when he gets in the Lords he'll try to keep me from voting. Of course a lord doesn't count for much in politics these days anyway, so he'd better be there than in the Commons. Now, why do you suppose he's to succeed our relation?"

I suggested that the relation might be a bachelor or childless.

"No!" said she. "Respectable married man, but no *sons*. Daughters don't succeed, and even if they did succeed to the title, you can bet they wouldn't let them help to make the laws. You see, if they had some smart women in the House of Lords, the poor lords would be made to feel their own stupidity!"

I asked her if she really cared much about the House of Lords, anyway, and she replied,

"Why, of course not. It's a perfectly putrid place! I only get furious about Peter Paul going there because it's an insult to my girl relations. Never mind! They're suffragettes, too. They're at the same school where I was, and they'll stop till end of term all right. I'd like to see their father try to take *them* out!"

The girl's next grievance was that, not satisfied with having broken up her last term at school—the father's doing—, her mother had refused to present her at court this summer. I was surprised that such a fierce little democrat should mind this, so, diplomatically, I drew out her views on the subject of royalty. She informed me that she cared nothing about royalty *as* royalty, that "of course, a king doesn't count in a constitutional monarchy," that Queen Victoria was "a preposterous person," having "the cheek to be a queen and not do anything for her own sex, and then saying that a poor old pioneer woman suffragist, so brave and heroic fifty years ago, ought to be horse-whipped because she made a speech about women's rights on a public platform!" She went on to say that Queen Alexandra was "well, you know—just a consort and that's all, but Queen Mary's a good old suffragette—why, didn't you know that Beatrice Harraden wrote to her about the way the government treated the suffragettes in prison— perfectly disgusting—and she used her influence to have them let out, without promises about keeping the peace, either, mind you—Queen Mary's just ripping!"

I thought I understood, then, why my young lady wanted to go to court—because "Queen Mary was a good old suffragette," but no, that turned out not to be the reason.

"Mother's afraid I'll disgrace the family at court—she's made some other excuse to father, but that's it."

"Surely not!" I said.

"Surely, yes I would, according to her idea of disgrace, for once let me get within speaking distance of the King, and I'll ask him what about votes for women."

When I reminded her that she had just said the King didn't count, she answered,

"He doesn't really, but, you see, to ask the King what about votes for women, would advertise the cause. Maybe they'll have to stop giving courts any more, like they've had to close the galleries and museums and the show gardens— you're lucky to see ours—we intend to make England shut up shop completely if they don't give us the vote."

I don't know how much you know about the plans for the summer suffrage campaigns, but this girl tells me there will be no golf links in the United Kingdom fit to play on, that Asquith and Lloyd George will be serenaded nightly under their windows wherever they try to sleep, that many bishops and deans are "marked men," and that throughout August, when, according to her prediction there'll be war in Ireland, (she is well up on the Ulster question) the women will make the lives of cabinet men a veritable hell on earth. Altogether, she predicts an August of considerable carnage. She has a little auto of her own and expects to use it for "the good of the cause," and I should think my host is in for a troublesome summer.

She tells me she trusts me not to talk to "Dad" on the subject, that he doesn't know she "got bitten" at the school, congratulating himself that he got her out "uncontaminated" and in time. It seems her mother knows she's "bitten," but keeps it secret from the father. I am wondering if there are many other English girls like this one. If so, our American girls, brought into contact with them, will have all they want to do to hold their own. And with girls of her sort growing into womanhood, and women like the teachers she describes at her school, I should think there is hope for old England in her women, even, if, as I seem to be finding, the men are deteriorating.

By the way, I have told my young friend that I know you, and have given her a card to you for use when she goes to London, and she says she will be "fearfully bucked" to make your acquaintance.

Sussex, May—, 1914.

. . . Through a chance remark of a *grande dame* here, I have learned what that girl meant in describing her mother as a "votes-for-ladies" woman. I was being shown over a wonderful garden this morning, and passed one of the gardeners, a fine upstanding man with whom I made acquaintance yesterday when I told him about some trouble a Southern friend is having with his magnolias. I found him to be a man of keen intellect and with knowledge which was, by no means, confined solely to the subject of horticulture.

When we passed the gardener, my *grande dame* said to me, "There is an example of the sort of thing that infuriates us Englishwomen. My *gardener,* who is my servant, has a vote, while I have none!"

I must say I wish she hadn't made that remark, because it throws me back to my old fear for the future of England as a democracy. Had she said, in passing her husband (I admit she couldn't have done so!) "You see what my husband is, and yet he has several votes, while I haven't even one," I could have measured the strength and justice of her protest. He is as near a nonentity as any man can be. He has no mind above riding and going about to kill something. His knowledge of the possibilities and responsibilities of the British Empire is less than that of an American primary schoolboy. He never earned a penny in his life. He doesn't even manage his estate or look after his tenants. A useless existence! But here was the trail of the Serpent of Caste winding through the mind of this charming and highly intelligent Englishwoman. Her *gardener* voted and she did not!

Washington, June—, 1914.

. . . Home again now, I have many things to think about. Memories of beautiful green country-sides, delightful hospitable people, old London with its everlasting lure, linger in my mind. I hope to return some of the hospitality, and the returning cannot come too soon for me, for I should like to show some of my English friends certain phases of American life of which I found them woefully ignorant. I should like them to return home, remembering something of our country besides wining and dining at our clubs and in our more prosperous homes, automobiling about New York, Boston and Washington, even something more important than visits to the homes of Longfellow, Whittier, Whitman, the Alcotts, Oliver Wendell Holmes. I should like them to realize that we have other institutions of learning than Harvard, Yale, Columbia and even the University of Chicago. I should like to introduce them to your little protégé, Millie Lucca, and explain to them what she stands for. In New York I hunted her up and found her in an evening school helping her father and mother with their lessons—that is she was minding the youngest baby while her mother studied, carrying it over to the mother for its occasional nourishment. Millie is fifteen and is in the High school. I gave her your parcel of books and she was delighted. She is a little girl of the finest sort, and her parents will make good citizens. The Americanization process is costing the tax-payers some money, but it is worth it. . . .

. . . I saw W. as soon as possible after my return. It happened that as I entered the room, he turned his full and all-smiling countenance upon me and I was encouraged to make a beeline for what I wanted. While I was putting very neatly my points, I happened to get a side view of the formidable jaw, and I knew it was all up with my proposal. That is where so many of us make mistakes about approaching him. Hereafter when I want anything from that quarter, unless it is golf, I shall be careful to get the side view first!

Well, better a well-fixed obstinacy than a too yielding temperament. It seems to me that we, like England, are particularly in need of strong leadership just now, and it may be that we have found it. . . .

CHAPTER V

JULY, 1914

A STRANGER, descending from an aëroplane upon London during these days of July, might think he had lost his way and had landed in the United States, for American flags are floating from hundreds of buildings.

"Oh, these Americans and their flag-waving!" he would say, and smile.

The American tourists are here. Their number is greater, so they say, than it has ever been in any previous July. This is why, according to the summer custom, the Star Spangled Banner flies so proudly in Oxford Street, Regent Street and other streets, to attract them to the shops. During the past ten or fifteen years the British shopkeepers have learned a lot about advertising!

Signs are everywhere displayed explaining that "American money is accepted here," and all goods are marked with their value in dollars and cents, immediately following the pound, shilling and pence mark.

The tourists are buying greatly and largely. The men are even "falling for" the English straw hats, recommended to them by the newspapers and the shopkeepers. The women are attending the bargain sales and getting wonderful values in the left-over spring stocks of hobble skirts and flaring coats. All London seems to be laying itself out to please the Americans, and, judging by the smiling and satisfied faces of the tourists, London is succeeding. Even the managers of some of the theaters that remain open during July and August, are agitating the question of distributing free programmes at the play, knowing how the most generous and extravagant of Americans can be moved to profanity by a sixpenny charge for a programme. If this is done, the innovation will not be permanent. The thought is only for the tourists. One house has already put out its sign, "WE DO NOT CHARGE FOR PROGRAMMES."

I cannot go near my windows now without seeing parties of Americans, for they always haunt the historic parts of old London, and the Adelphi is a favorite sight-seeing neighborhood. With their Baedekers and their opera and field glasses they go tramping over the cobble stones of the Adelphi arches and stand wrapt and enthralled at those parts where Dickens wandered while he gathered material for David Copperfield. They stand outside the Savage Club in the Terrace, waiting to see some celebrated brave come forth from that famous tepee; they gaze lovingly at the placque on the house next to the Savages which tells of David Garrick's living and dying there. Then round the corner into our street they come to run their fingers over Shaw's sterling silver door-plate and wonder if they dare climb the stairs to the lair of the lion.

Yesterday a tourist, an old friend of mine from Minnesota, sat at one of my windows which sometimes commands a view of Barrie, pipe in mouth, sitting at a table writing. It did that yesterday, and I called her attention to a form screened by a curtain. She watched, awed and fascinated, and then asked,

"Does he live there all alone?"

"No, he lives there with Lady Nicotine," I answered.

To-day I have had a telephone message from her.

"I somehow wish," she said, "you hadn't told me that scandal about Barrie—and you spoke of it in such an off-hand way, as though it didn't make the slightest difference to you, so long as you could live in a street of celebrities."

"I don't understand," I said.

"I mean about Barrie and that titled foreign woman."

Most of the wealthy American expatriates who live at the smart hotels or have their town houses here, have now left London, along with the English society people. They will stay awhile at the seaside and then join country-house parties on August 12th for the shooting, for this is the English way and whatever the English do, trust these faithful imitators to do. Because blood-lust is fashionable, the men become as like as possible unto "country gentlemen" for the nonce, and what the

smart Englishwoman does, the would-be smart American tries
to copy. The other day I met a member of this particular set.
She has a three weeks' old baby and is preparing to go away
"for a rest." I said something that showed I took it for granted
the baby would go, too, whereupon she exclaimed,

"Oh dear, no! I'm sending Baby to another place with her
nurse. Royalty and the smart English women always do that,
you know!"

Come to think of it, a great many of them do, but what a
pity Americans should try to copy this inhuman custom.

In the parks, the squares and all over the streets of every
part of London, children are playing at war. They have flags
representing Ulster and Southern Ireland. There are old brooms
and sticks for rifles, small barrels and pails set up on perambulators or chairs for machine guns, and folded newspapers or
wrapping paper serves for military caps. They are shouting
"Up with the Union Jack and Down with the Pope!" and "Up
with Home Rule and Free Ireland!"

The children are drilling because grown men are drilling.
London companies of Ulster and Nationalist volunteer are
openly preparing for civil war in Ireland, and even companies
of Amazons for both sides are being drilled by Anglican clergymen and Catholic priests. To those of us who have thought of
England as a land of law and order, it is all an amazing spectacle.

I am making a study of British laws and constitutionalism,
and I am continually puzzled. There has just been a conference
on the Home Rule Amending Bill held by the leaders of both
sides at Buckingham Palace in the presence of the King, and the
King delivered a speech. The papers report that he read it to
the leaders and then left the room to Asquith, Carson, Redmond and the other eight members of the conference. There
has been considerable criticism of the speech, and Asquith
announces that he himself, not the King, is fully responsible for
every word and every phrase of the King's speech, and what
are they going to do about it? In so far as I can understand
it, the Prime Minister wrote the speech and handed it to the
King, who "spoke his piece," as he was told to do, and there

you are. In that case, just why did they go to the Palace at all?

The government is treating the Ulster rebels in such a lenient, not to say, gracious, way, as more than ever to infuriate the leaders of the Women's Suffrage movement. Even those who, up to now, have obeyed the laws and taken no part in militancy are wondering if their motto "In quietness and in confidence shall be your strength" is really worth while. The men rebels are fawned upon, reasoned with, treated with, even when they defiantly march to Westminster with their banner, "ULSTER WILL FIGHT AND ULSTER WILL BE RIGHT!" Suffrage women marching quietly along the streets bound for the House of Commons in order to present a petition, are ordered away by the police and if they refuse to go, are forcibly turned back. The encounters between the women and the police are becoming absolutely too horrible to contemplate. For the past four or five years this sort of thing has been going on. I remember when that little actress, no bigger than my thumb, Winifred Mayo, was first arrested for joining in a deputation. A great burly policeman, one of London's biggest, charged her with "obstructing the police." Winifred, looking for all the world like a tiny, dainty bit of Dresden china, extended her hands toward the magistrate and said,

"Now, really would you believe it?" and not a man in court had enough sense of humor to laugh, though there was a titter among the women spectators.

Woment of title have attempted to take a Petition of Rights to the King at the Palace, and were not allowed within the gates. This refusal is not the King's, but the refusal of his ministers, who say *they* are the King's deputies, yet when the women try to approach them in a legitimate way, turn the police on them. When the members of the royal family go driving now, they have little balls of rumpled paper thrown into their carriages. The authorities and the newspapers then cry out "Women insult the King!" The whole idea is merely one of advertisement for the Cause and a determination that the seriousness of the position shall be understood by the King.

At the June gala performance at Covent Garden, a woman in the stalls rose and addressed the King, who was in the royal box. My impression is that she did it without instructions from the leaders of the movement and that she was too troubled and excited to measure her words, for she called out,

"You Czar of Russia sitting up there!"

Nothing could have been further from the mark, and the form of her address was unfortunate, for if there is any Czardom in England it comes from Downing Street and not from Buckingham Palace.

It turns out that the Democrat's little friend need not have feared that the Cause would not be represented and proclaimed at Court when her mother refused to present her. At one of the June courts, two young women, sisters, daughters of Sir Michael Blomfield, the noted architect, and granddaughters of an Anglican bishop, Mary and Eleanor Blomfield, stood straightly before the King and Queen, neglecting the usual curtsey, and said,

"Your Majesties, for God's sake stop forcible feeding in the prisons!"

Then these two particularly pretty girls, looking lovely in their court costumes, walked quietly out, leaving the King and Queen staring after them, the courtiers angry and certain ladies-in-waiting looking pleased. Now I hear that such ladies as desire are wearing their militant suffrage badges at court while in attendance.

Herein lies one of the sources of strength of the suffrage movement, that women of the highest society are engaged in it, so there is no place so exclusive and so sheltered that the voice of demand cannot penetrate. Gone are the days when, to believe in "women's rights," meant to be dowdy. Among the suffragettes are some of the most fashionable women in London. Some of the more energetic workers have been feeling rebellious against hobble skirts, which can be very hampering, indeed. Being unwilling to go back to old fashions, they are ordering skirts slit at both sides with buttons and button holes. They are now climbing fences, scaling ladders and trees with impunity.

Before the schools closed, I went to spend an afternoon at one of the girls' colleges. I found twenty-five of the girls in the playgrounds with four of the mistresses in their caps and gowns. They were learning a song for some of the closing exercises, one which I understand will be much used for the August serenading of cabinet ministers to keep them from sleeping too soundly. It was Crawford's parody on Sir Harry Bumper's Toast song from The School for Scandal:

> "Here's to the baby of five or fifteen,
> Here's to the widow of fifty,
> Here's to the flaunting extravagant queen,
> And here's to the hussy who's thrifty.
> Please to take note, they are in the same boat,
> They have not a chance of recording a vote.

> "Here's to the lunatic helplessly lost,
> Of wits, well, he simply has none, sir,
> Here's to the woman who lives by her brains,
> And is treated as if she had none, sir.
> Please to take note, they are in the same boat,
> They have not a chance of recording a vote.

> "Here's to the criminal lodged in the jail,
> Voteless for what he has done, sir,
> Here's to the man with a dozen of votes;
> If a woman, he wouldn't have one, sir.
> Please to take note, they are in the same boat,
> They have not a chance of recording a vote.

> "Here's to the lot of them, murderer, thief,
> Forger and lunatic, too, sir,
> Infants and those who get parish relief,
> And women—it's perfectly true, sir!
> Please to take note, they are in the same boat,
> They have not a chance of recording a vote!"

Among the girls I noted a beautiful creature with short hair of the loveliest auburn. One of the teachers told me that this girl's guardian had stopped her spending-money because of her lavish gifts to the Suffrage Cause. Then she went out and had her hair cut off, selling it for five pounds, in order to make a contribution to the August campaign. Teachers and pupils all saved their hair-combings to sell to hair-dressers to get money for the same purpose.

Henrietta came in this afternoon bringing a matinee ticket for Briggs, which meant that she wanted to talk without danger of being overheard. She got out her little silver-trimmed note-book and asked me to typewrite from her dictation.

She handed me a Bible from the bookcase and began:

"First Corinthians, eleventh chapter, eighth and ninth verses —hunt them up, that's a good girl," she said, while her fingers turned over the pages of her little book. I hunted and wrote:

"For the man is not of the woman, but the woman of the man. . . . Neither was the man created for the woman, but the woman for the man."

Again Henrietta called out, "First Corinthians, fourteenth chapter, thirty-fourth and thirty-fifth verses—hunt them up, child," and again her fingers swept through her little book. I wrote,

"Let your women keep silence in the churches, for it is not permitted unto them to speak; but they are commanded to be under obedience, as also saith the law. . . . And if they will learn anything, let them ask their husbands at home; for it is a shame for women to speak in the church."

"Now Titus, second chapter, fifth verse," said Henrietta, and I wrote:

"To be discreet, chaste, keepers at home, good, obedient to their own husbands."

"Now hunt in Timothy, first epistle, second chapter, eleventh, twelfth, thirteenth, fourteenth and fifteenth verses."

I found it and tapped out:

"Let the woman learn in silence with all subjection. . . . But I suffer not a woman to teach nor to usurp authority. . . . For Adam was first formed, then Eve. And Adam was not deceived,

but the woman, being deceived, was in the transgression. . . .
Notwithstanding, she shall be saved in child-bearing."

On through the Pauline Epistles went Henrietta, till it
seemed she had made a note of every verse which taught the
subjection of women. So swiftly did her fingers turn the pages
of her little book, so glibly went her tongue, that I had difficulty in keeping up, rapidly as I am able to handle my machine.

She took the Bible away, dived into her smart green leather
bag, brought out a prayer book, and read to me extracts from
the marriage service to match the verses from St. Paul. She
herself wrote the names and locations of churches scattered
throughout England, with dates of sermons preached from
texts which she had quoted, so I knew I was not intended to see
them.

Then she thrust her hand into her bag and pulled out cuttings
from newspapers.

"I want a lot of copies of these," she said. "How many car-
bons can you make?"

"Five at a time," I said.

"Will you do them three times, making fifteen copies?" she
asked.

"Yes."

"All right. We change now from Paul to British newspapers.
Now quote:

"Man assaulted girl of fourteen. Penalty, five pounds fine or six
weeks imprisonment. . . . Man indecently assaulted girl of fifteen, fined one pound and allowed a fortnight to pay in, and the
magistrate said 'We must protect these girls!' . . . Man of thirty
assaulted girl of eleven in a railway carriage, penalty one month's
imprisonment. . . . Man assaulted a little girl of five, given
sixty days imprisonment. . . . Offence against a girl of seven,
man to choose between three pounds fine or two weeks imprisonment. . . . Indecent and violent assault on girl of eighteen, ten
shillings fine. . . . Man assaulted own daughter aged eleven,
penalty one month's imprisonment. . . . Assault on young woman
in railway carriage, two pounds and costs. . . . Assault on child
of four in a dark passage-way, man fined two pounds and costs.

... Three boys, one after the other, assaulted a little girl—and were bound over for six months. . . . Assault on girl of eight, penalty two months imprisonment."

After each of these cases, Henrietta gave me dates and localities to write down, and proceeded with an hour's dictation of further details of assaults and attempted assaults upon children and the penalties inflicted. Finally, when she had turned the last leaf of her little book, I stopped, out of breath, and went out to the kitchen and prepared tea.

I wanted to ask what she was going to do about all this, but I did not. It is quite understood that, though Henrietta trusts me, she does not tell me everything. What she wishes me to know she tells without questioning on my part. When I had returned with the tea, she said,

"I've found out there is a conspiracy among a certain number of clergymen and politicians opposed to giving women the vote. The parsons are to preach in and out of season on such texts as I've been giving you. I've been around listening to their sermons and making notes of them. I've done it in the most quiet and 'ladylike' manner and haven't made a single interruption. Now, these men, who are supposed to be well educated, know quite well that anything Paul said on the subject of women, as on many other subjects, which were merely his narrow opinions, anyway, could not possibly have a connection with the present time. They know, too, that Christ never taught the inferiority or subjection of women. Women were Christ's best friends. He taught the moral equality of the sexes, and he told the men who brought to him the woman taken in adultery that those who hadn't committed adultery themselves might throw the first stone—and you can jolly well believe they slunk off at that!

"Now, to each one of the parsons in the Conspiracy who've been preaching sermons on these pretty little Pauline sentiments, I'm sending a copy of this report of only a few of the recent assaults on children and the trivial penalties the men are paying—I'm using the fifteen copies you've made to-night, and I wish you'd do some more for me. I'm writing a nice personal letter, in my own pretty hand-writing, asking them if they will preach a sermon on the text, "But whoso shall offend one of these little ones," and to make this report of how the little ones of England are being 'offended' a part of the sermon. If they'll do that, it might stir up some indignation and shame among people who have no idea of the state of things. I'm sending each parson a stamped addressed envelope for his reply, asking for a reply before August 1st."

Calmly now Henrietta drank her tea, even stopping to compliment me on my new cups and saucers. It seems to me I have never known a woman so full of beautiful sentiment and yet so practical and so lacking in all signs of hysteria as Henrietta. She is as healthy in mind as in body and never neglects her daily exercise in athletics. Unlike many English-women of her class, she does not go in for hunting or any blood sports although she has her own riding horse, and she tells me she even gave up fishing some years ago because the fish were too beautiful to kill. She never has a caged bird in her home, though I have known her to buy lately-caught wild birds from the bird shops and then take them to the parks and set them free.

"I've been seeing some horrors in some of the pretty little country churches, I can tell you," she said, after a silence that might mean many things. "I've looked on while filthy old reprobates were married to virgins, with what the vicars said was God's blessing. Last month I attended a christening ceremony where a libertine and a harlot stood as sponsors at the font and had the cheek to promise what an innocent baby should do and believe in the years to come. I heard one rich pampered parson, hand and glove in with two wealthy mine-owners, preach to some miserable devils of half-starved miners on the text 'And having food and raiment, let us therewith be content.' I've listened while women were told to 'submit themselves' unto their profligate husbands 'as unto God.' If God has a sense of humor, he must have many a good laugh over what happens in our State churches.

"You see, they *are* a part of the State, our churches, and therefore it is justifiable to attack them for political wrongs.

They are part and parcel of our political machinery— Why, they can't even change the marriage ceremony to make it clean and decent without the consent of Parliament—not that they want to change it, of course. So women who feel they must be married in church are still submitting to the insults of the officiating clergyman when he tells them he is marrying them as 'a remedy against sin,' meaning if he doesn't marry them, they are bound to commit fornication."

I had never before heard Henrietta make more than a passing reference to the Church. I have known, of course, that she was not a good "churchwoman," that she considered her religious belief her own private affair and that she had refused to be married in the little church on her father's estate, and had been married at a registry office in her traveling costume. Now this afternoon, her mind seemed to be continually reverting to the wrongs which the Church was perpetrating on women.

"The worst foes we women have in all England," she said, "are to be found in the Church, and, besides, look at the bishops living in luxury in their palaces, kept up by the State, while poor people starve. Some of the best women in the country have been quietly urging their right to ordination, because they believe they're called of God to preach, and they want to do it in their own church. Listen to this from one of the Church papers —'A little band of women have pushed the claims of their sex to such a point that they have lost all sense of proportion!' This eggs on one of the smart secular papers to burst out into poetry:

> " 'See the new woman of to-day
> A candidate for ordination!
>
> .   .   .   .   .   .
>
> And some may think that they can see
> In her desire to be a parson
> A kind of further guarantee
> Against more sacrilegious arson.'

"Now, doesn't that sort of stuff show how useless it is to be quiet and 'lady-like' in trying to get our rights? These women who have put in their claim to preach, in the *state* churches, mind you, supposed to belong to *the People,* aren't militants. They are just quiet, good women, with great souls, convinced that the church is as much theirs as the men's, and so fun is poked at them in this way. . . . Dark places, our churches! The stained glass makes them like dungeons. Their darkness is going to be lightened a bit. . . . Oh, their chained Bibles and expensive fonts and solid plate! I can fancy Christ going into them and driving out the priestly money-changers."

A silence fell upon Henrietta. She stroked Daniel and looked curiously at me. Finally she said,

"Be thankful you're out of it all!"

"Out of what, Henrietta?" I asked.

"I mean that you're not one of us—you don't belong. In a way, you stand outside it all, and you needn't be ashamed for your country."

"Do you mean that I'm an outsider because I'm an American? I don't *feel* an outsider!"

"No matter what you feel, or *think* you feel, you are an on-looker here, and you ought to be glad of it. The things that are taking place in this old country couldn't be in your new land. They'd be out of the picture. Lynching is in the picture, but not these things."

"Oh, lynching!" I said bitterly. "Talk about being ashamed!"

"Lynching's wrong, but it shows something in your men-kind that's not common over here. I'd like to be proud of being an Englishwoman, but I'm not."

"Yet I don't suppose you'd change your nationality to be an American or any other nationality," I said.

"No! That's it! There's something queer and uncanny about 'country'—I don't profess to understand it, but there it is. As I said, you don't belong, and you don't have to feel ashamed."

After Henrietta left I could not settle to any work. I have always known she trusted me implicitly and relied on me for certain help that only I can give her. This is the first time she ever spoke as though she regarded me as a foreigner. When she reminded me that I would be deported if I broke the law to help the women, I took it in good part. But to-night she told me I didn't belong! Nonsense! We are almost one people, anyway. I felt that on the Fourth of July when I went to the Embassy reception. There were the Stars and Stripes and Union Jack intertwined over the doorway where Walter Page stood receiving almost as many British as Americans. The British, there to help celebrate the day when the American Colonies broke away from them! It actually appealed to my sense of humor, and I mentioned it to Mr. Page . . . I'm glad he's here. He understands Anglo-American friendship for what it is . . . I remember how I first made his acquaintance and how it ripened into friendship. Years ago he rejected a book of mine in such charming language and with so many compliments as to its merits that I sent it back to him, saying I found his office boy had made a mistake—that he couldn't possibly have meant to send back a manuscript so chock full of good things as he said mine was. Would he read it a second time and confirm my impression that he had made a mistake? It came back again, with a still more complimentary letter— It had everything desirable in it except money, it seemed! I told him there was more satisfaction in getting a rejection from him than an acceptance from other publishers. I was spending a year in New York at the time and I went to see him and we became friends. I'm glad he's here. Still, on the Fourth he said in a quizzical sort of way, "Now, let me see, you *are* an American, aren't you?"

.   .   .   .

The days seem to leap away, despite the warm weather. A friend of Henrietta's, that nice young Labor man, called and gave me news of her, as he has been in the Provinces. He says there's nothing the Suffragettes haven't thought of, even to making a complete list of the mistresses of their chief opponents, and all the gay houses they may be inclined to visit during their August holidays. He thinks there'll be civil war in Ireland, but that's no reason why the women should give up their so cleverly-mapped-out August and autumn campaign. He saw an immense placard on a Berkshire church:

"Owing to the Dastardly Outrages by Frenzied Criminals who have no regard for God or Man, this Church will, for the present (though with the greatest regret) be kept closed, except at hours of Divine Service."

He said that altogether sixteen churches have already been destroyed or damaged by fire. At one of the churches a bird-house was taken down and removed to a safe distance before the place was fired. In another, a chained Bible was unfastened and a collection of Suffrage literature of a religious trend, put on the chain, with various quotations from the sayings of Christ. At another church, noted for its windows and curiously carved alabaster font believed to have been brought from the East by Crusaders, a woman was seen making an inspection of the eaves where swallows have been nesting for the past century. She was heard to call out to another woman, "I told you they would all be gone weeks ago. It's too late for any young ones." This church is now being guarded night and day. In still another church, a rare bit of stained glass representing St. Paul has been smashed to bits.

.   .   .   .

I have a letter from Henrietta. She is coming to town for a meeting. She says she has had her hair cut off, and "just for fun" she tried on one of Jim's suits and finds she makes a "rather ripping looking young man." Certainly I believe she would, though I have always considered her distinctly and distinctively feminine in appearance. . . . She has had letters from several of her conspiracy parsons and they tell her they do not consider the subject she suggests for a sermon a suitable one to be discussed in the House of God. . . . Will I "take on" Daniel during August? Yes, of course, I'd take him on permanently, if allowed.

.   .   .   .

Henrietta took me to the meeting, one of the last before the scattering of the Suffrage forces into various country and sea-side and mountainous places. They will not rest, these women. Holidays are their busiest times. School teachers, shop assistants, musicians, doctors, hard-worked for ten or eleven months at their professions, give their holidays to the Cause all as a matter of course.

Henrietta had a new hat and it completely hid the back of her head so I could not see that she had short hair till she took it off. Yes, she could make a "rather ripping looking young man." But last night that description wouldn't fit. As she stood beside me at the meeting, she looked saint-like, inspired and inspiring. I saw her face light up all gloriously as she joined in the singing at the end:

> "We will not cease from mortal strife,
> Nor shall the sword rest in our hand,
> Till we have built Jerusalem
> In England's green and pleasant land."

(THE END OF PART ONE)

PART TWO

The Alien (1914–1918)

(*From Notes, Letters, Diaries*)

CHAPTER VI

THE RUSH

THE Americans have rushed the Embassy. A week ago they were scattered in their thousands all over the British Isles, Baedekers in hand, kodaks and field glasses swung over their shoulders. Now they have concentrated on London.

The Baedekers are thrown away or packed deeply in trunks, for anything of German name or origin is unpopular these days. Kodaks may not be used without special permits and field glasses are not needed.

The small, somewhat shabby Embassy offices in Victoria Street are not large enough to hold the crowds, so extra rooms have been taken in the Savoy Hotel, just around the corner in the Strand.

I have myself formed one of the crowd for I have urgently wanted to see Mr. Page. I met one of his assistants and told him I had come about a Passport.

"For a friend?" he asked.

"For myself," I replied.

"But why here?" he asked.

"Where else?" I returned.

"Are you an American—a real honest-to-God one?"

"What sort of an American is that?" I asked.

"The genuine article—not the kind we've been having come here—that's married to an Englishman or something— You know!"

"Well, I'm an 'honest-to-God' one, I should say. Mr. Page knows me."

"Yes, I know, but somehow I always thought you were English. Must you see him to-day? It's terribly hard on the chief. You've no conception of the rush we're having, and if you're not sailing right away—and you won't be able to do that, I can tell you, if you haven't engaged passage—couldn't you wait a few days?"

"Oh, I'm not going back to America, and I can wait a while," I said.

He was gone, and I stood about in the crowd, people packed together like sardines or like guests at a White House reception. The air was thick with accents from all over my native land, and they were as various as those of an English crowd gathered from as many shires. There was the soft Southern, the clipped Middle-western, the somewhat slower New York and the hesitating Yankee drawl. I stood near two young women, smartly dressed after the Austrian fashion.

"Yes, left Germany before the English declared war. Say, I did like the Germans—such nice manners! The officers are too sweet for anything. . . . Yes, must have been a dozen of 'em right at the train and they gave every one of us a bouquet —didn't know our names or anything, mind you, but just because we were Americans, you know. I call it real gallant and friendly. I'll bet we don't get bouquets when we leave England! The Englishmen, somehow, unless they're engaged to a woman, don't think of things like that!"

"Going home?" said an oldish man to me. "Nothing like your own country, is there?"

Where had I seen him? Oh yes, at a dinner or luncheon, celebrating an American Thanksgiving or something of the sort. A nice sentimental speaker— "I tell you, my friends, blood's thicker than water, and if ever the old country needs a hand, why—"

Certainly I remembered him, and I immediately wondered what kind of a "hand" he was going to give the "old country." I soon found it would be a good-by handshake, if he could manage it.

"Well, well, I don't know if I'll know New York—haven't seen the blessed place in thirty eight years—thought I'd spend the rest of my days over here—got a nice place out in the country—good shooting— By the way, Madam, do you know anything about this law somebody was telling me they have over there now—lose your citizenship if you stay away for four years—or is it six? Fine law, I say! I like the British view—once an Englishman always an Englishman. But I've got my birth certificate. Got it years ago when I went to Russia— Couldn't ever travel there without passports, you know."

"You're damned lucky, then," said a man near by, in a low tone. He was middle-aged, and I remembered seeing him return from a trip to another room. "They're asking me to *prove* my citizenship."

"Have you been away long?" I asked. It was the kind of occasion on which one didn't seem to need an introduction.

"Twenty-three years," he laughed. "Wouldn't mind spending the rest of my life on this side, but I don't want to be mixed up in their old wars. I'm an American all right, but now they want proof, as if my word wasn't good enough. I went to the Consulate and tried to register. They wanted proof. I come here to get some sort of paper that'll take me back to the United States, and now *they* want proof!"

"Yes," I said. "You see a good many people might want to be Americans these days. There are British subjects who are trying to claim American citizenship on all sorts of pretexts. Mind you, I'm not questioning your claims to citizenship, but you see it's hard on the American officials just now."

I was thinking of two Irishwomen and one Englishman of my acquaintance who, having spent some years in the United States, took out first papers, and then decided they did not wish to become American citizens, and returned to Great Britain. Yet now, none such loyal Americans as they! They *thought they were* American citizens— Didn't know anything about two sets of papers! They can't get over, and the Englishman has turned conscientious objector and the Irishwomen have gone to Dublin.

Through the crush at one of the shipping offices I thought I recognized the excitedly wagging head of Mrs. de Plays Bingham, and wondered if she were properly "fixed" for voyaging back to her native land. I fancied she was wishing back the ten thousand pounds that clever Lady Emmeline must have got out of her. Lady Emmeline is bound to be very popular during the war and most forward in all good works. I heard yesterday that she was going to start a hospital or nursing home with the money she has been getting from aspiring Americans, who, by the way, she laughingly refers to as her "new milch cows." I'm sure it will be a place for officers and not for Tommy Atkinses!

A voice called me back from contemplation of the war activities of Lady Emmeline and her kind.

"Yes, I am certainly going home as soon as I can get there —steerage or any old way. This country's bound to be invaded —Why, didn't you know? Yes, force of Germans landed on the East Coast, but a British man o' war spied 'em and trained the ship's guns on 'em—every one killed. But next time the Germans might be luckier—Pro-British? Yes, certainly, but that doesn't blind me to their unreadiness. Only man that knew anything in advance was Churchill. He didn't demobilize the Fleet at all after its show off Spithead."

"Yes, had an American mother, didn't he? Lady Randolph. Married a youngster after her first husband died— Smart woman, smart son!"

"What? I surely *am* going back! I've got passage for self and wife and son, thank God! What I say is, all American friends of England who've been living here, ought to go home now and not stay and eat the food the British will need for themselves. Bound to be a shortage. . . . What if the German ships get all around and blockade these tight little islands? They can't grow enough for themselves, it stands to reason. . . . Sorry to take the boy out of that fine school, but, as I said, eating food that belongs to the real genuine British—it's not the act of a gentleman. . . ."

"What do you think? Had to take a room with three other women and second class at that—offered to pay for the whole stateroom myself, but no! Well, no use grumbling— That's what war does!"

I prayed God that war might do nothing worse to any of us!

"All I can say is that they were mighty good to me at my hotel, honey." It was one of the soft Southern voices. "Accepted my check like gentlemen. Yes, the English are gentlemen. I hope they'll win."

I went nearer the door. The queue seemed interminable. A red-eyed woman was holding tightly the hand of a small boy. She pushed toward me. "Do you think we'll get home?" she said.

"Of course! How long have you been here?"

"Since June. I didn't get a return ticket because I wanted to go back by way of Canada and see the St. Lawrence. We live in Iowa. My grandmother came from Dorset. We've been to see the old house. I hope the English will win, but I'm glad we're not in it. If the Germans invade England, I should think the Americans would have to come over, wouldn't you?"

I found the people in the queue were mostly tourists, and I hoped the shipping companies were giving them first preference. I felt great sympathy for them, over on holiday and caught in the war. It was natural they should return home as soon as possible. But the people who had lived on this side for years and then suddenly found they were such good Americans that they could not stay away from their own country—those who had built homes here, paid taxes here and none at home, made their livings here and lived here on the money they had made in America, educated their children here, were rearing them as English boys and girls, had fallen into English ways and made sport of the tourists who, as I often heard them say, came "a culture-hunting"—all these angered me. England at peace they loved. England at war they forsook.

Cowardice was driving so many back, physical, moral and financial cowardice. There were gold-hoarders among them just, as, of course, there were among the British who were smart enough to get in stocks of gold before the Moratorium. Food hoarders, too. Quitters!

And all over Europe in the capital cities of the nations at war the position is the same. In Italy and France there are Americans who speak English with an Italian and French accent, offering thousands of dollars for steerage passages back "home." Italy, of course, is still "out," but it's better for Americans to get away while her ports are free.

I came home by way of Victoria station. I am keeping a lookout at the stations to see what I can do for the Belgians who are constantly arriving, and I always carry chocolate and biscuit in my bag for them. Refugees were coming in and companies of troops in khaki were going out. I was giving chocolate to one of the Belgian kiddies when a young subaltern saluted me.

"Somebody told me you were 'Enid'," he said. "Send us boys some messages over there, will you? We'll be sure to get you, somehow. Good-by—I've only a second—"

Even before I could grab his hand, he was off and jumping onto the moving train. I shouted my farewell and "God bless you!" He nodded, saluted again and the train was gone. Who was he? I shall probably never know.

Another train. Hundreds of Tommies were boarding it. They were looking very jolly and singing. Forgetting the rest of the Belgians, I threw into the car all my remaining chocolate, some cigarettes and a collapsible aluminum drinking cup. "Share it! All I've got to give you!" I called, and the train moved out.

At the entrance to the station, more boys in khaki, at the gates still more. No martial music accompanied them. They were marching in time to the tune of

"Put me among the girls!"

Now several hundred recruits turned into the gates. They were of all sorts—black-coated, smocked, over-alled. There was music, yes! They marched to be trained to kill and be killed to a music hall air,

"Get out and get under!"

If anyone had started to sing "Land of Hope and Glory" or "Britannia Rules the Waves!" I verily believe they would have died of embarrassment and blushes. The British fighting men, somehow, are like that.

I did not know there were so many thousands of beautiful boys in all the world as I have seen in London during these past few days. So full of joy, so full of fire, such eyes! We are accustomed to hear and read so much about the beauty and innocence of girlhood, but somehow it seems to me there is something in the faces and the eyes of boys, like these I am seeing now every day, that no other beauty can approach. I laugh and wave and throw them flowers or anything I happen to have when they pass me in the streets but afterwards I cry.

. . . .

Anna —— has been in. I hadn't seen her for two or three years. Long ago she was an American, or that is the way I put it, because she has grown so English. I remember her marriage and her coming over here to live. Her American husband had business here, and her boy was born here, and when he was two or three years old, his father died and Anna stayed on because she liked the quiet life and smoother ways of England. I really had supposed she had become naturalized long ago.

She was in a state of hysteria because she had just discovered that her boy was a British subject. He had been at one of the great English schools and came home last week prepared to enlist with a number of other boys of his own age.

"Why," said she, "Son, you can't enlist. You're an American!"

"The hell I'm an American!" he shouted back. "I was born here, and I'm an Englishman!"

"But your father was American and I'm American, and that makes you an American," his mother insisted, oh so joyously, thinking that could prevent him being accepted, even if he did try to enlist.

The boy went out and enlisted in the Royal Flying Corps and Anna followed to prevent his being taken. To her utter amazement she has discovered that the boy really is a British subject because of his birth, and as for herself, her status is very doubtful, indeed. She has never been in America since the boy's birth and he has never seen that country. From every point of view he is an English boy.

"I didn't know, I didn't know!" she wailed when she was telling me the story.

"But even so, I don't see how you could have tried to prevent the boy's doing what nearly every other boy of his bringing-up is doing or soon will do," I said. "You live here for twenty years, you have your child born here, you bring him up as an Englishman, put him to school with English boys, and then when he acts in accordance with his bringing up, you try to hold him back! What kind of a boy would he be, even if by some fluke or technicality, he were proven to be American and were willing to accompany you back to America, which would be a foreign land to him and almost the same to you?"

I felt great pity for Anna, but it was just the same sort of pity I feel for my English friends with their boys. What is the difference? Mothers' hearts are breaking all over Britain. My own heart is aching for them all.

.　.　.　.　.　.　.　.　.

I was not one of the wiseacres who expected war. I never had patience with those British friends who for two or three years have been going to Germany and, returning, have assured me that they were really preparing for "der Tag" over there. I have a keen memory of how tired I grew of the sound of poor Lord Roberts' voice at the dinner of the Society of Authors a year ago when, invited to be the star after-dinner speaker of the occasion, he spoke for a full hour on the need of "preparedness." Hadn't Queen Victoria been the great royal Anglo-German matchmaker for the very purpose of preventing trouble between the two countries?

I have never had any feeling of dislike for Germans. Even now I must say it, although so many of my friends are just discovering that they always did dislike and distrust Germans! As a nation, they have always seemed to me to be a kindly people. Last year when I went to Germany and Austria-Hungary, I made several such good friends among the German women delegates at the International Women's Congress at Buda Pesth. Once when I was lost in Paris I remember it was a kind German visitor there who got me back to my pension when a Frenchman was taking me the wrong way. . . .

How war absorbs, swallows, sucks in everything! The troubles in Ireland seem so little and so trivial these days. The volunteers who, on both sides, were training for shooting one another down, are already enlisted in the service of the Empire. In the House of Commons John Redmond has called out "God save England!" and the sturdiest anti Home Rulers have called back, "God save Ireland!"

There is not a suffragette in prison now. They were all let out without so much as a promise to "keep the peace." Wouldn't it have been funny if the Government, ever without a sense of humor on this subject, had asked them for that promise! The suffrage leaders are mobilizing the women of Britain for all sorts of work.

I have "taken on" Daniel again, though I told Henrietta I didn't know how long I could look after him.

"You said you weren't going away!" she said.

"I didn't! I told you I wasn't going back to America!"

"Well, where else can you go, I'd like to know—you being a neutral?" she inquired.

"I'm not a neutral— Don't call me that again if you expect our friendship to last!"

"I know you are with us, but *technically* you are a neutral, dear," she said.

"Well, maybe that 'technicality' may turn out to be just the thing to help me along," I said.

"Queer," went on Henrietta, "how all the old plans, all the old hatreds, have gone, isn't it? The man-made government that treated us women so shamefully now calls on us to help. 'Ship in danger— All hands to the pumps!' they shout, and to the pumps we women go."

Henrietta is on the job as a motorist. She's a wonderfully swift and careful driver. Jim enlisted the very day war was declared. Only once has she mentioned the great August campaign she had planned against the churches and the parsons who preach the subjection of women. "I've got that list you made out, you know, but things will be a bit delayed!" she said, and she laughed grimly.

Henrietta's beautiful suburban house is full of Belgians. She has taken in eight refugees and is feeding and clothing them.

"And they're complaining of the cooking!" she laughed.

"They say English cookery isn't tasty, and I'm not disputing with them on that score; but the point is that I'm having trouble with my cook because the 'gees' are going down into the kitchen and trying to cook things themselves— What with eight Belgians and one English cook all in one kitchen—well, you can imagine what it's like in the way of excitement. I thought of offering one of the 'gees' the cook's place, for the sake of peace, but it seems I mustn't do that."

"Why not? It would seem just the thing."

"Hurt their feelings! It's understood they are to be treated as guests and not as servants, and I'm willing, but I didn't bargain for guests to complain of the cooking— In England it 'isn't done,' you know!"

Henrietta isn't the only Englishwoman who's having this sort of trouble. She has a "professed" cook at a high salary, but the cooking is English and not continental. The way the British have taken the Belgians into their homes is, to my mind, an example of the most beautiful selflessness. Everybody knows how the Englishman values his "castle," and the privacy of home is a fetish among Englishwomen. Yet hundreds of them have turned their homes into free boarding-houses, doubled up in their bed-rooms, when they've never done such a thing before, turned their drawing rooms into nurseries for Belgian children. And now, quite a lot of the Belgians don't like English cookery and say so!

Well, if I "took on" a Belgian refugee, and she complained, even of Briggs' cookery, I'd fire her—the Belgian, I mean.

.   .   .   .

I'll have to be more careful. Briggs says "a lady who was calling at the other lady's flat" stopped at our door yesterday and listened "with a funny look," when I had the gramophone going with one of my German conversational records. I'll have to get a box of lower toned needles. . . . How much I've forgotten since the days at college out in Wisconsin when I was the star German scholar and my translations of Goethe and Schiller were the admiration of all the girls and the faculty. I remember the Juniors' concert when I sang "Time was I had a beauteous fatherland" in the German, like one, so they said, almost to Leipzig born. How did it go? Every verse ended sadly with the refrain,

"Es war ein Traum!"

What a pity I haven't a record of that. . . . Well, I'll see what I can do with "Die Wacht am Rhein!" I must shut the window. . . . Now for the record . . . I will learn to sing it with real feeling. . . .

.   .   .   .

It was too funny the other day when I met Mrs. Pennell's Augustine in Of Alley, coming from her marketing. She has taken quite a fancy to me and we converse most pleasantly with gesticulations, mainly, for she doesn't know a word of English and my French vocabulary is very limited. I used to consider it a most idiotic arrangement that made me study German rather than French at the college. When I've been in France it has put me to a great disadvantage. However. . . . But about Augustine. I had been to the Strand to buy a paper to see the latest about the Fall of Liege, and got to thinking hard and almost ran into her. She dropped some of her vegetables out of her apron, where she so often carries them and I exclaimed, "Lieber Gott! Was willst du, Augustine?" Poor Augustine stared and began to run toward the Pennell flat before I realized that I had been thinking aloud. It was really too bad, she being the only representative of the other half of the *Entente Cordiale* whom we have in the neighborhood. What she's told her mistress I don't know. . . .

I'm sure my pronunciation must be abominable. There's that little old Alsatian who used to live somewhere around Soho. I remember his manner of speaking was as beautiful—when he could be induced to talk German—as his hatred of Germany was awful. Years ago he used to say France would have her revenge. A few lessons from him would be the very thing, if I can find him. . . .

The poor dear old thing! I haven't been able to find him. It seems he moved out Walham Green way, and I traced one house where he lived. Some neighbors said he'd gone away and others declared he was interned as an enemy alien, but

I think that can't be true. A German subject, of course. He was born before the Franco-German war and the Germans took him and his family over along with the country. I remember his telling me how his mother taught him to pray for the good God to avenge Alsace.

So now I'm at a loose end. I have my old books and dictionaries, but I must depend on the gramophone for pronunciation. . . . I've told Briggs I'm studying Russian—Russia is very popular, what with her "steam-roller," though rough ground is impeding its hoped-for smooth progress over the Western road.

 .   .   .   .

I saw Miss S—— in John Street to-day and she asked me if I had let my flat yet and how long a lease I had. I asked her what she meant, since I had never thought of letting my flat. She explained that she took it for granted I would go back to the United States, and when I said I certainly wouldn't, she replied,

"Well, if *I* had another country, I'd surely go to it. We are in for a big and awful thing."

"Yes, I believe it," I said, "and I stick!"

She is the fifth person who has asked me if I had let my flat and when I am "going home." I'm getting rather tired of it.

At the P——'s last night, my host said, "And when are you going home?"

I really thought that he meant to hint that the hour was late. I jumped up and apologized and asked for my hat and scarf. Mrs. P—— pushed me down in my chair again, explaining that the night was very young.

"Well, when I'm asked so pointed a question as that—" I said, looking around at her husband.

The laugh was on me. It turned out that Mr. P—— was merely inquiring when I was sailing for New York, and he and his guests expressed surprise at my staying on during war time.

Of course, many people do not know I am an American, the subject of my nationality never happening to have come up in their presence. I find that some who think they detect a slight "accent" have thought I was a Canadian. Some have written to congratulate me that my "colony" is showing "such splendid loyalty to the motherland." These correspondents say that they detect "something fresh, with prairie breeziness" in my writing. There are still others who take me for an Englishwoman who has traveled much in the Dominions and so I am a little "different!" But most of my readers take me for granted as an Englishwoman.

. . . .

Mr. Page asked me what I wanted a Passport for, and I said "to travel with." He asked "Where?" and I said "Anywhere," adding that, of course, he knew I was a newspaper correspondent, and he said "Yes." He made a remark about "traveling" not being so simple as in ordinary times, and I said "No." He then said that, being a Neutral, I must be careful not to do anything that would get my country into any complications, and that he would send me an Emergency Passport, if I really felt I needed one.

I'm as good a Neutral as he is, and certainly I need a Passport.

. . . .

The Passport has come. I find I can go traveling with it all over the British Isles! It's a *neuter* document.

I have written to Washington and asked The Democrat if he will use his influence to get me a Passport that has some "kick" in it.

He has cabled back,

"Writing you fully concerning your request."

CHAPTER VII

A SPOKE IN THE WHEEL

THE Democrat's promised letter has followed the cablegram:

Washington, September—, 1914.

. . . I am sorry to have to put a spoke in the wheel which you thought would so smoothly roll you around to Germany as "an American newspaper correspondent, being technically a neutral!"

Have you lost your sense of humor, or is it that you think I have lost mine?

No! I will not use my influence to help you to get any other passport than that with which your Ambassador has supplied you. Moreover, if you now determine to try some other means of getting one, I shall feel it my duty to our country as well as to you, to protest against its being granted.

I was not surprised that as soon as war was declared by Great Britian, you felt you must change all your plans, in order that you might do something for the country where you have for so many years earned your living. I certainly would have been surprised if you had, like certain other expatriated Americans whom we both know, insisted upon catching the first available ship that would take you out of the danger zone. That sort of thing, of course, "isn't done" by persons of your temperament, whether they be American or British.

Up to a certain point I sympathize with your "What can I do for England, that's done so much for me?" attitude, but not to the extent of thinking that you owe no duty to your own country, to say nothing of a duty to yourself.

I will grant that you have done valuable "detective journalism" during your career, but I trust I shall not too much wound your self esteem when I say I doubt your ability successfully to carry on work as a spy in Berlin, because of your literary popularity in Germany. I quite understand your keen desire to collect some bouquets from German officers, after the manner of those American women, to whom you refer. They are, by the way, already at work here upon a propaganda scheme, which is going to get them into trouble with the government.

Your pathetic complaint that your German publishers owe you money, leaves me cold. Your attempt as a "technical neutral" to go and collect it for the benefit of British minesweepers, would not, of course, be "trading with the enemy" from the *technical* point of view, but I advise you to let your dues accumulate with interest, even though you may, after the war, have to accept them at a much depreciated currency!

Your desire to help the Allies in general and Britain in particular is laudable, but I don't see that you owe them your life, for that is what it would come to—that you would be shot as a spy.

Even though you were willing to take that risk, it would not absolve you from the crime (I speak plainly) of involving your own country in disastrous complications, for the sake of trying to help a foreign country. . . . Of course, you have laid your plan before me in idealistic terms. You say that you would help Britain because the cause of all humanity is at stake, and you appeal to me as one humanitarian to another.

When it is certain that the cause of all humanity is at stake, that fact will be made as plain as the city that is set upon a hill and cannot be hid, even from such blind people as you seem to consider us over here to be.

You say that you *must do something,* and as you cannot nurse and will not knit, this plan is your one opportunity to help. I have more confidence in your native ability and originality of resource than you seem to have. You had better put your wits to work. I have never regarded you as a woman of but one idea or as one who would put all her eggs in one basket.

I am sending you a copy of the President's Neutrality Proclamation. Many of us find ourselves unable to follow his advice in regard to our *thinking.* When he tells us we must be "impartial in thought as well as in action," we look upon it as a hard saying and hear it with a you-be-damned feeling, and I have told him I have no intention of turning myself into a political eunuch. In the matter of Great Britain's entry, it is of good omen that one can see no gold mines nor diamond fields lurking in the background. It is, however, well to keep our sanity and exercise our logic. British honor and British safety pointed the same way. For this, all friends of Britain have cause to be glad.

You may now retort that besides being as good a neutral as Walter Page, you are as good a neutral as I am! However that may be, I am convinced that our country's wisest present course is one of close watching and patient waiting. I cannot think of anything more damaging to the cause of the Allies than our precipitate entry, Roosevelt's declarations notwithstanding. I love Teddy with an abiding affection, but I am glad he is not now in the presidential chair, although, even if he were, he would not be able to convince the majority of our people that they have anything to do with this war.

We are not prepared for war at this moment. Let that be sufficient answer to your indignant inquiry as to why we did not intervene, even if there were no other reasons. I cannot see our present duty in the way you seem to see it. Having lived away from your country for so many years, do you not think that we on the spot are better able to keep our ears to the ground?

Two of my young relations have trekked across the border into Canada, lied lustily concerning the place of their birth, taken the oath of allegiance to George the Fifth and joined the Canadian Army. I asked G—— if he understood he had thus lost his American citizenship and was now a man without a country, and he replied that he didn't know it till after he had done it, but that he would have done it anyway. . . . I am glad Canada has taken the straight course, which was across the ocean with her troops. I have tried to make M—— understand that Canadians have no right to expect to eat their cake and have it too. His attitude is "What have we Canadians got to do with it, anyway?" I reminded him that he seemed to for-

get that Canada had not built those dreadnoughts she had proposed, and would be helpless in case anything happened to the
British Navy. He seemed to think that our Navy wouldn't
"stand for" the shelling of Canadian coast towns, and I'm
not sure that it would. . . .

And now, returning to yourself. Look for your work. I'll
warrant that you'll find it very close to your hand. When you
are sure you have done your duty over there, it is possible that
you can make yourself exceedingly useful here. By all means
keep your gramophone in tune and go on brushing up your
German!

Always your true friend,......................."

ACH!

CHAPTER VIII

THE PASSING OF BRIGGS

IT was the Christmassy spirit in Briggs that aroused the fighting spirit in me.

She stood in the doorway with the string-bag which she used for marketing, and, handing me a long list of things to be got from the stores, she said,

"For the Chrisnnas pudding, Madam!"

"I'm going to buy a Christmas pudding this year, Briggs," I said.

She gasped. I knew what was coming.

"Madam, I 'ave never—" she began, whereupon I rose in my wrath from the typewriting machine. I had felt for some time that a scene with Briggs was due. I had been bottled up for a long time and I knew the cork was likely to pop out at any minute. It was unfortunate that it should pop in regard to a thing that had to do with the season of good will, but there it was!

"That's all right, Briggs," I said. "I know you have never before lived with a lady who bought her Christmas puddings. I am aware it 'isn't done' in the best families. I know the husband must take a stir at the pudding-in-the-making before he goes to his office, and the baby brought down from the nursery to have his podgy hand held while he, too, takes a stir, and the pudding must be boiled so many days and put away to cool, and then re-boiled and so on ad infinitum—"

Briggs stared. She is accustomed to simple language from me and her stare just caught me up before I had added, "else there'd be nothing but death and damnation in the family for a whole year!"

I continued smilingly and plainly. "I know of a place where

they're making thousands of the best Christmas puddings ever, to send to the boys at the front, and what they have left over they're going to sell to ordinary folks, and I'm going to take three—one for us, one for some children whose father is at the front and one for you to take to your mother."

Here Briggs found her voice. It was faint and tearful, but decided, nevertheless. "My mother never 'as heaten a bought Christmas pudding," she said. Then she took out her handkerchief and mopped the tears from her cheeks.

Suddenly her face brightened, a smile shining through the tears. "If it's the money, Madam, I would rather pay for the ingreejunts myself than not to make a Christmas pudding. I 'ave never been in service where I did the cooking that I didn't make the Christmas pudding."

Briggs is generous. Often, to my great embarrassment, she spends her money on flowers and little gifts for me. She came to me four years ago. Up to that time I had been unable to keep a servant longer than a few weeks because they couldn't conform to my ways and I wouldn't conform to theirs. I got behind with my work. Editors glared fiercely at me when I apologized for delayed articles on the ground that I was having a servant problem, in spite of the fact that, years before, it had been supposed that I, going out "In Cap and Apron," had solved the servant problem of England for all time.

So, when Briggs came on the scene, I decided to give her a long rope and hide most of my domestic light under a bushel. There was no other way to keep her. But those were not war times.

In September I raised her wages and said, "Now, Briggs, I think there are going to be terrible times in England, and we have to be very economical indeed. I've got Neuritis and the doctor has put me into 'woollies,' and they cost a lot of money, even in peace times. I can't afford to have them shrunk at the laundry, so will you wash them out for me?"

But, on the ground that she had never lived in a family where "washing was done in," that "proper families" sent not only their own, but their servants', laundry work out, Briggs refused the increased wages and declined to have part or parcel in my "woollies," except for the mending of them, which I must say she always did very neatly. I then became so "improper" as to wash them myself, and the aggrieved look on Briggs' face became almost unbearable. To "maid" a lady who did her own laundry work was a hurt to her dignity from which she never recovered.

Briggs had always made tea according to the old-fashioned formula, which I have known to be nonsense—a teaspoonful for each person and one for the pot. When war came on I said,

"Briggs, we really mustn't think of giving the pot any tea at all for itself. When you were out the other day, I made tea for a visitor and I found that one heaping-teaspoonful made two cups of tea for each of us. I stirred the tea in the pot, you know, before I poured it out. I did it in the kitchen, of course."

"Oh Madam, I 'ave *always* made tea with one spoonful for the pot, and proper people never stir their tea in the pot. It looks so——"

"I didn't let the lady see me, Briggs," I laughed. Then I added very determinedly, "Now, remember, one teaspoonful in my tea pot, and one in yours hereafter!"

The next thing I knew Briggs was going without her own afternoon tea altogether, a deprivation that I knew was worse than death to her as an Englishwoman.

I drew her into the study and tried to reason with her. I explained that although we were not yet restricted in the amount of food we might buy, later on, no matter how much money we had, we were sure of legal restriction, and that tea, of all things, would be the first limited commodity. I told her how it must be brought to Britain from India or China, how British seamen were now risking their very lives to bring it to us. I tried to induce her to take a cup of the tea I had made without an allowance for the greedy pot. She would not touch it.

Butter is not now restricted, but it surely will be. I had never eaten margarine, but hearing of a new and special kind, made under the cleanest and most hygienic conditions, I bought a half pound secretly, took it out of the labeled wrapper, placed it in the silver butter-dish, and Briggs served it for my luncheon and her own. She is very fond of thin bread-and-butter, and I noticed that she ate a plentiful supply that day. Knowing that it would be inconvenient for me to continue to buy margarine on the sly, I told her what I had done, and suggested we should go on in the good way, giving the money we saved, by not buying butter, to one of the war funds. That night Briggs ate dry bread for her supper, and asked me to give all her butter money to a war fund.

Briggs, like large numbers of her countrymen and countrywomen, has always been accustomed to take three lumps of sugar in her tea. Now, three large lumps of sugar will not usually dissolve in a small cup of tea. It cakes at the bottom, and I had always noticed a thick coating of sugar in the bottom of Briggs' cup when I have been in the kitchen at washing-up time. I may say I have noticed it in the cups of my guests, also. Knowing that sugar would soon be on the restricted list, and that many persons took a certain number of lumps merely from force of habit, I bought a new patent sugar-cutter, which divides the loaf evenly in two. I set Briggs to work at it, and the next day found she used six of the small lumps and still had the coating at the bottom of her cup.

Then I gave up in despair. I knew my back was to the wall, and when came the dispute over the making of Christmas pudding, I fought it out with her to the end, which meant to give her notice, and help her to get another place.

Yesterday I was invited to visit a class in domestic science. It is made up of poor girls who are being taught cookery and the arts of housewifery, the main object being to have them learn economical methods. The teacher, a charming woman, a graduate of a fashionable and expensive "school of cookery and household arts," is giving her time as a part of her war-work. She began her lesson on dish-washing with the question,

"Now girls, what is the first thing to do?"

"To pour out the hot water in the pan and make it soapy," chorused the girls, and one of their number was chosen to carry out this instruction. She filled the dish-pan half full of boiling water, took a whole bar of soap, stuck a fork through it and began to wriggle it around in the hot water. What little soap was left, came out in a soft, runny condition and was laid aside.

Almost I shouted my protest against this waste of good soap. Why was there not a soap-shaker with bits of saved soap that could not be used for other things? But being a guest, I kept silent, while the teacher smilingly bowed to the girl to indicate that she had begun her dish-washing correctly.

Next, the dishes were placed in the pan, and, when they were washed, the dish-water was full of grease and bits. The water was thrown down the sink, and I knew a plumber would soon be needed. My own plan is always to wipe off the dishes with soft paper before putting them in the pan.

Then the floor was swept with a broom which did not go into the corners and was made in such a way that it banged against every piece of furniture—the sort of broom that Briggs always insisted upon using. I have only saved my best furniture from being ruined by myself using a vacuum cleaner and forbidding Briggs to use the broom in my study and bed-room.

In the class, I watched the potatoes being peeled and was shocked at the thickness of the parings. I saw apples prepared for tarts amid the greatest waste, noted pastry-boards left with a quarter of an inch of pastry sticking to them; saw meat roasted with dripping put in the pan, instead of a little water to keep it from burning and scenting up the room.

I came away disheartened. If teachers of domestic science taught poor girls to work in this way, what could one expect of the Briggses? I am discovering that the English, though adepts at "doing without" when necessary, are a wasteful people. The Americans are *extravagant,* but not wasteful. There is a difference.

The evening paper gave me no good news from the front, although news is so censored as to put the best foremost. Somehow, because of my experience with Briggs and the cookery school, my feelings seemed to become a part of the miserable November fog which enveloped me as I turned in at my own doorway and found Briggs weeping because she had got a new situation, subject to her "character" being satisfactory.

"The lady," said Briggs, between sobs, "would like to know if you would kindly call on her and bring my character, instead of her coming to see you, because she 'as 'ad a haccident with her hankle."

There are crucial moments when Briggs' aitches are worse than usual. This was one of them.

"Do you think you will like the lady, Briggs?" I questioned, kindly.

"Yes, Madam."

"Then, why do you cry?"

"I don't want to leave you, Madam!"

"But you won't learn to do things my way, and with a war on, things have got to be done my way."

"The war will be hover in a few weeks. I 'eard somebody say it standing in front of the Palace the other night. Oh, Madam, I want to do right, but I 'ave never—"

Impatiently I waved her aside and rang up her prospective mistress to inquire when I should call.

When I called, the lady sat in front of her drawing room fire, her bandaged foot stretched upon a stool, her knitting needles performing wonders in the way of a badly-shaped sock. I knew her to be connected with the nobility, and I was quite prepared to find a woman who, though "one lady alone," would keep more than one maid. Briggs, it seemed, if her character were satisfactory, would act as cook-housekeeper in "full charge," with a "tweeny" maid to do the rougher work.

"Now, will you be quite frank as to why she is leaving you?" she asked. "She seems to be fond of you, but says there is a difference of opinion about a Christmas pudding and other matters of cookery."

I explained my position, adding, "I have heretofore let Briggs go her own way, because I was really too busy with my journalism, to insist on having mine, but with a war on, I am determined to prepare for the worst, and Briggs won't learn to prepare."

"You mean you expect England to be invaded?" she asked looking at me half amusedly.

"No!" I said.

"Blockaded?"

"Not precisely."

"What then?"

"I expect that a large number of food ships will be sent to the bottom, because that seems to be the only thing Germany can do on the sea. I expect we shall all need to exercise the very greatest economy in food, and if I keep a servant at all, I demand that she shall follow my instructions in the matter of economy."

"Is Briggs wasteful?"

"Not in the ordinary acceptance of the term. She is just pig-headed and conservative, and won't try any new ways even to see if they are better than her old ways. I am a good house-keeper and an economical cook."

She smiled. "Your servant told me you were an American. That explains it!"

"Explains what?"

"The whole position. English servants and American mis-tresses never hit it off. I've known a number of cases. Unless the Americans are very wealthy, indeed, like your heiresses married to our aristocracy, there is always trouble in the kitchens. I take it that you know too much about housekeeping," and she laughed softly.

Then she questioned me cautiously about Briggs' morals. Did she drink, have "followers"? Was she honest, respectful in her manner, was she kind and attentive in illness, and could she, on occasion, act as "maid" in assisting her mistress to dress? I gave her most satisfactory replies, while the knitting needles clacked vociferously. I found that she, like Briggs, ex-pected the war to be over in a few weeks, probably before Christmas, although it would be well to send plum puddings to the front, as the troops would, possibly, not be demobilized before January. She knitted, she said, because it seemed to be the only thing she could do to help. If the British troops didn't need her socks and scarves, why then they could be given to

Balkan soldiers, who were always fighting about something, or, she added, "to your own men down South, where there are, I understand, always revolutions going on."

I corrected her "understanding," telling her I thought she was referring to South America, and she said, "Perhaps, but is not that your country, where the negroes used to be slaves on the great cotton plantations?"

We parted with her assurance that she knew she and Briggs would get on together. She did not believe it was necessary to change all one's ways of living because of the war. She had implicit trust in the power of the British Navy, and I told her no one could have a greater love and admiration for that institution than myself. Yes, certainly, she would have her usual Christmas puddings made, and if I could spare Briggs before her month's notice was up, she could start in at plum pudding making immediately, although even now it was rather late.

As I left her flat, the newsboys were calling the glad tidings of the capture of the Emden raider by the Australian navy, but in the Strand I heard news of the sinking of British merchant ships.

Briggs has gone. The flat is clean and in order. Perhaps her new mistress is right— Perhaps American women, except the wealthy ones, do not "hit it off" with English servants, and I shall probably have to do my own work. Well, *I can do it!* I shall have but little money coming in, and such war-work as I have planned to do will, of course, be unpaid.

Come to think of it, I remember that I have no friends here who get on so well without a servant as I do. If they lose their servants, they take on charwomen, who mostly do nothing but dirty up the place, but my friends say they *must* have help, even such as live in the "one lady alone" state. Once in a while I also take in a charwoman, not for the work she can do, but for the sake of recreation and character-sketching!

I have been thinking of the farm-house out West. I remember how I had to stand on an up-turned box to reach the table when Auntie taught me how to make the Christmas mince-pies, bread and doughnuts. Sometimes there was a cake, when we could afford to use the butter, most of which we always sent to Milwaukee to be sold on commission. . . . I remember I had "egg-money" for my very own to put away in a box. I owned Jerusha Jane. They gave her to me for a birthday present when she was a tiny fluffy chick. She was a wonderful layer and had the most delightfully musical cackle which I would follow to a retreat she had in the hay stack. Auntie called her "the college hen" because her eggs were sold for my college fund. . . . I think I could not have been more than eleven when I stood on the box and learned so much of cookery.

Then I learned to make soap. It was very expensive at the village general store, so we made soft soap from the bits of fat and lye, which we put in a great iron pot out by the ash-pile. I had to watch the pot to see that it didn't boil over. We used to buy a little hard soap, of course. I think it was Castile. I had a cake of it in my bedroom, which was over the kitchen. The pipe came up through the floor from the kitchen stove to take the chill off. . . . I used to put the big water pitcher close to the pipe at night to keep the water in it from freezing, but if the "smothered" wood embers did not keep through the night, there would be a layer of ice over my pitcher, and then I would have to thaw it out. . . .

A tabby cat used to lie under the kitchen stove, which stood up on high legs, and had an extending black hearth on which we set the buckwheat cakes to keep warm. In the summer the stove would be "taken down" and then "set up" in the shed, and the kitchen made into a nice dining room. When I was twelve, I helped Auntie to paper the kitchen with a paper which had bright bouquets of poppies and corn-flowers, tied with double bow-knots. That would have been on a Saturday, and on Monday at the district school we were all told to write a composition on "What I did on Saturday," and I wrote about helping to paper the kitchen. The teacher asked me to write a second copy of my composition, so she could keep it. She said it was very well written. . . .

A rat-tat at the flat door. I must go, for I have no Briggs to answer the door now. . . . It was the postman with a packet from Thomas Hardy, an autographed copy of "Tess of the D'Ubervilles," and a note to say he hopes my Authors' Belgian Christmas Fund will be a great success.

CHAPTER IX

THE FUND, A GEORGIAN TEA-POT
—AND NEUTRALITY

H. G. WELLS sat in my kitchen and nursed his good right hand.

"Writers' Cramp!" he said, and waved his left hand toward the books he had been autographing. "All this reminds me of the children's song,

> 'Will you walk into my kitchen?'
> Said the spider to the fly.
> ' 'Tis the won-der-full-est kitchen
> That ever you did spy!' "

"No! The spider had a parlor!" I contradicted.

"Well, the real point is that you're the deceptive spider, and I'm the innocent fly. You enticed me here to autograph what you called a 'few' books, and I've done several dozen, and my hand aches."

"The generosity of your publishers!" I said. "I asked for a few, and they sent me all these," and I indicated the neat pile into which I was packing the books after I had run the blotting paper over his inscriptions.

"It *is* the won-der-full-est kitchen, at any rate!" he said, looking up from "The Passionate Friends," on the fly-leaf of which he had written, "From a Passionate Friend of Belgium—H. G. Wells," followed quickly with "For Belgium, which is setting the world free!" in the front of his book, "A World Set Free."

"And yours is the Wonderful Visit!" I replied. "Here, autograph it," and I handed him his book of that name.

He was soon followed by Sir Arthur Conan Doyle, come

to autograph and inscribe six dozen big and little books. In most of them he wrote, "With Homage to Belgium," but when he had reached the forty-seventh, he wrote "With Belgium to Homage!"

When he had finished what he laughingly called his "stint," he, too, looked about the kitchen and declared himself to be in glorious company.

Daily now, celebrated authors climb to my kitchen, writing their names in the books I have gathered there ready for the Authors' Christmas Belgian Fund.

Truly, it *is* the wonderfullest kitchen! I do not suppose that in all England, if in all the world, to-day, there is so wonderful a kitchen, or one, the contents of which will so surely descend to future generations for treasuring and safe-keeping.

Once I had a study and a bedroom, all proper and tidy. Now they are given over to packages, and old and new clothing for Belgian refugees. In my bedroom are seven beautiful silk-lined overcoats. I made a request in a newspaper for a really good warm overcoat for a Belgian gentleman of high degree (name not mentioned) who had escaped from Brussels clad only in trousers and dressing gown, and now seven English clubmen (also of high degree) are wearing their last winter's overcoats because they sent me their new ones— They thought it nicer to offer the Belgian gentleman coats which had never been worn! The coats have nothing to do with the Authors' Fund, of course, neither have the toys for Belgian kiddies, nor the groceries for Belgian families, nor the fine, dainty underclothing for Belgian maidens. As for the study—it is Bedlam.

Certainly poor Briggs is well quit of me and my war doings. I can fancy her tears and her indignant asseverations of "Madam, I 'ave never—" if now she saw the kitchen dresser, where once, with so much pride, she kept the shining china and glassware. Its shelves are stripped of their natural belongings and bear the weight of dozens of autographed books from many of the greatest living authors. I have covered the deal kitchen table with baize and an immense blotter, and here the authors sit to do their autographing. I do a minimum of cookery, so there shall be no steam to injure the bindings. When I have time I run over to Soho for French or Italian meals, but mostly I live on nuts.

Belgium in her terrible need has so appealed to all of Great Britain that one has only to say "For Belgium!" to get almost anything one may ask. What, with a suddenly reduced income, I had to think quickly how I should get money to help the Belgians not to a "merry," but to a less horrible Christmas than the Germans seem determined to give them. My thoughts went to my literary friends, some of whom, like myself, are already feeling the effects of the war on their annual incomes from books and other writing. So I wrote and telephoned to my friends, and to many other authors whom I knew only by reputation, and explained my scheme. I asked each one to send one book, autographed and inscribed with some sentiment about the invasion of Belgium, and a promise to autograph others that I felt sure would be given me by their publishers.

First I sent my appeal to the Adelphi authors. Then I wrote to Rudyard Kipling, Thomas Hardy, John Masefield, Alfred Noyes, and a hundred others. All day and most of the night my typewriter clicked with the letter-writing. Authors came and books came, and now the wonderfullest kitchen!

When a sufficient number of books were given and promised, I got three friends to help, one whom I call the "Lightning Calculator" because she knows figures, finance and literary values; one "The Best Seller" and the third, whom I call the "Beggar," because of her success at cajoling shopkeepers and others into giving presents to good causes. Of course, we needed a shop in a busy street for the sale, so the Beggar went forth and soon came back with the Grand Trunk Railway offices in her pocket, Brangwyn-painted ceilings, immense plate-glass Cockspur Street show-windows, and all. Then to insure the transfer of my prospective takings-in quickly and safely to Belgium, I offered them to the Daily Telegraph, to be added, as a separate account, to its Christmas Present to the King of the Belgians for his People. Honorary bankers and an Honorary auditor were next secured, and then came offers from friends to come on in daily relays as salesmen and saleswomen.

Among them are several authors and an ex-lady Mayoress of London. For the running of errands there is a Belgian boy scout, who has just escaped from the Germans by whom he was taken prisoner, British Boy Scouts and Girl Guides, and Daniel, who will carry baskets and other parcels not too heavy for his own weight and stature.

I am spending the evening and shall probably spend most of the night in the kitchen. The books are to be packed in boxes and small parcels in alphabetical order according to the names of the authors. Here among the Fs I find a slip of paper as a reminder that I have not yet got the book from Anatole France for which I wrote him some time ago. There is difficulty in reaching him, for, at the age of seventy, he has joined the French army as a private, and though I have scouts at work "over there," I am beginning to be afraid I may not hear from him till the sale is over. I have taken a big "chance" on Anatole France, and even if no book comes from him, I shall not allow myself to be sorry for having, as it were, "put my money" on him. It was this way: I was told when I started collecting books that the sale would go off with a "real bang" if I could get royal patronage, and the name of a very likely Royal Person as patron was given me, with instructions as to the proper proceedings. I followed instructions to the letter, which included sending a list of the authors whose books I already had and another list of those from whom I had requested books but who had not yet sent them. In this latter list—in fact, heading it, was the name of Anatole France. Back came a message saying that the Royal Person approved of my list with one exception—Anatole France must be taken off the list and his book not placed on sale if I obtained it, because the Royal Person did not approve of his religious, or non-religious views!

Immediately I answered by telegram to the "middleman," who was arranging the matter, "Prefer Anatole France. Please consider patronage off."

I go on, packing the books. I have the Gs—John Galsworthy from across the street, sends four, one of them inscribed "To

that nation to whom more than our gratitude is due—Belgium."
He sends also a check to pay for 250 copies of "Dik: A Dog
of Belgium." Here's Kipling, with his "Just So Stories for
Little Children," merely autographed, but surely I shall get
a goodly sum for that, and his publishers shall be somewhat
worried, after the one is sold! Here is Reginald Wright Kauffman—one American author, at any rate! I have not tried to
get at authors in the United States. The time has not been
sufficient, but Kauffman was over here when I made my S. O. S.
call to any American authors who might be in England. In his
"Daughters of Ishmael" he has written an unpublished poem:

> "You did it, Little Belgium, You!
> You stopped the Dyke with half your sons,
> You did what no one else could do,
> Against the Vandals and the Huns.
> The eternal future in your debt,
> From now until Man's latest day—
> How can the wondering world forget,
> And how, remembering, repay?"

Among the Ls is William J. Locke. What kind and helpful
advice he has been giving me about the Fund! Now, Masefield, and Henry Newbolt with "Drake's Drum;" Alfred Noyes,
Eden Phillpotts, Quiller Couch, Charles G. D. Roberts with his
beautiful wild life books.

Now Owen Seaman, editor of Punch. That makes books
from two Punch editors, for dear Sir Francis Burnand, retired now at Ramsgate, has sent me an old, old copy of his
famous skit on Colonel Burnaby's "Ride to Khiva," published
in Punch in 1870. And such a kind letter from Sir Francis,
reminding me of the early days of what he calls my London
"escapades" which made an occasional page of wholesome fun
for Punch.

Now comes May Sinclair for the S packet: Clement Shorter,
who first published my London Flower Girl experiences;
Temple Thurston, who has sent his books around from the
Terrace by hand. Here's Horace Annesley Vachell—I can't
seem to find another V, so I'll put him along with Izrael Zang-

will who long ago named me "Merely Mary Ann" after one
of his books because I, like Mary Ann, went out to work as
a housemaid. I can put William Watson's manuscript poem
in this parcel, also, because there are not many Ws. Here's
Stephen Philips' manuscript verse, written in his rather care-
less way on a torn half sheet of paper— Surely that must take
pride of place one day at least in the show-window. Beatrice
Harraden, with her "Ships that Pass in the Night" must
go back among the Hs with Thomas Hardy, and here's Sir
Arthur Pinero, with his "Mind the Paint Girl." Jane Barlow
and Miss M. E. Braddon must go over into the B box, along
with Lord Brassey and that jolly plain sailor man, Admiral
Lord Charles Beresford, who has sent his beautifully bound
Memoirs and his "Echoes of the Fleet." Mrs. W. K. Clifford
and Joseph Conrad I must put in the C box, while Jane and
Mary Findlater, Sir Gilbert Parker, A. E. W. Mason and
Lady Ritchie, daughter of William Makepeace Thackeray, must
be properly parcelled. Maurice Hewlett has sent four books—
I'm depending on him for several guineas, while Viscount
Bryce's "American Commonwealth" I shall try to sell to some
good American. Arthur J. Balfour is also likely to have his
"Foundations of Belief" taken to America, where he is so
greatly liked. Earl Curzon has written in the front of his gift
"I would sooner that a single copy of this book were sold for
the relief of the suffering in heroic Belgium, than one hundred
copies in the open market."

It was Sidney Low who published in the old St. James's my
"Almighty Dollar in London Society." I reminded him of it
when I sent to him for the book in which he has so beautifully
written:

> "O Belgian dead who found your grave,
> In that wronged land you could not save,
> Not vainly have you fallen to give,
> Your faith, your fire, to those who live!"

Late this evening came one of Arnold Bennett's books, on
the flyleaf of which he has written, "I wish this book would
last half as long as the glory of Belgium will last." I have had

to send Stephen Gwynn's book, "The Fair Hills of Ireland," to the British Museum, to get the inscription translated, because it is written in Gaelic. I wonder if he sent me this puzzle in revenge for a manuscript of mine he once had to read (and recommend) when he was a publisher's reader in Fleet Street! Joseph McCabe is in America, lecturing, but he has sent over some autographed and inscribed slips of paper which his wife has pasted into the books she has brought. In his new book on Treitschke is the inscription, "For Belgium, my old University Country, now teacher of the world."

It is two o'clock in the morning and the books are not nearly all catalogued or packed. Those friends who are to be "salespersons" will come in to-morrow—or rather, later to-day—and help me to finish. The dresser shelves are still only half cleared. Familiar names of friends and acquaintances stare at me from the bindings. Here are books that I read when I was a girl in the farm house kitchen, that kitchen I helped to paper. Some of them were written when the authors, now full of years and honors, were in the early days of their writing. I wonder what I would have said on those evenings, when I read aloud to Auntie by the light of the kerosene oil lamp, which every day I had so carefully to clean, if some one had told me that in the year 1914 I should sit in this other kitchen, fingering copies of those same books, counting their authors as my friends, turning them into a Christmas fund to help a country of which I then knew nothing, except that it was on the map of Europe!

To-day I had a letter from my little cousin, Mary Elizabeth, who is now taking the course at the State University. She says she is earning all her board and room rent in the town by washing dishes, making beds, rolling a baby in a perambulator, for the wife of a lawyer who does not keep any "help." So it seems Mary Elizabeth's father is not well-to-do at all, as I had supposed, when she told me she would be going to the University in two years from the summer she came to see me in London. . . . Of course, I ought to have thought of that. There must be far more chances for a poor Western girl to help herself through the University than there were when I went to college. . . . I worked five hours a day in the domestic department the first year. That was the year the chinch-bugs got in the wheat, and Jerusha Jane was growing old and did not lay every day. . . . We were all so worried about my "higher education," especially as Auntie felt I ought to have special tuition in English literature. . . . I am tired. I am glad I have a good box spring and a soft hair mattress to sleep on, even if there are only a few hours left now before I must be up and moving the books over to Cockspur Street. I remember the bed at the farmhouse was terribly hard, though I didn't realize it then. I slept soundly the sleep of youth on the wooden slats and the feather bed under the home-made patchwork quilts, made at the neighborhood "quilting bees"—no soft eider-downs nor all-wool blankets in those days!

Well, I love my present day comforts all the more for being able to earn them. My life as a journalist is an absorbingly interesting one. It has brought me into contact with all sorts and conditions of people. It was through my journalism that I first made friends with the great British authors whose books are now on my kitchen dresser. Come to think of it, I remember that some of them must have been almost as poor as myself when they were boys and girls, though their parents belonged to what is called the "professional classes," but I don't remember hearing any of them speak of working their way through college or university. . . . I don't seem to be able to connect them up with the kind of life I lived on the farm in those long-ago days.

. . . .

The sale is on in Cockspur Street. The Beggar herself has decorated the windows with the Belgian colored ribbons and the silky white mull. She merely mentioned to a great wholesale house in St. Paul's Churchyard that these were desirable things, after they had given her thousands of yards of twine and many reams of brown wrapping paper! Suspended from the center of the main window hangs the sign, painted in orange, black and red:

THE AUTHORS' BELGIAN CHRISTMAS FUND

PATRONS—

Her Grace the Duchess of Newcastle,
The Right Hon. the Earl of Meath,
The Right Hon. the Earl of Lytton,
The Hon. Harry Lawson, M. P.
Monsieur Alfred Lemonnier (Editor *L'Independance Belge.*)
Honorary Organizer and Honorary Secretary,
Elizabeth Banks ("Enid")
Who Is Your Favorite Author?
You Can Buy His or Her Books, autographed and inscribed.
Do You Love Dogs?
Buy "Dik: a Dog of Belgium," written by Elizabeth Banks
with Dik's portrait by Herbert Dicksee.

The Christmas sale is over. I have never known such full and strenuous and interesting days as were the last two weeks before Christmas. Every day brought its special excitement.

Besides the ordinary Christmas shoppers, autograph hunters were numerous, and several "dealers," whom we did not know were dealers till they got away with some of our treasures, came and bought books in order to speculate with their autographs. I argued with one of these gentry for half an hour and never "spotted" him. He asked for *any* book by Sir James Barrie. I explained that Sir James, in reply to my request, had written me a most charming letter, regretting that, because of an arrangement with his publishers, he was not at liberty to autograph his books for sale, and so he sent a check which he asked me to accept, instead of books, to help along the Fund.

"That's too bad," said the customer. "I'm devoted to his writings. That letter, now, perhaps you would sell it to me for a souvenir— What about five guineas?"

"It was a private letter— No, I couldn't sell people's letters without their permission."

He smiled ingratiatingly. "I understand, a question of etiquette! But the check would have his autograph— His signature, you know. Have you deposited it, yet?"

"No," I said, "We weren't going to the bank till the end of the week."

"Then don't! You don't say what the amount is, but I'll pay your fund double the face value of it. Barrie won't mind your selling it, I know, though he's so chary of his autograph. I want it for a keepsake."

I felt tempted. He saw my hesitation and smiled encouragingly. "I'll wager you don't get many offers like that for checks!"

"No, we don't," I said. "Sir James is the only author who asked me to accept a check instead of books."

He saw I was undecided. I was wondering if I might not get Barrie's permission to sell the check.

"I'll tell you what I'll do," said he. "I'll come again tomorrow. Meantime, don't deposit that check. Just think it over. If it isn't too large an amount, I might treble it!"

He was gone, and coming over to me from her cash-drawer, the Lightning Calculator gritted her teeth and said *"A dealer!"*

"Then give me Barrie's check," I said. She handed it over, I endorsed it, rushed out of the door, onto a bus, went to Harrod's, the honorary bankers, and deposited it. I don't believe in dallying with temptation.

When I returned, I picked up a book of Jeffery Farnol's from the counter, cleared a space in the front of the main window, and opened it at the title page, which he had autographed and inscribed with the words "SURRENDER BE DAMNED!" It had the effect of attracting a queue—and I felt better.

The next day the Lightning Calculator received the dealer. "That check's deposited," she said suavely, "but we'll sell you some Dik books—*not autographed!*"

But not even one of my penny stories would he buy.

We were all of us amateurs, but gloriously enthusiastic, and there were busy days when we never stopped for luncheon, working on till tea-time or supper time, feeling faint with hunger. When this news got abroad—and all sorts of news did get abroad, since there were reporters coming every day to get a "daily story," various persons used to come in at noon, bringing baskets of sandwiches and cakes and even hot coffee. Others would give us their cards and insist upon taking us out to hot meals at the nearby restaurants. These latter were often officers on leave from France who, as they said, were "great friends of Enid's." Bless them! They were getting my "messages," though I had never seen them till they came to the sale. There were other days when some of the authors whose books we were selling would come in and take us out to luncheon in relays. Among these were Morley Roberts and Leonard Merrick, who tried to make us understand that starving was not really one of the things that we owed to the Belgians, as we could not sell effectively on empty stomachs.

Leonard Merrick, by the way, was the cause of the making of a new rule in regard to author salesmen and saleswomen. One afternoon when it was too foggy to expect many customers, we all went out together for a late luncheon, leaving Leonard and Hope, his wife, in sole charge, the Calculator being careful to show them the list of minimum prices for books, and warning them not to sell below it. When we returned, we found five customers waiting at the counter, while Leonard and Hope were busily tying up parcels, their faces shining with delight. As these were their customers, we stepped back unobtrusively until the three women and two men passed out of the door with their little packages.

"Great rush as soon as you left!" said Leonard. "That company of five came in, each wanting a book to give away as a Christmas present."

"And we sold each one of 'em a book, too!" put in Hope, proudly. "They were awfully anxious to help the Belgians— That's why they came here instead of to an ordinary bookshop— They couldn't pay but six shillings each for a book—"

The Lightning Calculator almost jumped over the counter, in consternation.

"We haven't any six shilling books— What in the name of all the Allies do you mean?"

"So we told them," smilingly interposed Leonard, "but they said we ought to have, as plenty of people would patronize us at that price for the sake of Belgium, when they couldn't pay fancy prices, so Hope put five books on the counter and said they could have them at six shillings each—and here you are!"

He marched to the cash-drawer and held up a crisp one pound note and some silver.

"Whose books, all autographed, did you sell at six shillings each?" I asked in a muffled voice.

"Mine!" answered Leonard gaily. "They didn't know I'd written them, you see!"

"You've meddled with the Minimum!" shouted the Calculator. "You're the first one who ever dared to meddle with my Minimum!"

"But only with my own books—I knew I mustn't sell the other books below the Minimum."

"All the worse! Haven't you any pride, Leonard Merrick?"

"Not a bit, when it comes to getting thirty shillings for the Belgians! Can't I autograph more books if anybody asks for them?"

"Yes, he *can!*" interposed Hope.

"And yes, he *will!*" declared the Calculator, "but I'll see that he doesn't sell any more—depreciating the market value of our star authors' autographs! And no more authors sell their own books!"

I went to the telephone and ordered copies of "Conrad in Quest of His Youth," "The Actor Manager" and "Whispers About Women" to be sent early the next morning, and she whom we call the Printer hurriedly made a large-lettered sign which we placed conspicuously on the counter:

"Mr. Leonard Merrick's Books all Sold. Others will be ready to-morrow, Autographed and Inscribed by the Author. Price One Guinea Each."

Then, having proved his incapacity as a salesman, Leonard was thereafter relegated to the harmless, if uninteresting, task of wrapping parcels.

There was another day when one of my intimate friends came in and, picking up three books by a "popular" author, said, with a smile, "I see these books are not properly autographed."

"Oh yes," I said, showing her the fly-leaf, "but the autograph is valueless. Ten of them were sent here by the author without invitation. They are never asked for."

"My dear," she whispered, drawing me aside, *"I* wrote them! I've been working as a 'ghost' for —— the past four years, and I shall soon be able to turn out one every three months —seventy-five pounds apiece for me, and several thousand for ——! Nobody notices the difference— In fact, there isn't any difference. I've studied the early style and I manage beautifully. Of course, I trust you, and, of course, I won't insist on re-autographing those books!" and she went out of the shop laughing.

One day we had copied out in big letters and placed in the window, the unpublished verses Morley Roberts wrote in the "David Brand" which he contributed. The verses drew a crowd:

> "Only a scrap of paper,
> Only a nation's word;
> These are the things they tell us
> Gentlemen think absurd.
>
> Only a twice-signed Treaty,
> A poor, thin guarantee:
> The vow of three great nations
> To let a small one be.
>
> No more than this, this only,
> And that's why the five words sting,
> Where gentlemen serve their country,
> And a gentleman—though a King."

It made a lot of Britons feel newly furious at von Bethmann Holweg, and it brought in a buyer for the books and lots of buyers for "Dik: A Dog of Belgium," especially among the refugees to whom the shop is becoming a sort of Mecca. Some of them belong to Belgium's "first families," as I can tell by their speech and manners. They bring their children, too, who hold out their pennies saying the one word "Deek!" or, rather, that is the only word I can understand. Officers and Tommies and Jack Tars also come in for Dik, and they tell me it is very popular at the Front, where it is sold in the Y. M. C. A. huts. One day a sailor, from a mine-sweeper in the North Sea, came in to buy some copies of the story for himself and his mates to read "between sweepin' up" as he said. I asked him to explain how mine-sweeping was done, so he drew on a sheet of paper a diagram illustrating the process, with a rough drawing of "Mollie," the cat mascot of the boat, and signed his name to it. I let it be known that I intended to exhibit this drawing in the window with a note to say that it would be sold for two guineas as a war keepsake-curio, when word came to me that this must not be done, as it might be giving valuable information to the enemy!

My particular little "office" was a cleared space behind a screen in the great general room, where I could hear, but not be seen. One evening, while autographing Diks, snatches of the voice of the Best Seller in conversation with a customer, floated over to me from the counter.

"It's the last Galsworthy we have— We're trying to get a third Hardy— Sending 'The Dynasts' for him to autograph— Yes, a beautiful Christmas present if you can bear the thought of giving it away— Oh, to your wife? That's different—keep it in the family, of course— You see, when both the author and the artist autograph the Diks, and they are tied with Belgian ribbons, they make a lovely Christmas card. It's Dicksee's dog masterpiece. The Duchess of Newcastle, one of our patrons, started the fashion, and now we're selling faster than we can get them autographed and trimmed— Other books besides Dik? Oh yes— Here's a copy of her first book—difficult to get—out of print— She'll autograph and inscribe it while you wait— Well, yes, she *is* an American, but people here never think of that—"

I could tell that a customer, with a distinct American accent, was asking questions about the originator of the Fund. I noted the hesitation in the voice of the Best Seller as she haltingly admitted the fact of my nationality—"but people here never think of that"! My throat seemed to be contracting, the hand with which I was swiftly autographing Diks, trembled— Then a rush of the Best Seller to the edge of the screen—

"Quick! American millionaire! Almost buying us out! Terribly interested in you—asked me 'What is her state?'"— Now what does that mean? Didn't like to ask him— Does he mean your state of mind? If so—! Well, autograph this, and if you add something about being an American, I think he'll pay special extra for it!" Hastily I autographed the first book I ever wrote, adding "From the farmlands of Wisconsin" in brackets, and off flew the Best Seller. I saw, through the cracks of the screen folds, that she was wrapping up two parcels, while she said,

"Easier to carry in two than in one— Thank you very much, indeed— Yes, bad news—can't expect to win all the time— but you ask the Tommies if we're 'down'earted' and listen to what they say!—Being British—"

The American was gone, and the Best Seller skidded across to me with her hands full of bank notes. "Great sale!" she cried, waving the notes, "and he's coming back for a Kipling if he'll autograph another— Just one— Ask him— Seventeen is only one more than sixteen after all! Ha! Any American accent that comes into this shop must pay up! Let them help with their dollars if they won't help by—"

There must have come a queer expression into my face, for the Best Seller paused and grabbed my hand lovingly. "Why, you must know, my dear, I wasn't thinking of you— You give *yourself*— You're one of us— We never think of you as—"

She rushed off to other customers. Business was flourishing.

"Well, yes, she *is* an American, but people here never think of that!" kept singing itself over and over again in my head, and in my heart. She meant to comfort me when she repeated what she had said to the customer—to comfort me—!

I know there is an undercurrent of unpleasant feeling in England since the publication here of President Wilson's Message to Congress of December 8th. There have been several leading articles about it. I remember that in one of them there was this: "Wilson warns the American people to be ready to meet the horde of 'cultured' savages, should the need arise.

It will not arise! Free Europe will be strong enough to secure
her own liberation!" They do not feel unpleasant toward any
other neutral country. The forming of a sort of Neutral Triple
Alliance between the Kings of Sweden, Norway and Denmark
has even brought words of commendation from the British
press! As for Italy's indecision, whether it is a waiting to see
which way the cat jumps, or merely a delay caused by the slow
delivery of marching boots from an American factory, that
elicits neither carping criticism nor stinging humor.

The voice of the Best Seller roused me from my reverie.

"I'm so hungry I'll be eating the paper clips! I've sold the
Beresford books— Lord Charles ought to be skipping in with
his sailors' hornpipe and dance us all out to the Ritz for a large
meal— Oh well, I suppose he's delayed—I say, Scout Achilles,
bring us in some soup and biscuits from the A. B. C."

Toward the end of the sale there came an express package
from the Midlands, containing a beautiful Georgian tea-pot
and a note:

"Dear Enid: I can't write books, but I do so want to help your
Fund. This has been in my family ever since the time of George
the Third. My mother gave it to me for my wedding present. It is
my dearest household treasure—but sell for what you can get, and
add the price to your book-shop receipts."

A friend had just come in while I was unpacking it.

"Why, that's the kind of a teapot Mrs. Page has been looking
all over for!" she exclaimed, taking up the beautiful bit of
silver.

"You mean the Ambassador's wife?" I asked.

"Yes. Hold it for an hour. I'm going there now and I'll
telephone you from her house," and she swung out of the door
and into a taxi. Within the hour came a personal message to
me asking if I would send the teapot to the Ambassador's residence, and I decided to take it myself. None of the others at the
shop had heard the conversation, and as I went out with my
parcel, I merely said I knew of a possible buyer of the teapot.

"You ought to get ten guineas, and a bargain at that," called
the Calculator after me, and I agreed with her.

Such luck! All the way there I fairly chuckled in my delight. If the wife of the American Ambassador bought that teapot—and the message seemed to imply that it was a sure sale—what an advertisement for the Fund, what a story for the newspapers!—

"Mrs. Walter Hines Page, wife of the American Ambassador, has bought the beautiful Georgian teapot, which has been exhibited for sale at the offices of Canada's Grand Trunk Railway by the Authors' Belgian Fund organized by Elizabeth Banks, the American journalist."

Yes! *American* journalist! "Never think of my being an American—" Well, I'd *make* them think of it now!

I fairly raced up the steps of the Page home, carrying my precious parcel into the library, unwrapping it for the Ambassadress, who viewed it with shining eyes.

"Oh!" said Mrs. Page. "I've wanted one all my life. I can use it here and take it back home and use it there."

"Then you'll buy it, Mrs. Page?" I asked. "I think I ought to get ten guineas for it—fifty dollars—don't you?"

"Quite reasonable!" she laughed. "I just want my husband to see it before I decide positively. He'll be here from the Embassy office in a few minutes now. He knows how I've wanted one."

Walter Page came in and shook hands. I told him something about the Fund and its book treasures, and I noted his interest as I mentioned the prizes in autographs and manuscript poems. I told him that some of the Embassy men had been in and bought books. Then Mrs. Page, all impatience, broke in with:

"This Georgian teapot! She's selling it because somebody gave it to her Belgian Fund—I've told her if you—"

Mr. Page took up the teapot, the teapot which was made in the time of that German King of England whose pigheadedness drove the American Colonies away. Walter Page is a man who appreciates beauty in art and I could see his pleasure in handling and looking at the thing. Then, suddenly, I noticed a change in his expression. He put the teapot back on the table and seemed, in an instant, to turn from the friendly literary man into the careful, cautious diplomat. He looked at his wife, made an excuse, and left the room.

Then a servant summoned Mrs. Page, and, telling me she would be back in a minute, I was left alone with the teapot and a foreboding of misfortune.

Mrs. Page returned to the library. Her face was full of disappointment.

"My husband thinks we ought not to buy the teapot," she said. "You see—" Her voice trailed away.

"Oh!" I said. "I suppose it's because—because—"

We looked into one another's eyes, I was almost crying, and I believed she was, too. Gently she helped me to wrap up the teapot, shook hands and told a servant to call me a taxi. Once inside it, I gave the front glass a bang with my furious fist, and the driver, thinking I wished to speak to him, stopped. I motioned him to go on.

For I knew why the wife of the Ambassador from the greatest neutral power to the Court of St. James's, must not buy a teapot from a Fund which was helping the Great Little Belligerent, fighting for the world's freedom. The news of the sale with the name of the purchaser would be noised abroad, even if I myself did not give it to the next reporter who called for the "daily story," and the simple buying of a Georgian teapot would become a non-neutral act to the extent, perhaps, of creating international complications!

As I entered the Grand Trunk doorway, the Calculator called out, "Did you sell it?"

I controlled myself and spoke casually, "No, it turned out not to be the kind of a teapot the lady could buy, after all."

"Well, don't cry!" she teased. "Two other women are battling for it, one by telephone and one sitting here praying fervently that you wouldn't sell it."

I handed over the teapot.

CHAPTER X

A FLYING MAN IN FLANDERS

IT is May, and I am afraid, always afraid, of the Terror-by-Night.

Whenever I give myself time to think, my thoughts are of Count Zeppelin's promise of an Air Fleet over London this spring, and then my teeth chatter and my legs shake.

About this fear of mine, I am perfectly frank. I will not try to save my pride and self-esteem by fooling myself with the delusion that I am only afraid for London, this city that I love, which for years has cast a spell on me, calling to me, always drawing me back, whenever I have gone away. My fear is a *personal* fear. I am afraid of being struck by a bomb—and not killed. I am not afraid of death. I am afraid of getting maimed and incapacitated for earning my living.

To-night London seems all-glorious. I look up at the sky and see a dark blue starry mantle thrown over her. Except for the stars there is darkness everywhere, for the street lights are shrouded with smeary green-painted glass, and they cast only a little blur that could hardly be called a light. Every blind in the Adelphi, and all over London, is drawn tightly, and before I stand at my window to look out, I must turn off the electric light.

On just such a clear night as this, we have been assured, the first Zepp raid on London may be expected. Already they have visited the Coast towns and have dropped bombs within thirty miles of London. The newspapers keep us well posted on what happens in the outlying districts. They tell us the names of the towns, the names of the persons injured and killed, the names of the streets and the buildings that are demolished.

I find my only remedy against nervous collapse, or possibly death from pure fright, is to keep busy. All the afternoon and this evening until a few minutes ago, I have been writing letters to the boys at the front—the officers, the Tommies, the bluejackets, the marines and the airmen—none of whom I have ever seen. My letters are in reply to theirs, some short, some long, some with heavy blacked-in spaces, showing the censor has been at his deadly work. I try to decipher the blots, holding the sheets this way and that up to the light, and then I have to confess that the censor knows his job. I have learned something in regard to the censorship that I think must be a bit of comfort to the boys—that no one man or set of men, is entrusted with the Secrets of Hearts. It seems that various officers take turns at censoring, and that the man who censors to-night will himself be censored to-morrow night.

Besides the letters, I get many of those little Field Service Post Cards, with their coldly-set printed forms, topped with the announcement: "The sentence not required may be erased. If anything else is added, the post card will be destroyed." If several days go by when I do not write, from sheer inability to find the time, there will come the little post card with the one clear line, so pathetic in its appeal, "I have received no letter from you—lately." Then I fly to my typewriter, be it never so late, and send a long letter, to be accompanied by some chocolate or cigarettes, reproaching myself for having neglected, even for a few days, a soldier boy who so honors me with his friendship and trust.

To-night, because my mind is so full of the fear of Zepps, I am thinking of my airman correspondent whom I call "the Flying Man in Flanders." Never having seen him, I have been trying to "visualize" him from what he tells me of himself and from what he does not tell me, except between the lines. I know he is very young and of what is called "good family." He is too young to have read any of my earlier work, and he took me for an Englishwoman, as a matter of course. I have told him of my fear of Zepps, and he has confessed that he does not know how he would feel "down on the ground in London," but that he never fears them when he is flying.

I have not heard from him this week. A few minutes ago

I drew the blinds and turned on the light to read the last word I had from him, a post card:

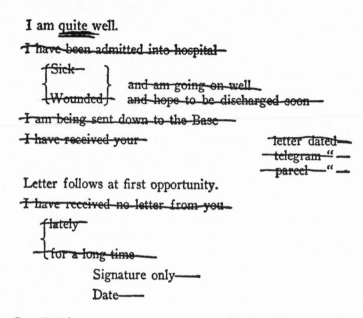

I am quite well.

~~I have been admitted into hospital~~

{Sick~~ ~~Wounded~~} ~~and am going on well~~
~~and hope to be discharged soon~~

~~I am being sent down to the Base~~

~~I have received your~~ ~~letter dated~~
~~telegram "~~
~~parcel "~~

Letter follows at first opportunity.

~~I have received no letter from you~~

{~~lately~~
~~for a long time~~}

Signature only——

Date——

So all I know to-night is that the Flying Man was "quite well" with the "quite" emphasized to reassure me and that I am to have a letter "at the first opportunity." I wonder if the letter is something special? I am waiting for it.

.   .   .   .

The last post is in, and the letter has come from the Flying Man in Flanders:

"Dear Enid:

I am censor to-night, and so I must be *very careful*. Everything depends on how you act in regard to the matter I am going to tell you about. I don't know what steps you will take. I only know you are the only person to whom I dare write about it, and something tells me I must write. I leave the whole matter to be dealt with at your discretion, but I need hardly mention that *my identity must never be disclosed*. Now, for the facts.

On the evening before the Zepp attack on Southend, information reached us at 10:30 p. m., first message that *one Zepp* was out. Before midnight we knew *how many* were out, and they were moving on *us*. The necessary preparations were made, but suddenly they changed course, and made for England, without coming near us. Now, what arrangements were made in England, I don't pretend to know—but one thing is obvious, that the cleanest and safest way to dispose of a Zepp is to sink it at sea *after* it has dropped its bombs, for then, with the exception of a trifling amount, it is harmless to ships beneath.

But I am not going to say What is the Navy doing? Other considerations may have prevented them from observing for Zepps. But what I am going to ask is, *What is the Royal Air Service doing?*

The facts are these: At Dunkirk they have a large quantity of the latest and best machines (Here I may say they take preference over the Royal Flying Corps for delivery of new machines). I know the exact number, but suffice to say that they have a supply of Fighting Machines, armed with the latest in quick-firers, a large number of Rolls Royce cars, and everything that money can buy them. They know that Zeppelins have gone to England; they know they will come back minus their bombs; they know the *shed* that one will make for on its return, i. e. they know its course, and yet they let them come safely back in daylight without making the slightest attempt to find them. I *know* this, because one of our Squadron out on a long-distance reconnaissance *saw* one of them, making its shed, but he could do nothing, as he was a reconnaissance machine.

Just one other point. When you go flying at night, it is very, very difficult to find your bearings (As proof of this you will remember the German Wireless reported some weeks ago having bombed Hazebrouck and Cassel, when their bombs dropped on other towns. Now, this is the point—the PRESS at home are telling the Zepp crews exactly where they have dropped every bomb, and I may tell you that wherever a bomb is thrown, a chart is marked.

All the Zeppelins have been doing up to now is to get correct bearings—first of Tyneside for defences, and Armstrong, Whitworth and *now* for London. So that should it happen that particular buildings in London get bombed, you will have to thank the patriotic press of England.

I suppose you will say "Why does the Censor allow it to be published?' Well, that's another story, but *ignorance* has something to do with it. When will the people at home wake up to the dangers in their midst?

You probably know the Authorities changed and altered lights for the purpose of fooling hostile aircraft at night, but with the *aid of the newspapers,* the Hun is overcoming what was a difficulty to him.

I cannot write anything personal in a letter like this. We are sick about it here. We don't advertise like the R. N. A. S. but we do try to do 'our bit.'

Forgive me for troubling you with all this, but it is all for the cause we both have at heart—the downfall of the Hun. . . ."

When I had read the letter, I knew that the first important thing was to prevent the hand-writing and signature from being seen by any other person. I knew this boy could be court-martialed for what he had done. He had not only taken it upon himself to criticize the British Admiralty, saying what it should do and what not do—these civilians who stayed at home and directed affairs—but he had written a letter, which he had purposely put off till he himself should be censor, to a person he had never seen, a *neutral alien!* He had given her information which he declared to be of life and death importance, for the saving of London's chief treasures in structural art. She was to use the information *at her own discretion,* she a journalist, who could turn the whole thing into a sensational story for the American newspapers!

I copied the letter on my typewriter, burnt the original, and tried to think out how I should get the boy's advice to the Admiralty without myself becoming involved in questionings and investigations.

After midnight I rang up a man I knew I could trust to get the information to the Admiralty. His reply to the telephone was short and snappy, for he had been hauled out of bed to answer the call. I told him I was sending him something very important early the next morning and asked him not to leave home till he had received it. I sent him a copy of the letter, telling him I could answer no questions in regard to the name or the rank of the young airman, and stipulated that, under no circumstances, was he to mention that his own information had come through me.

In due time I had his reply. "I've done it! Give this to that boy at the front, tell him I wish I could know his name—and God bless him." He enclosed a little keepsake, which I promptly forwarded with explanations of what I had done.

June 1st, 1915. The first air raid on London came last night. The noise of the bombs woke me up. In my terror, I did nothing I had planned to do in case of a raid, except that I grabbed Daniel in my arms and rushed down to the second basement, where the cellars are. I went in my night-gown, bare-footed, carrying my dressing gown and slippers in my hand.

The housekeeper was not nearly so frightened as I was. My teeth chattered so that I could not speak, and she gave me some brandy. Poor little Daniel trembled in my arms, but tried to comfort me by licking my face. As the noise of the bombs and the guns went on, I could hear the voices of people on the pavement above the cellar. A woman's voice shouted, as though in protest against persuasion,

"I tell you I'm going to see them, if I can!" and then there was a cry of

"To the Arches! The Arches!"

The Adelphi Arches, built up by the Adam brothers from the Thames, have for some time been proclaimed to be the safest shelters in London in case of air raids.

In the morning papers, instead of the columns of intimate description that have appeared of the raids that have taken place outside London, there is merely this:

"THE ADMIRALTY. TUESDAY MORNING,
ZEPPELINS ARE REPORTED TO HAVE BEEN SEEN NEAR RAMSGATE AND BRENTWOOD AND IN CERTAIN OUTLYING DISTRICTS OF LONDON. MANY FIRES ARE REPORTED BUT THESE CANNOT BE ABSOLUTELY CONNECTED WITH THE VISITS OF AIR SHIPS.

FOR THE PUBLIC SAFETY.

THE PRESS ARE SPECIALLY REMINDED THAT NO STATEMENT WHATEVER MAY BE PUBLISHED DEALING WITH THE PLACES IN THE

NEIGHBORHOOD OF LONDON REACHED BY AIRCRAFT, OR THE COURSE SUPPOSED TO BE TAKEN BY THEM, OR ANY STATEMENT OR DIAGRAM WHICH MIGHT INDICATE THE GROUND OR ROUTE COVERED BY THEM. THE ADMIRALTY COMMUNIQUE GIVES ALL THE NEWS WHICH CAN PROPERLY BE PUBLISHED.

THESE INSTRUCTIONS ARE GIVEN IN ORDER TO SECURE THE PUBLIC SAFETY, AND THE PRESENT INTIMATION MAY ITSELF BE PUBLISHED BY THE PRESS, EXPLAINING THE ABSENCE OF MORE DETAILED REPORTS."

CHAPTER XI

AN ALIEN ON THE EAST COAST

I DON'T know how the story of why I went to the East Coast would have been treated by a Military Tribunal under Martial Law, because I have never attended a sitting of such a Tribunal.

I, an Alien, living in London during war time, went to an East Coast town, a proscribed area, without getting permission, without papers to prove my identity, and without the slightest idea that I was doing anything wrong.

However, I can fancy what a smart cross-examiner, prosecuting for the Crown, in the ordinary Courts of Justice would do with my story and, incidentally, with me. For it *was* an absurd story. I can see the sarcastic twist of the prosecutor's lips, the withering glance of his eye, as he addressed the Jury:

"Gentlemen of the Jury, let me show you how utterly foolish and unbelievable this woman's tale is, the story she has told here in the witness box of how and why she happened to come here. She is a journalist—I believe it is said of her that she is the best known 'detective journalist' on this side of the water. She, an American, has spent years in this country 'exposing' various things of which she does not approve, and selling her 'exposures' to many of our English newspapers at very special space rates, using various aliases. You have heard me ask her if she has any other aliases than those of 'Enid' and 'Mary Mortimer Maxwell,' and she has confessed to still another, while absolutely refusing to tell what it is, on the ground that it is a sacred war-time secret between her and a certain London editor, whose name she also refuses to divulge. We know that throughout the purlieus of Fleet Street, that street which has so aptly been called 'The Street of Adventure,' she is known as 'The Trinity'—sometimes as 'the Triplets.' Since she confesses to still another name, making three besides her own, might I not suggest that she should be called 'the Quadrangle,' or shall I say 'the Quadruped'?

"She once disguised herself as a housemaid, and with her unproficient methods of doing household work, wrought havoc in some of our best English homes; she has washed clothes in what she has described as 'insanitary laundries'; spoilt good British-manufactured tweeds and linens in dress-makers' shops where she has posed as an 'apprentice' desiring to learn the trade; she has sold flowers at Piccadilly Circus, bringing down upon her head—quite deservedly, I think—the fists of the legitimate flower-sellers who go early to Covent Garden to buy their wares; she has swept crossings in Regent Street and Baker Street; she has worked in Yorkshire and Lancashire cotton factories and bred discontent among the regular workers in the matter of their wages and manner of living; she has pretended to be an American heiress and told stories of our noble families that were better left untold— All these things she has done with a certain adeptness that would go to show that, at any rate, she is possessed of considerable intelligence, and yet she says she was unaware that she had no right to come down to the East Coast, that she even forgot she was an Alien!

"And what is the reason she says she had for coming here? There it is, Gentlemen of the Jury! If you have been able to understand what she calls her 'sole explanation,' your understandings are better than mine. She says she was 'all on edge' in London, owing to Zeppelin raids, during which times she hid herself in the cellars and the arches of the Adelphi; that she had no sleep for more than a month, because it was necessary to stay awake to know when the raids came; she says she thought she would 'go mad' if she didn't get a 'change' from London; so, for a *nerve cure,* she came down to the East Coast—where we never have air-raids, oh no!—and ordered a room facing the sea in a hotel which she knew suffered from bombardment in the early months of the war. Gentlemen of the Jury, loyal and enthusiastic citizens of this part of the East Coast, would even you recommend this town as a health resort in these times for a nerve-racked woman who is afraid of Zeppelins?

"She says she expects to write articles about how our fishing-smacks are turned into mine-sweepers; that she has also in mind a pretty little story about a cat-mascot on a mine-sweeper, which she is going to have printed at her own expense and sell for the benefit of mine-sweeping sailors!

"But, Gentlemen of the Jury, the richest part of her story is this. She says that yesterday morning a reporter for a London newspaper rang her up and asked for a telephone interview on the subject of why she, having lived so long in England, had never been naturalized—a most reasonable inquiry, Gentlemen of the Jury, and she declined to be interviewed, saying 'that was too long a story,' whereupon the reporter offered her a column or even two columns in which to make her explanation, which newspaper hospitality she declined to take advantage of! Then when the reporter incidentally spoke of her as 'a neutral' she dared him to come round to the Adelphi and say it to her face, and when he jestingly said to her, 'Then *you* are not "too proud to fight?"' she shouted over the telephone, 'Torquemada! Turn the screw!' and rang off.

"And then, Gentlemen of the Jury you heard her say 'I was so worked up that I wanted to get as near to the War as possible, so I came to the East Coast.' And again, Gentlemen of the Jury, you heard her reply to my question as to whether that was actually the truth— 'Of course it is! Truth is stranger than fiction! I write both, so I ought to know!'"

I can see the judge, a kindly man, peering scrutinizingly at me over his glasses, a question in his eyes, while I am riddled to bits by the prosecuting barrister. I can hear myself saying to him,

"My lord, I admit that it sounds a ridiculous story, but it is true!"

I can see a gentle smile in his Lordship's eyes and read his thought. "If she is as clever as all that, she would certainly have made up a more plausible tale than this. It is too absurd *not* to be true!"

.   .   .   .

But it did not happen just that way when I broke the rigid laws of "Dora," although the circumstances were precisely what I have imagined the prosecutor to be telling to the Jury. I had consulted my doctor about neuritis.

"Nothing at all the matter with you but just nerves," he said. "Better go away from London for a change. What about Devon? The West Coast is full of sunshine, and it's quiet and safe."

All very well for doctors to prescribe such "changes"! When I take holidays, I have to "work my way." I must find things to write about in order to pay the extra expenses for railway fares and hotels. What newspaper would print articles about things that happened, or didn't happen, in a sunshiny place, quiet and safe on the West Coast? Then the requested interview as to why I didn't get naturalized proved to be the last straw. I sent word to the big hotel facing the sea in the East Coast town for a room to be reserved, packed my bag and took the next train.

The manager of the hotel received me most graciously. It seemed that he "breakfasted with Enid every Sunday morning." He handed me a form to fill out, such a one as I had not seen before, not having been to any hotel since the war began. I found that if you were British born you had only two or three questions to answer, but if you were born outside the British Empire, you must tell all sorts of things about yourself, so I spent some minutes conscientiously describing myself.

The manager stood holding my coat and bag. He was himself going to show me to my room, and informed me that he had ordered dinner kept hot for me, which I thought was particularly thoughtful in him, it being after nine-thirty when I arrived.

"*You* don't need to do all that writing," he said. "Just these questions for *you*," and he pointed to the lines.

"But it says I *must*, if I'm not British born," I answered.

"Enid not British born!" he exclaimed.

"I'm an American," I said.

He looked astonished. "Then, of course, you have your papers with you," he said.

"What papers?"

He explained that I, as an Alien, was expected to have special identification papers, besides the permission of the Authorities to enter the town, a Proscribed Area in war time. When I told him I had no "papers" of any sort, he looked very grave.

"I must report you at once to the Police, you know. I am so sorry. I cannot provide you with a meal or a room until I have the permission of the Police."

Already he was at the telephone. I could hear his part of the conversation. It was a very troubled, sympathetic man who turned and said,

"They say you must come to the station without a minute's delay. It is very serious. I am so sorry I can't let you have dinner before you go."

He called a carriage, handed me in and placed my bag on the seat beside me.

"Just keep the bag," I said. "I'll be back as soon as I've explained to the police."

"Better have it with you, in case— I'm not sure what is to be done." He shook hands with me, and, as quickly as the darkness of the streets would permit, I was driven to the police station. I handed my card to a young police officer in the outer office.

"The manager of the hotel telephoned to you about me. I understand you want to see me," I said.

He looked at me with all the solemnity and stern gravity of extreme youth and inexperience.

"Well, what did you come down here for?" he asked.

"To get a change from London and to write about the fishing-smacks and things," I said.

"Papers, please!" and he stretched out his hand threateningly.

"I haven't any. I didn't know I had to get permission to come. I had no intention of breaking the law. I just came."

" 'Just came'! If you live in London, you must have identity papers, being an Alien."

"In London the authorities don't treat Americans like Aliens. Other Aliens have Identity Books. We don't. We go where we wish, without reporting."

"Even if that's true—and it sounds queer—your going

where you wish doesn't include the East Coast—most danger-out part of England—spies all around—what's to prevent your being here to spy?— You're not even an Allied Alien, and British subjects themselves have to get permission to come here."

His youthful eyes searched me through and through. His face was so gloomy and suspicious that I felt I must try to cheer him up. I smiled broadly, took a chair without invitation, and said,

"Now let's talk about it pleasantly! I've merely made a mistake."

"Mistake! You don't seem to know what you're in for. Even if you're innocent, it's a hundred pounds fine or six months' imprisonment, or both!"

"I haven't a hundred pounds, and I'd hate to go to prison. Really, now, don't you see this isn't the way to treat a lady?"

I didn't like the look of things, but I thought if I could only make this young man more cheerful, there might be something gained.

"Don't you ever smile?" I asked. "Isn't there anybody here who smiles?"

"Perhaps you'd like to tell your story to the Chief Constable, and see if he'll smile!"

"Yes," I said, "If you'll just hand him that card I gave you, I'd like to explain to him."

He went to another room and returned, glooming and threatening.

"The Chief Constable will see you!" he said, in some such manner as one would say "The Lord High Executioner is ready— Say your prayers!"

At the doorway of another room a man extended his hand. "Really, I'm so sorry to give you all this trouble," he said, as though he, not I, were the culprit. "Will you sit down and tell me all about it?"

I looked into the face of a perfect English gentleman—a face not glooming nor glowering, but greatly troubled.

"I had never thought of 'Enid' as anything but an English-woman," he said, turning my card in his hand.

"Many people don't," I answered. "Sometimes she doesn't, herself!" I got the smile I craved, and felt more at ease.

"Just tell me how you came to do such an extraordinary thing as to come here without permission and without papers."

"That's it," I said. "I didn't know it was extraordinary," and then I told him exactly how I happened to go to the East Coast.

"You say you haven't any papers to prove your identity. Is there anyone in the town who would vouch for you?"

"I have many friends hereabouts. I had expected to visit some of them, but they have never seen me, so they couldn't vouch for me or swear that I am whom I say I am. They are friends through my writings."

"You make things very hard for me. The law is very strict on the East Coast. I must conform to the law, as well as ask you to do so."

"That young man outside said I was liable to imprisonment for six months, or one hundred pounds fine, or both. Must you impose that penalty?"

"I have another choice, if I am convinced that your story is true. It is to send you back to London to-night by the next train, and to make sure that you go to the address which is on your card."

Again he studied the card, and he looked so sad that I felt more sorry for him than for myself.

"Shall I stay here at the station till the next train— It will be a wait of several hours, won't it? I've had nothing to eat since lunch time. The manager of the hotel said he must not give me the dinner he had ordered kept hot."

He started. "This is worse for you than I had supposed! Do you mean to say you're hungry?"

"Frightfully!" I laughed. "Have the police dogs got any biscuits?" I did not tell him that my head was aching and that I was holding up with the greatest difficulty to keep from fainting.

"Can't you suggest anything at all I can do to prove your identity— You understand I don't doubt it myself?"

"Would it help any if you rang up the Referee office in

London, and asked them to describe 'Enid's' personal appearance? I'll pay for the trunk call."

He looked relieved, and hurried to the other room where the telephone was. "I can do that," he said.

"What did they say?" I asked, when he returned.

"I decided not to telephone. I thought it wouldn't be pleasant for you."

"No, it wouldn't. They'd have a nice joke on me when I got back. By the way, I did not mention that I have a passport in London."

His face brightened. "What about telephoning someone to send it to me so I could have it to-morrow morning?"

I said there was nobody to whom I could telephone. It was securely locked in my desk with other private papers.

"I see I must go back to London to-night," I said.

"No! Stop here for the length of time you intended. Report to me the day you leave and the train you take. As soon as you return to London, register your passport to me, so that I can report to the Authorities that I have examined your 'papers' since that is all the papers you have. I will just ask for your word that you will send me the passport."

I said, "Yes, I will send it," and thanked him, as he escorted me out to the waiting carriage and instructed the driver to take me back to the hotel. The manager was at the door and helped me out. He was looking happy. "The Chief Constable telephoned me you were on your way, to be sure to have your dinner on the table and to give you a good cup of tea with it," he said.

I stayed there nearly a week. I wandered about where I would, paid some visits, and sometimes in my walks I saw the Chief Constable, an English officer of the law and a gentleman, one whom I can best describe as a genius at understanding.

I slept in a room at the hotel next to one which had been wrecked by the bombardment when the Germans shelled the so-called "fortifications" of one of the most beautiful summer resorts in the world. I seemed to make up for all the sleep I had lost in London. Peacefully and dreamlessly I slept in my room overlooking the sea in the most dangerous part of England, while a little way in the distance, the silent gray Fleet of Britain kept watch, protecting me, a neutral Alien, living in the land of my fathers.

On my return to London I registered my passport to the Chief Constable, receiving it back from him with the kindest possible letter, which made me know I had made yet another English friend in an entirely unexpected way.

I have said nothing to any one about my experience as an Alien at the hotel or the police station, but it has seemed to me that something is due from me to many readers in other parts of England who may be sad and disheartened during these terrible days of death and disaster, a message of hope. So I have written for the Referee a Sunday article, paying my tribute to the beauty, the bravery and the high courage I found on the East Coast:

THE LADY OF THE ROUND TABLE

"The Blinds of Hope."

AN OPTIMIST OF THE EAST COAST.

It was on the East Coast, facing the sea—the cottage where I stopped as guest.

The cottage was built in those days when they built to last—solid, substantial. I knew it had stood there upon its hill for more than a century. I felt that a century hence it would still be there, quite as weatherproof, quite as comfortable, as it was now.

Everything about the place seemed to be in keeping. There was nothing transient, flitting there—except myself, the visitor. The maidservant who opened the old oak door was middle-aged—indeed almost elderly, and I knew she had served her mistress for many years. One could not fancy this maid giving "notice." One seemed to see her going on with her duties, contentedly, conscientiously, till she or her mistress should pass away.

Up the solid staircase, with its old-time balusters, the maid conducted me to my room, and somehow I felt that she disapproved of my new-fashioned fiber suit-case which she carried and placed

* Reprinted from the Referee.

conveniently by the window ready for unpacking. I knew the boxes and bags which her mistress used when she made her infrequent visits to her friends were of good strong leather, time-worn, but just as fit for service as on the day when, years ago, she had gone to that cottage a bride. I began to feel half-ashamed of my own modernity.

. . . .

My hostess was one of my newer friends, and I had never visited her before; so, left alone, I looked about my room with interest. Like the whole cottage, it gave the impression of solidity and permanency, yet it was dainty and furnished in exquisite taste.

The bed was an old four poster, hung with dimity to match the curtains at the window. The bedspread was of fine net with sprigs of flowers showing through; the sheets and the pillow-slips were of finest Belfast linen. A Chippendale chest of drawers stood in a corner and there were chairs to match it. A Sheraton bookshelf held books, beautifully bound, for my reading. A candlestick of old hammered brass, highly polished, was on the table by the bed.

I looked at the pictures on the wall. They were prints and engravings of times gone by—perfect of their kind. The china on the mahogany washhand-stand was of some old English ware of value. One or two pieces had been cracked and, for safety sake, had been made secure by riveting.

Wherever I looked about the room I saw the evidence of taste, of beauty, of harmony—and something more. There was an indefinable atmosphere of lastingness about the place. Here seemed rest, peace. From the window I looked far out over the sea. I knew that somewhere was the silent Fleet keeping watch—or were the guns booming and I unable to hear them? It was strange that here on the East Coast I felt so secure, so far removed from the War, while in reality I was nearer the War than I had ever been before.

I sat down by the window and looked out. After a while, because the sun shone so brightly in my eyes and so blurred the clearness of my outlook over the sea, I drew the blind until it reached half-way over the window and discovered a thing that made me stare.

The blind was made of paper!

. . . .

A paper blind in such a room as this! Bewildered, I passed my fingers carefully over the dark, thick green stuff—paper—and looked about at everything else—so dainty, so well-made, so lasting. Where I had thought all was harmony the paper blind struck a discordant note. Who could have believed that the same woman who had furnished the room and even picked out and doubtless draped the graceful dimity at the sides of the window had superintended the putting up, with pole and fixtures, of this thing which even now showed a frayed, torn edge—a paper blind!

So I sat pondering over this strange freak in the character of a woman of taste and breeding and one who I knew was not hardly pressed for money. Then I saw my hostess at the door.

"I knocked, but you were so absorbed in studying something that you didn't hear me!" she said, and her voice was so sweet and silvery that it made the paper blind seem worse and worse.

She came over to the window. "The sun is a little glaring, isn't it?" she asked.

"Yes," I said, "and so I drew the blind a little."

"Ah!" she exclaimed, fingering the edge of the blind. "I see it's getting frayed, and there's almost a three-cornered tear in the corner here. Well, I'm glad, for somehow that gives me courage to believe what my sailor boy wrote home last week. He's away off there, somewhere, somewhere," and she pointed to the sea. "He added a postscript to his last letter: 'Mother, now we sha'n't be long!'"

She looked at me keenly and half-humorously. "You don't like my paper blinds, I see; but come down to tea while I tell you about them, for the whole house is curtained with paper blinds."

"Will they last?" I asked, not knowing what else to say.

"Indeed not!" she laughed. "They're not meant to last. They are the Blinds of Hope!"

We sat down at the tea-table by the sitting-room window, over which was half-drawn a replica of the blind upstairs, except that there was most certainly a patch pasted on what might have been a pin-hole.

"Now, I'll tell you about the Blinds of Hope," she said. "You know that down here on the East Coast we must be very careful that not a streak of light shines out over the sea?"

"Yes," I said.

"Well, I have always had Venetian blinds at my windows. I am very fond of them, especially if they are painted green; but they cannot be absolutely and hermetically sealed, and I knew I must get something heavy and lightproof in the place of those I had. At first I tried to find something in the heaviest and most expensive linen, with the thought that I must have blinds that would last. You can see from the way my house is furnished that I adore pretty things, but I want them substantial.

"Just as I was about to order the material for the heavy linen blinds I changed my mind. It seemed to me that if I had substantial blinds, warranted to endure for years, with my Venetian blinds put away in the storeroom, I should grow to thinking the War would last always whenever I looked at the blinds. Now, I understand my own disposition well enough to know that I mustn't allow myself to get melancholy—for my boy's sake and the country's sake and my own sake. So I told the saleswoman I would take paper blinds instead of linen. She looked surprised, for she knows my penchant for durability. 'Yes, Madam,' she said; 'but, you know, we don't warrant them to last. They are good and thick and lightproof until they get torn. They are just War blinds.'

"So I bought them and had them put up at every window. Whenever I draw them up or down (and I always attend to the blinds myself) I think that they are just War blinds, not warranted to last nor meant to endure; and I believe—yes; I am convinced— that the War will not outlast my paper blinds.

"You see now why I call them 'the Blinds of Hope,' don't you?"

.   .   .   .

And now I find myself thinking often of the sweet philosophy of my East Coast friend. In times of downheartedness it comforts me. Perhaps you, too, need comforting, and so I have told you the story. Is the morning gray, the evening threatening?

Come! Let us draw up, draw down, the Blinds of Hope!

ENID.

CHAPTER XII

STORM-DRIVEN

Extract from an article in the NEW YORK TIMES *of November 21st, 1915—*

". . . She arrived here two weeks ago on the British steamship Minnehaha. Although she is an American she says she refused to sail from England under the American flag because she considers that flag has shown its inability to protect those who have a right to its protection. . . . She wrote to President Wilson telling him that she intended to sail by whatever ship she pleased, but that, in her phrase, it was 'up to him' to see that, according to the provision on her passport, she was enabled 'safely and freely to pass' from one country to another.

"She now ascribes the fact that she did pass 'safely and freely' from England to the land of her birth, however, to the efficiency of the British Navy, which she says she saw with her own eyes all around her for several hours, in the shape of torpedo boats and mine-sweepers, making sure that the waters were free from German submarines. . . .

"In her workroom in a hotel near Broadway, she explained that one of her several missions here, private and public, was 'to see for myself whether it was true that Uncle Sam had lost his spinal column. I didn't want to condemn him on mere hearsay, you know!'

"The walls of the workroom are covered with British recruiting posters. . . .'"

CHAPTER XIII

"DETACHMENT!"

(Washington, December, 1915.)

I SAT in the gallery of the House of Representatives, and waited for one of the things I had crossed the ocean to hear, the President's Message to Congress.

While I waited, I looked round about me. In the Diplomatic Gallery sat the Teuton-in-Chief, his face immobile, inscrutable. There were many eyes turned his way, watching and, apparently, wondering. He gave no sign of embarrassment. Of all the occupants of the gallery, he looked the most unconcerned, though it was said there would be a message in particular for him.

The hall was more closely packed than I had ever seen it in the old days when I used so often to be in one or another of the galleries on my journalistic missions for London newspapers. I happened to have a reserved seat, but it was in no way superior to the seats in the ordinary public galleries where, in order to get a place, all the people had to do was to be there early enough, on the first-come first-served principle. Involuntarily I thought of the openings of the British Parliament, with their attendant pomp and pageantry, and the impossibility of all but an especially chosen and favored few gaining an entrance. All about me, men and women were talking.

"He'll get what's coming to him!" and there were nods in the direction of the Teuton-in-Chief.

"The Hyphenates will get it, too!"

"He's going to tell how we need more ships."

"What d'ye mean—war ships?"

"Carrying ships—merchant ships. We've got to have 'em, if we keep our end up in trade."

"What's that? . . . I tell you, that speech was written three weeks before the Lusitania was sunk, and delivered three days after. . . . Of course, somebody ought to have called his attention to how the 'too proud to fight' thing would sound before he went to Philadelphia. . . ."

" 'Call his attention!' Wait till you see his jaw, and then tell me if anybody would ever dare to 'call his attention,' or instruct or advise or even suggest! There, he's coming—watch the jaw!"

"THE PRESIDENT OF THE UNITED STATES!"

At the clear-sounding announcement which penetrated to all part of the hall, everybody stood up for just a second. Woodrow Wilson bowed, a half grave, half pleasant expression on his face, the people bowed in return, and we were all seated again.

For the moment I was so carried away by the simplicity of the thing that I forgot everything else. I had attended many great meetings and been in many important assemblages where noted men and women spoke from platforms, and just as noted ones were in the audience, but I could remember no scene of such impressiveness as this. Again I thought of the opening of the British Parliament, the King and the Queen attending in state, the peers in their robes, the peeresses in their rich dresses and jeweled coronets, the King reading a speech which someone else had written for him, one which might or might not represent his own views—the common people cut off from all sight and sound of their Parliament at work.

". . . We have stood apart studiously neutral. It was our manifest duty to do so. . . . It was the manifest duty of the self-governed nations of this hemisphere to redress, if possible, the balance of economic loss and confusion in the other, if they could do nothing more. . . ."

The MESSAGE was being delivered, the message for which not only the American nation, but the world, waited.

". . . In this neutrality to which they were bidden, not only by their separate life and their habitual detachment from the politics of Europe, but also by a clear perception of international duty, the States of America have become conscious of a new and more vital community of interest and moral partnership in affairs, more clearly conscious of the many common sympathies and interests and duties, which bid them stand together. . . ."

Pan Americanism! Now followed an exposition of the Monroe Doctrine, and in the faces of all those about me, I noted sympathetic and determined agreement. Only the face of the Teuton-in-Chief was still expressionless. It was as though, like a machine, his job were merely to click down notes of great import to be read by some one else.

The cultured voice went on, the steadied, measured tones seemed to drop words, one by one, as though to a baton, beating time.

". . . No one who really comprehends the spirit of the great people for whom we are appointed to speak, can fail to perceive that their *passion is for peace*. . . . Great democracies are not belligerent. . . ."

Peace Poison, this! Were Americans the only people who had "a passion for peace"? Had not all Great Britain this same "passion"? Peace with honor, peace with security, peace with freedom— Was not this the peace for which so many of my men friends were fighting, the peace for which my women friends were working, giving their sons, their husbands, their lovers, all they cherished most in the world?

Through my mind there rushed fragments of the talk I had with Roosevelt, or rather the talk he had with me, for he did most of the talking, just before I took train from New York for Washington. When I went into his room at the Metropolitan Magazine offices he remembered me instantly. We had made friends during his last administration, when, as a Washington correspondent for English newspapers, my business sometimes took me to the White House. Across the ocean I had now carried him a colored reproduction of Bernard Partridge's great Lusitania cartoon, which had first appeared in Punch and was now being used as a recruiting poster all over Great Britain. He was as pleased as a school boy to receive what he called "a present from London," and while he nearly shook my hand off in assuring me of his gratitude, I burst out with,

"Oh, I'm so ashamed these days, so ashamed!"

Then he flashed all his teeth upon me and laughed heartily.

"I'm mighty glad to see you're a good American still!" he said.

"Why," I replied, "that's what many people are saying I am *not,* and what I'm not at all sure of, myself!"

His teeth flashed again. "Of course, you're a good American, or you wouldn't feel ashamed— If you'd turned English, you might feel disgusted with us, but you wouldn't feel *ashamed.* Don't you see?"

And then he talked. Mercy, how he talked! I had heard picturesque language from men before, but nothing like this! Every once in a while he burst out with the muttered exclamation "Jelly fish!" His teeth stopped flashing and got in some fine work in the way of gritting and grinding, as he more thoroughly examined the poster, and then pounded his desk, as again he hissed "Jelly fish!"

I had gone to see him, feeling heartsick, homesick. I left him feeling that I had been given a tonic, but when I arrived in Washington, and told the Democrat I had been to see "Teddy," he said,

"You should not have seen him before hearing Wilson, and I say it as one who loves Teddy. I hoped you would listen to Wilson's message with an open mind, not as one suffering with hate-sickness."

"Hate-sickness!" Could it be possible that I, who had always so prided myself on my ability to look at all sides of a question, had really become narrow and prejudiced in my outlook, so that I could not even properly listen to a speech by the President of the country which had given me birth? What was he saying now, that so many people were leaning forward so intently while others were craning their necks toward the Diplomatic Gallery?

"Jelly fish?" Interrogatively Roosevelt's stinging epithet seemed to be thumping against the drums of my ears as I, too, leaned forward, the better to watch his face, to hear his words. . . .

". . . plans of the Department of War for more adequate national defence. . . . The program which will be laid before you by the Secretary of the Navy is similarly conceived. . . . We have always looked to the Navy as our first and chief line of defence. . . . But armies and navies of war are only part of what has to be considered if we are to provide for the supreme matter of national self-sufficiency and security in all respects. . . ."

I dug my nails into the palms of my hands and shut my teeth and my lips firmly together lest I should lose my self-control and cry out in protest against such narrow vision. That world from which I had come was drenched in blood, men of many nations were going down to death for freedom's sake, and this man spoke with such detachment! "National *self-sufficiency!*" Again I saw the flash of Roosevelt's teeth, again I heard the gritting and grinding. I felt sick— Was it hate-sickness? Well, then so let it be!

"Listen with an open mind," as the Democrat had said? What was wrong with my mind, I should like to know! Wilson had said it—*"national self-sufficiency"!*

Now again the drop, drop, of the words, one after another. People about me were craning their necks toward the Diplomatic Gallery.

". . . There are citizens of the United States, I blush to admit, born under other flags, but welcomed under our generous naturalization laws to the full freedom and opportunity of America, who have poured the poison of disloyalty into the very arteries of our national life. . . . We should make use of processes of law by which we may be purged of their corrupt distempers. America never witnessed anything like this before . . . seeking to make this proud country once more a hotbed of European passion. Such creatures of passion, disloyalty and anarchy must be crushed out. . . ."

Again he took up the subject of "national efficiency," and I saw the message would end on that note. "We serve a great nation. We should serve it in the spirit of its peculiar genius.

. . . We are not partisans, but heralds and prophets of a new age."

He had gone back to the Executive Mansion, the floor and the galleries were emptying to the hum and buzz of comments. I remembered that three years ago I had heard his great speech at Carnegie Hall, the speech that had carried many people off their feet, or, rather, one particular sentence of it, one cleverly turned phrase, one word that had brought such cheers from a great multitude as I had seldom heard. He had ended with,

"Fellow citizens, if you elect me to the high office of President of the United States, I promise you I will not be your master, but your . . ."

Breathlessly I had waited for the word. I had been impressed with his oratory, his mastership of phraseology, and now I thought he was going to spoil everything by using the hackneyed cant about being but the "servant of the people," when in slow measured tones came the word—"spokesman"!

"I will not be your master but your *spokesman!*"

It was a stroke of genius.

And now, three years later, had he kept his promise? Could it be that he was the spokesman for the whole American nation? Was everybody thinking now only of self-efficiency, security, while the rest of the world was on fire? I had left the gallery and gone down to the East entrance of the capitol, and was standing on the steps when the Democrat joined me.

"Well?" he said, as we descended the steps together.

"Detachment! I did not know there could be anyone in the world at this moment so absolutely detached!" I replied, bitterly.

"Detached? From what is he detached?"

"From everything that matters!"

"Woodrow Wilson is President of the *United States,* if that is what you mean by 'detachment.' It is *you* who are detached! I am reminded that last year when Henry James became a naturalized British subject, in answer to the question as to why he wished to change from an American citizen to a British subject, he gave as one reason that the American people thought of the war in terms of 'humorous detachment.' It was, of course, Henry James who was 'detached' from his country and everything that was American by almost a half century of residence abroad. For years he had not been an American, but a detached onlooker, and he did the square thing by himself and by England only a few months before he died."

For a few minutes we walked through the Capitol grounds in silence.

"I don't think I am 'detached' in the way that Henry James was 'detached,' " I said, and I knew my voice was trembling. "Roosevelt told me that the shame I felt proved I was still a good American. To-day, when I saw the simple democracy of our government officials, and realized that the great state buildings here in Washington really belonged to the People, when I saw all sorts walking so easily and freely into the galleries, and compared the capitol here with the Parliament House in London, I felt more American than I have felt in many years."

"Yes," he said, "I was hoping it might have that effect on you. Let us say you are only *semi*-detached!"

"What I feel about Wilson is that he hasn't kept his promise to be the 'spokesman' of the American people. Why, since I got back to America, I haven't met a solitary person, man or woman, who doesn't feel ashamed and say the Americans ought to be in the war. The people who may not particularly love the British are, at least, pro-French. Why even the children are clamoring for French toys for Christmas after their parents have explained to them the awful plight of the children of France. I've met just one German sympathizer, the German-born young cousin of one of my friends—and they're trying to keep him out of the way of *their* friends, because he keeps saying that Britain is starving Germany."

"Let me see— You've been meeting what over in England they call 'the professional classes,' doctors, lawyers, college professors, artists, literary folk—people of New York, Philadelphia, Baltimore, Boston, who, until the war, have been going over to France and England quite often, and you've been on this side four or five weeks haven't you?" he mused.

"Yes, naturally!" I said.

"Well, Wilson isn't President of just these people of these
coast cities. I'm afraid you've forgotten how large your country is and the number of its inhabitants."

"No, I haven't," I replied, "but isn't it strange all the people
I have been meeting feel rather as I feel?"

"Not at all, when you pick out that kind of people to meet!"
he laughed. "By the way, I've forgotten just how long it is since
you were in your own part of your own country, the Middle
West, and when you last had a ride in a 'lumber wagon' along
rather bad roads. Why don't you go out there and mix among
the People Who Don't Understand?"

"I haven't the time. I must be back in England before the
end of this month, and, besides, I don't think I could keep my
head among such people. I don't suffer fools gladly."

> " 'If you can keep your head, while all about you
>   Are losing theirs—' "

he quoted. "That's what Wilson's doing— Tell me, do you
think Teddy's name for him is quite descriptive?"

"No, I certainly don't think he has any of the known quali-
ties of a jelly fish. I don't believe he's weak. It's his apparent
strength—or shall I say stubbornness?—that frightens me."

"Yes, he is stubborn, and with many men, stubbornness is
only another name for weakness, but it isn't so with him. I
don't agree with him in all things, but I recognize what is big
in him. Does it occur to you that it takes real bigness to stand
being thought a coward? How, again, does Kipling put it?—

> 'If you can bear to hear the truth you've spoken,
>   Twisted by knaves to make a trap for fools'

"But we were talking about the Middle West. The farmers
and the villagers of Wisconsin, Michigan, Minnesota, Illinois,
who, though I call them the People Who Don't Understand,
are not fools. Ignorance doesn't necessarily mean foolishness.
With your missionary zeal, you should set your mind first to

understanding *them,* and then trying to make them understand. And, besides, in regard to you, yourself, it might be the making, or rather the *re*-making of you. Think about it!"

What is the use of thinking about it? I can't go out to the Middle West. I must be back in England very soon now.

CHAPTER XIV

"WORKING MY WAY"

IT was the second night after my return to London from New York that I had what I call the Dream of the Children.

In my dream it was night, and I was awakened from my sleep by a loud ringing and knocking at my door. Jumping out of bed, I opened the door into the public hall and I found the stairways crowded with children. They were of all ages and conditions. Some were little friends whom I recognized, but most were strangers, and they were calling out to me in many languages. Some of them were carrying live kittens and puppies, others had dollies and woolly toys. Two tots were dragging a huge clothes-basket filled with all sorts of household wares and cooking utensils. The children's faces were white and drawn with terror, their little legs trembled so they could hardly climb the stairs, and their voices shook as some in English cried out,

"We have come to you because it's a war!"

Then I pushed them back from my door, crying,

"Don't come in, children! My flat is near the roof. We'll go to the arches where it is safer!" and I tried to drag them after me.

"Not the arches and not the cellars any more!" cried they, "It's a new kind of war, and we mustn't be down below!" and then, intermingled with the children's cries, I heard the street policemen shouting,

"Clear the cellars! Clear the arches!"

The children pushed into my flat, and on and on came what seemed to be an unending stream up the stairs. They were wearing the costumes and speaking the languages of many nations. What most of them said I could not tell, but they

147

held out their hands to me, speaking with their eyes, eyes of such terror and appeal. In the midst of the babel of foreign tongues I could distinguish only one word, "American!"

Now my flat was full. Children were everywhere, and still more pressed up the stairs and through my doorway. In the midst of what seemed thousands of children, I stood weeping and helpless, while outside there was the noise of guns and the hissing of flames. Lights, brilliant and terrible in their fierceness, dashed against my study windows, at which the children shrieked, yet, strangely enough, the windows remained unbroken and all of us unharmed—while more and more children crowded into the flat. The little foreign boys and girls chattered unceasingly, and finally I said to a little English girl who held my hand,

"What do these children say?"

"They say you will save us, because you are an American," she replied.

I dreamed again. I was in a great house of many rooms and corridors, wide and lofty. Save for myself there seemed no one there, and I wandered from room to room and floor to floor, in search of the sound of a human voice.

Down many stairs, holding on to ancient balusters, I went, opening doors on every floor, only to find each chamber empty. Finally I came to the underground foundation, where still the ceilings were lofty and the doors curiously carved and decorated. Opening one of these doors, I, at first, could hardly see the furnishings and surroundings, because of the comparative darkness. Then, as my eyes became accustomed to the gloom, I made out the figure of a man, sitting crouched in an arm chair before an inglenook fireplace in which there were dead embers.

I could see the man's back, only, but there was that in its attitude which showed the depths of misery and despair as plainly as though I saw a sorrow-lined face. And the back seemed to me very familiar.

Before such agony I stood in reverent quiet, afraid to advance, afraid to retreat. I waited until I could gain further courage, and then I stretched out my hand and placed it on the man's shoulder.

"Mr. President," I said, "there is no one in all the world for whom I feel such sympathy as I feel for you."

Then the face of Woodrow Wilson turned toward me, a face upon which seemed to be written the woe of all the ages, and he said gently,

"I didn't know *you* felt like that!"

"Is there anything I can do?" I asked.

"Yes," he said, "you can *write!*"

Then I awoke to a new day.

.   .   .   .

I have resigned from the Referee.

.   .   .   .

Henrietta came in to-day for the first time since my return.

"One would think," said she, "that you might make up your mind to settle down a bit in London, instead of planning to go off again. No sooner do you return from America than you say you must go back there!"

Straight and smart in her khaki uniform, she stood before the fire and looked troubled.

"Say what you will," she went on, "it *is* safer here in London, with all the air-raids, than crossing the ocean. You're the puzzle and worry and despair of us all—terrified of bombs from above, and yet risking the submarines from underneath, and you say you're not afraid of them!"

"I'm not," I returned. "Perhaps that's because I feel so sure that Britannia rules the waves, though she doesn't rule the air!"

"You know I never pry into your business, but do you mind explaining why it is that you feel you must go out to that place —what is it you call it?"

"Middle West," I said.

"Well, is it your idea that by going away off there, you could help to bring your country into the war?—because, if it's that, go, in God's name, and be quick about it!"

"Oh, Henrietta, I don't know. Perhaps it's just my damnable curiosity at work. I seem to want to get re-acquainted with the people with whom, as they say out there, I was 'raised.' I'm such a bad American, you know!"

"Yes," she agreed. "I've sometimes thought that, but it has never seemed to trouble you before."

"It didn't!" I replied.

"Do you think by going out there, you could help any better with the war?"

"I don't know, except that it might put more life and spirit into me, and so into my work. But, frankly, it seems to be a mere matter of my wanting to understand things. And besides, I had such a strange dream."

Then I told her about the children.

"What do you make of it?" she asked earnestly. Henrietta is not one to jeer at things she does not understand.

"I don't know, but I keep seeing all those children as plainly as though they were here, and I keep hearing them tell me that I will help them because I am an American—and then I remember I'm such a bad American."

Henrietta gazed into the fire, then at me. She generally has the knack of making me feel that she understands me without saying so. She did it now.

I noticed that she was looking not so worried as in the days when she tried to live in her country house along with the Belgian refugees. Before I went to America she had handed it over to them "for the duration" as she said, and got her English cook a situation in one of the hostels. She gives the Belgians a certain stated allowance for their food, and finds they can save something out of it to help the funds for their needy country. They are far more economical than the same number of average Englishwomen would be, and they are doing their cooking to suit their taste. They quarrel among themselves, but Henrietta doesn't mind that. She herself is living in a London service flat, with her old nurse, who has been in her family something like forty years. When I am in London, I can now "borrow" Daniel on occasions to keep me company, but there is no longer any question of the necessity of my "taking him on" when his lady's work is out of town.

The Belgians worship Henrietta as a *grande dame,* but there was one of her actions which I think they still talk over among themselves with considerable puzzlement. They arrived at Henrietta's house just before the commandeering of horses began in that neighborhood. They were awakened very early one morning by a muffled noise which turned out to be a rifle shot, and two of the strongest of the Belgian men were ordered to help Henrietta to dig a pit, wide and long and deep, for the burial of the still warm body of Nance, her beloved mare. Then, speaking rapidly to them in French, she made them understand that when the commandeering officers should make inquiries, they had only to say they knew nothing of Madame's riding horse.

What manner of being was this Englishwoman, they asked among themselves, who so calmly gave up her husband and brothers to fight, but refused to let her strong horse go into the war? This happened more than a year ago, and I believe that Henrietta's Belgian guests, though still astonished, have kept the secret of what became of poor Nance.

At the beginning of the week, I started out on a round of calls among my most dependable London editors. I did not find them keen to invest money in unwritten articles about the Middle West, although several of them had kept me busy writing from New York and Washington, and are still printing articles I sent on before I returned.

"Middle West— You mean Chicago?" asked one of the first to whom I applied.

"No. The country parts of Michigan, Wisconsin, Illinois, Minnesota—among the villagers and the farmers," I said. "You know the United States isn't entirely made up of large cities."

"Well, you always make things interesting," he said, without great enthusiasm, "so when you go, you might send me a column or two."

When I go! A column or two! I knew I couldn't go, except with an assurance of expenses covered, for I've lived entirely up to my income since the war began. A column or two would not help much in paying for a trip to the Middle West. I had returned to London, as per agreement, to finish up certain important work by the first of the year, work commissioned before I made my hurried visit to America. I had now done this, and was offered further commissions, which would keep me in England for the next several months, but I had declined them.

All my life, whenever I have wanted to do anything, go anywhere, I have been obliged to "work my way, rather joyful in the knowledge that I was able to do it. I began when I was about ten years old and wanted the Youth's Companion to come weekly to the farm-house. It took me six months to earn half the year's subscription which I was to share with another little girl, daughter of our nearest neighbor. I minded a baby for a young farmer's wife whenever she wanted to accompany her husband on a Saturday to the nearest town, where they sold apples to special customers in special streets. I wrote a "poem" for a little playmate to put on the gravestone of her beloved dog. The "stone" was a white-painted board, and together we printed on it, in black letters, the epitaph. I didn't want to charge her, for I, too, had loved old Jack, but I reasoned out that her father had no mortgage on his farm, and, besides, I would lend her the Youth's Companion if my partner in the enterprise would consent. I got ten cents for my "poem."

Next I earned fifteen cents for many hours' labor on many afternoons when school was closed, in "shooing" mild-eyed cows away from an unfenced field, before the owner had his rails ready for enclosing it. I discovered the hidden nest of one of our best laying hens, helping Auntie to arrange for a "sitting" on a mixture of larger eggs than the brooding little creature was always able to lay, and for this service I was given two extra eggs to add to those of Jerusha Jane, which enabled me to take three cents from the "College Fund" to add to the Youth's Companion box. I sold six buttons from my adored "button string" to a girl whose collection lacked real distinction, and received two cents in payment. I think that all my trading transactions were strictly honest except one, which was the writing of a composition for the young son of our richest neighbor and letting him pass it off as his own, but I could not resist the twelve cents he promised me for my "ghost-work."

When I was a bit older, I next worked my way to music lessons on a small parlor organ, by doing odd jobs, such as wiping dishes, dusting chairs and cleaning lamp chimneys for the minister's wife who lived in the nearest village of five hundred souls and whose husband came fortnightly to preach in the little district school-house.

My next effort at working my way was during my first year at college, and since then, down the years to the present time, I have worked my way to first one thing and then to another, including a wonderful trip over Germany and Austria-Hungary the year before the war.

In this way, I have become a fairly well and widely-traveled woman, because when I have wanted to visit any place or country I have been able to work my way by means of journalism. My plan has always been to go to an editor and say,

"I am going to—. Don't you want some articles about people and things there?" and only occasionally have I found it impossible to pay my expenses in that way. I have learned that it is more diplomatic to go to an editor and tell him I am going to a place, than to ask him to send me. It does not sound so frightening to ask for a commission for special articles as to suggest his being responsible for the trip.

So yesterday I went to the editor of a paper that publishes a great many of my "Mary Mortimer Maxwell" articles, and told him I was going to the Middle West. Then, "Will you take some articles from there?" I asked.

"You mean commission a series?" he asked.

I nodded.

He shook his head.

"Don't care anything about the Middle West."

"You ought to!"

"Why?"

"Well, for one thing, it produced 'Mary'!"

"But 'Mary' must never mention that. She's English— lightly, brightly so, but pure English!"

" 'Mary' can do the articles on the Middle West, telling how it impresses an Englishwoman."

Again he shook his head. "What makes you do so much gadding in war time, when you could just as well 'stay put' here in London? Look here!"

He handed me a list of subjects hastily scribbled on a pad. "Do those for me," he said cheerfully. "Pay you well. I saved them up for you while you were gone. I've been a sort of 'Mary's little lamb.'

> 'And waited patiently about
> Till Mary did appear' !"

"I can do these in ten days, before I go to the Middle West," I said. "If you won't commission a series, I'll find another editor who will."

"What's his name?" he asked pessimistically.

But I couldn't tell him. I was feeling rather doubtful about his name!

A sudden inspiration came to me.

"Will you let me see a map?" I asked.

"War map?"

"No. A map that shows up North America well."

As he handed me an atlas, he said, "I won't commission anything from Mexico, either!"

"I never said you would! If you'll let me go into another room to study this map and then come back, I believe I can interest you in something else—another scheme."

In the next room I spread the map on the table near the window and studied the line between the United States and Canada, noting particularly the places where the boundary ran along the Middle West and it would be but a step to get from one country into the other. Could I interest this man in Canada as a source of special articles on recruiting, wheat-growing, self-denial for the sake of the great British Empire?

"Will you commission articles about Canada?" I asked, when I went again to his desk.

"Do you know Canada?" he asked.

"Not yet, but I'll get acquainted with it."

"How?"

"By going over there and traveling about. I'll write you some ripping articles from Canada."

"I thought you were determined to go to the Middle West of the States," he said.

I showed him the boundary line on the map and explained how I could go back and forth.

"But the Middle West part need have nothing to do with you," I said. "I can manage that on my own, if you will commission enough from Canada."

Then I sketched out what I thought would make for good reading matter, descriptive of Canada and Canadians, somehow working up everything in connection with the war, and I saw that he was interested.

"I'll take a hundred guineas worth of those goods!" he said, and when I left the office, I had a check in advance.

A hundred guineas made me "safe," but there wasn't much of a margin.

I went to the office of a weekly paper which printed a good deal of my work.

"I'm starting for Canada within two weeks," I said. "Can you use some articles about Canadian women, their war work, Canadian men, mining?"

"Why, of course, as long as you happen to be going, so there won't be extra traveling expense," said the editor.

I left that office with a commission for six articles about people and things in Eastern Canada. "And if you go out to the West, I'll take six additional articles about that," was the editor's parting remark, as we shook hands.

I must certainly go West.

.   .   .   .

Now I have finished up the special list of articles for "Mary's Lamb."

My trunks are packed. I sail for Canada to-morrow, "working my way," as usual.

My way toward what?

CHAPTER XV

THE LIKENESS OF THE LANGUAGE

(Notes from Letters to a British Imperialist)*

Manitoba–Minnesota–North Dakota.

M Y dear Sir John:
As I sit here with a part of me in the British Empire and a part of me in the United States of America, I am reminded of your request for my "honest impressions of Canada." I remember, too, that you said, "What I most particularly want to know is this: Are they loyal to *us?*"

A Canadian friend has driven four stakes into the ground here at a point where the Middle West of Canada touches the Northern part of my native land. It is even more interesting and complicated than that, for I am writing this letter in two States, Minnesota and North Dakota, and in the Canadian Province of Manitoba. My friend has ingeniously contrived a board with four hollows which fit solidly upon the stakes, where I can rest my typewriting machine. So here I am perched upon a three-legged milking stool from his barnyard, watching the growing Canadian and American grain all about me, grain that next year will be shipped over yonder to you—and accursed be the Hun who tries to sink it!

My Canadian friend's farm is partly in Manitoba and partly in Minnesota. His wife is American, his four children took turns being born in the two countries, and the whole family speak with the strongest "American accent" I have ever heard.

---

* Realizing the danger of the loss of letters by the German torpedoing of mail boats, the author kept copies of much of her correspondence with British friends during the time of her stay in Canada and the United States.

The house itself is on the Manitoba side of the line but his children attend an American Consolidated School because it is nearer than the Canadian school. Except that the house is much more attractive and has more conveniences (such as telephone, water laid on, electric light, vacuum cleaner et cetera) I could almost imagine myself back in the old Middle West farm home of my childhood. The cooking, the methods of doing the housework, the magazines, books and many of the newspapers are all American.

And now for my first "honest impression of Canada" which you bade me give you. It is the impression of a certain subtle sort of democracy of spirit that one takes in with every breath. The thing is not political, but social. For me personally this "something" is working an amazing change. I feel as though I had been spiritually sick and were being gradually restored to health. Canada and the Canadians seem to be re-making me and turning me into an American again. In Canada many things are happening to me which immediately remind me of something else. I analyze the sensation and find that I am being flung back to the years of my childhood and girlhood, and am experiencing over again in Canada the things I experienced in the United States. The people are the same, the customs are the same. Involuntarily and automatically I discover myself doing things I used to do before I ever set foot in England, and because of this very "throw-back" in my habits, I learn that I am making myself immensely popular with Canadians. As I know you for one who chooses to deal in facts, even if they are not nearly so agreeable as fancies, I am going to write plainly in this letter and in the letters that will probably follow it.

You have asked me "Are the Canadians loyal to *us*?" meaning, of course, not only to England, but to the Empire as a whole. When, a few months ago you commissioned me to get for you this information, I did not smile. But I do smile now, for, when I think of you, British of the most British and Imperialist of the most imperialistic, having asked an American woman to tell you this, there is stirred within me a grim sense of humor. If you had, years ago, come yourself to Canada and studied the country and its people, you would now have the understanding which I have got of the essential *nationhood* of Canada, and you would have no difficulty in comprehending the answer I now make to your query.

Canada is loyal to Canada!

It was not so very long before the war that you visited the United States, studying that land, its people and its customs, yet, like many another Englishman, you did not think it worth while to step across the Border and study what in your letter you call "the brightest jewel in the Imperial Crown." You and others like you have treated Canada as many a man treats his wife and many a woman treats her husband after the legal union has been affected. "She's mine!" "He belongs to me!" And then begins a course of indifference and neglect.

But I will not continue to rub it in. What's done is done, and, still more, what's undone must now remain undone till the war is over. You, who know so much of the furthest flung Empire, know nothing of Canada except in an academic way, which, to my mind, is no way at all. I will do my best to enlighten your ignorance in the way I usually enlighten ignorance in my capacity of journalist, by telling you some little stories.

The other day I listened to a visiting Englishman who came over to help the Canadians in their recruiting. He was addressing a gathering of intelligent citizens in a big hall. I could see he was a fine man—a good Imperialist like yourself—and he spoilt everything and made himself hated by referring to Canadians as "you patriotic Colonials" and calling their country "our proudest possession."

One of the first acquaintances I made in Canada was a dear little old lady who was born and reared in Nova Scotia. She gave me tea in proper English style, showed me oil paintings of her ancestors, all of whom, she proudly informed me, had been United Empire Loyalists when the American Colonies defied George the Third. They said they would not fight against their King, so they trekked across the border, leaving lands and houses, even jewels and wearing apparel, behind them, and took up their abode in the Canadian wilderness. The old lady proudly showed me a little axe, which at first I mistook for the small hatchet with which the youthful George Washington had hacked down the infamous cherry tree. Remembering that it had never been found by the Americans and preserved, well-oiled, to keep off the rust, in the National Historical Museum, I thought one of her fleeing ancestors had stolen it and carried it off as booty. Luckily, before I had given voice to that impression, she told me of the thousands like it which a grateful and appreciative government in England had shipped across the ocean nearly a hundred and fifty years ago for the noble pioneers to use in felling the giant trees of the virgin forests where they were to build their new homes. I thought to myself that the British politicians of those days knew as much about Canada as many of the present gentlemen of Westminster know of Canada to-day. She did not notice that I handled the toy amusedly, rather than reverently, as I asked, "Wasn't it rather small for the purpose?" Solemnly she confessed that it must have been, but she said that it "showed the spirit of dear England," a land, which, by the way, she has never seen.

But, Sir John, I warn you that all Canadians are not like this dear little old lady in simplicity, and you ought to study how not to send inefficient little axes over here like the gentleman who tried to help recruiting along by alluding to Canada as "our proudest possession."

In Ottawa I had my first experience of meeting a person who really seemed to believe in the Divine Right of Kings— You know how long I have lived in England, and I never met one there! This man was Wilfred Campbell, the poet, whose work I have loved for many a year. As I was introduced by a common friend who mentioned that I had just arrived from England, Mr. Campbell took me for an Englishwoman. Oh yes! Over here, on both sides of the Border, they do declare that I speak with an "English accent"!

I asked Mr. Campbell if he were a descendant of the Empire Loyalists and he said that he regretted that he was not, but I soon found that he had made a deep study of their lives and adventures. It was thrilling to listen to his stories of the bravery shown and the hardships cheerfully endured by those who sacrificed everything for their conscientious belief in the right-eousness of the royalist cause. One has to admire them, while thinking them mistaken, which I am bound to tell you seems to be the attitude of most Canadians I have met. Some Canadian school teachers have a bit of difficulty in teaching the history of Canada to their pupils when they ask whether the American Colonists were wrong and the Empire Loyalists right. Several teachers I have met tell me they have formed the habit of evading a direct answer by saying, "We must admire and respect the people who do what they *believe* to be right, and who are willing to suffer persecution for loyalty to a Cause."

Well, to go back to Mr. Campbell, it seemed to come about naturally enough that the poet should have a number of stories to tell of the revolutionary leaders on the American side. These stories, I understand, were taken over by the Empire Loyalists although they left their homes and jewels behind. It was easy to see that he had no great admiration for George Washington and I was just beginning to enjoy hearing some, to me, brand new stories of the Father of my Country, when the friend who had brought about the introduction gave Mr. Campbell a hint as to my real nationality, whereupon there followed embarrassment to the poet and a good laugh for me, with my assurance that I hadn't taken offence. Both men agreed that if I *would* insist upon living in England for years and years and cultivating an "English accent," I must take the consequences!

And now I think I hear you saying, "But you admit that they *are* loyal to us!"

Wait a bit! In the same city of Ottawa I met another distinguished man who happened to have read many of my newspaper articles under the pen-name of "Mary Mortimer Maxwell," who, as you know, is supposed to be an Englishwoman.

"Are you disappointed," I asked, "to find that 'Mary' is not a genuine Englishwoman?"

"Quite the contrary," he replied. "You Americans speak our language. *Now we can talk!*"

And we did talk. Sir John, that man did not talk of "dear England" nor even of the British Empire. He talked of Canada, her resources, her hopes, her destiny, and of why she was fighting in this war. He explained to me that the English people did not speak what he called "the Canadian language," and he dwelt upon the misunderstandings which naturally followed what he called "this unfortunate fact." Could it be, I wondered at first, that I had met one of the "Annexationists," a Canadian who desired separation from the British Empire and a joining up with the United States? But no, this man was thoroughly opposed to annexation, though he talked affectionately of our "neighbors over the way." I said to him, "Tell me frankly why Canada is in this war which, of course, as a self-governing Dominion, she was not forced to enter," and he answered, "Canada is in it for the same reason that other nations are in it, to protect herself." He said nothing whatever about Imperialism. In the course of our talk he lost patience with me because I hinted at a feeling of shame that the United States stood outside.

"Why should the States come in?" he asked. "I don't blame them for keeping out as long as they can. We *had* to come in, but the States have nothing to do with it *so far*."

I met this man in the earlier days of my visit, and I now perceive that he is representative of a very great many Canadians. It is a mistake for the British to believe or to pretend that all Canada is being swept by a wave of sentimentalism and emotionalism in the matter of the Mother Country. The Canadians are a practical and common-sensible people, with an immense amount of State Pride very like to that one notes in Americans. I find that they dislike the term "British *subject*," preferring to be called "Canadian *citizens*."

Out here I have yet to hear a word of criticism or blame of my native land for not entering the war, and I am beginning to feel that I, an American by birth, had better keep quiet on a subject of which I seem to be woefully ignorant, and learn from the Canadians how to look at this thing justly and dispassionately. My Manitoba farmer friend who put up my writing table here said to me this morning,

"See here! What do you know about your country, anyway, when you go off and live for years in foreign parts? *We* know the Americans better than you do. We live next door to 'em, and we keep quiet and watch your Uncle Sam—we watch and listen while he saws wood."

I am really trying to grow in grace and understanding. Here on the Border I wander about, getting on first one side and then the other, noting the same sort of people, talking and living and working in the same sort of way, and I assure you that I often have to stop in my walks and inquire of passers-by which country I am in, and I ask people whether they are Canadians or Americans, and they ask me what part of England I come from. Back and forth I go, and I've now got to the point where I am unable to tell which is back and which is forth.

· · · · · · · · ·

Winnipeg, Manitoba

. . . I think I must be losing my "English accent," for now I seem to be able to pass as a Canadian, unconscious of any effort on my part.

When I arrived at this Wonder-Town I rang the bell of a pretty little house which had been recommended to me for lodgings. The pleasant-faced middle-aged woman, who answered, said yes, she did let rooms, and that she had a vacant one on the second floor, which means one flight up in this country. In reply to my question if I could have it and for how much, she said,

"Well, come in and sit down and rest in the parlor. You do look tired out."

I can assure you that I felt tired, too. The things I have done during the past month to get acquainted with Canada! I have worked in the fields, been down in the mines in ore buckets and, pretending I was a homesteader, I have staked out a claim. I sat gratefully in the rocking chair by the window and looked at the pleasant woman, who was wearing a nice white dress with a colored print apron to protect it, and I saw her studying the labels on my bags. She asked if I had come a long way and I said that I had come from London. She asked if I'd lived in London long and I told her I had, and then she named several people whom she said I must surely know. There was Jones, the hardware dealer, and Mrs. Emery, who was so prominent in church work, and the Blacks who lived in the white house on the corner of two streets of which I never heard, and I explained pleasantly that I didn't happen to know her friends, remarking that London was a large place.

"Well, yes," she said, "middling large. I used to live there when I was a girl, but I left Ontario before I got through the high school."

Then I knew that to this woman "London" meant a town in the Province of Ontario, so I said, "I meant London, England."

She looked at me sharply, her lips pressed tightly together and she folded her arms determinedly across her chest. Finally she said, the words dropping separately from her mouth like cold cinders,

"Once—I—had—an—Englishwoman—boarder!"

It was not the thing she said but the way she said it that surprised me into making no reply to her declaration, and there seemed to be nothing for me to do but to wait for her next observation. In a minute or two it came, fiercely, defiantly.

"I said then I'd never take another one!"

You have often complimented me on my journalistic instinct and my ability to turn the everyday happenings of my life to good account in my profession. This time I was tempted to forget everything except that I was dead tired and wanted to rest, and almost I said "But I'm an American, though I live in England." Then I pulled myself together, remembering that I was in Canada to learn. I even remembered you, Sir John, and your demand to know if the Canadians were "loyal to *us*," so I picked up my "English accent" again, smiled sweetly and said in my most appealing way,

"I fancy" (You know people say "guess" on this side instead of "fancy") "you must have had an unpleasant boarder from England, but there are unpleasant people in every country. I assure you I'm a very nice person, indeed. Just what did the other Englishwoman do that you didn't like?"

She searched my face, and my eyes fell before her. Here was I at my old trick again, obtaining information under what some of my English critics used jestingly to call "false pretences"! The woman went on.

"What did she do? Why, she asked me to clean her shoes—boots, she called 'em—and she was a tall healthy woman and took long walks and got 'em muddy. She ordered hot water brought to her room every morning and again every night—and the bath room next to her with boiling water all day and all night! She didn't get her orders obeyed, I can tell you! And then—and then—"

Now she seemed to be too full for utterance of her indignation. She hit her left wrist with the palm of her right hand. Perhaps it was not polite for me to press her, but I simply had to know what supreme indignity that unhappy Englishwoman had heaped upon the Canadian woman.

"And then—?" I said questioningly.

"She called us *Colonials!*"

I think I must have appeared duly shocked at this, and even then, before I was allowed to spend the night in that house, I had to use all my tact. I talked hard and I worked hard for the honor of your country and your countrywomen, and I promised I wouldn't commit any of these crimes. I "did" for myself so efficiently that the next morning my landlady was knocking at my door and inviting me to have breakfast with her—she who, as she had distinctly informed me, kept only a rooming house and never gave meals. Over one of the many fascinating pre-digested cereals with cream which one finds in Canada, I asked incidentally,

"What became of the other Englishwoman you were telling me about?"

My hostess sniffed. "Oh, when the war started, she said she must go back and work for her dear country. Somebody in Winnipeg had a letter from her only the other day saying she was working on the land—*working on the land,* mind you, and never knew how to clean her shoes till she had to learn to do it here!"

"Yes," I said. "I know some Englishwomen, now working on the land, who never used to button their own boots, much less clean them, before the war."

I've made a great hit with this particular Canadian woman, but I put it to you plainly, Sir John, why should it be necessary for me to do this sort of missionary work in one of the British dominions? Why am I able to do it? Is it not because of the likeness of the language between the Canadians and the Americans, the language which, despite my long sojourn in your country, I am becoming more and more delighted to find I have not been able to forget? Is it then the part of my country to explain Great Britain to Canada and Canada to Great Britain? Well, I am willing to do what I can in this very necessary work, but one of these days the war will be over and there will start again emigration from England to Canada, and it would be well that Canada and her people, her ways and her institutions should be better understood by those who desire to come here. It is high time that English school children should learn something more than that "Canada belongs to us" and that "it is a cold country." Besides, it doesn't "belong," and it isn't a cold country, except in spots and at times.

And speaking of schools and the difference beteen the English and Canadian "languages," during a "stop-over" at a flourishing town on the way here, I became acquainted with the Mayor who told me this story: An Englishman settled just outside the town as a "gentleman farmer"— The fact that he announced his occupation in those terms did not add to his popularity. He said to the Mayor, "How is it you haven't any public schools here? What am I to do about my boy's education?"

"What do you mean?" asked the astonished Mayor. "We've got the best public schools this side the Border. There's one of them!" and he pointed to a magnificent brick building in one of the finest streets.

"That's a public elementary school," replied the Englishman. "My wife's laundress sends her girl there."

"Why, yes, of course!" said the Mayor. "My girls go there, too and my boy used to go. If your boy is too far advanced for the elementary, send him to the public high, where my Tom is now."

"But my farm laborer's son goes there," objected the Englishman.

"Yes, of course!" answered the bewildered Mayor. Then he

looked sharply at the Englishman and said, "See here! I don't know exactly what you're trying to get at, but it strikes me you're out of place here."

A week later the Englishman's farm was on the market. He found it unpleasant to live there.

And here's another school story. Before the war a nice Englishwoman came to a Canadian town that prides itself on its schools, noted that there wasn't a private school in the place and sent out circulars to the rich and prominent citizens calling their attention to this fact, and suggesting that they, as "British subjects," would probably like to finance her to open a school for the "daughters of gentlemen." She explained how such schools were managed in England and offered to send over to get young "gentlewomen" from Girton and Newnham to assist her. She also returned to England by pressing invitation from the citizens of the town. The man who told me the story said that except for her sex, she would have received an invitation to go to the devil.

Now, Sir John, *I ask you,* as they say here. I really do!

I lately attended a recruiting meeting in a town park. The recruiting sergeant was telling of the need for more men, and threatening conscription, when a great broad-shouldered fellow called out,

"Why should I go over there and fight for England?"

"Who the 'hell asked you to fight for England?" called back the sergeant. "I asked you to go and fight for Canada. Isn't she worth fighting for?"

I heard a story in Toronto of a line-up of unemployed Englishmen outside a place where free stews were being given to them. It happened before the war and the Englishmen were determined to stay in the cities instead of going to the farming parts. Said one down-and-outer to the one behind him, "Well, I will say they're kind to us chaps over here!"

"Why shouldn't they be?" asked the man behind, stretching out his hand for the plate. "Don't they belong to us, and 'aven't we made 'em what they are?"

. . . .

Edmonton, Alberta.

. . . You ask me if I have yet seen the celebrated sign of which you have heard, topping factory or farm-yard gate, stating that "NO ENGLISH NEED APPLY." No, I have not come across it, and I think these war times would not be likely to bring it to light, but I can well believe it has been seen by many a traveler in these parts. Yesterday I asked an Alberta farmer "Is it true that you Canadians dislike the English, and that when you employ farm workers, you prefer the Scotch, the Irish and those of other nations?" This man is himself of pure English descent, his grandparents having come here with five pounds only as capital.

"Yes, it's true," he said. "The English come here trying to teach us our business. They talk continually about the way they do things 'at 'ome.' The men we take on the farms and the women we try at housework are all the same. They actually treat us as inferiors and tell us to our faces that we ought to be grateful to them for trying to teach us. My wife has tried several English domestic workers. She didn't expect them to know how to cook and work like the Canadians and the Americans, but she expected they'd be willing to learn, but they said to her 'We thought you'd *like* to know how things are done at 'ome!' "

This man has been telling me what good citizens the Icelanders make and also what successes the German-Americans are when they come over to Canada from the States, having learned American ways, which are the same as Canadian ways. He mentioned also the success of the Scotch emigrants in becoming Canadianized.

It is a bitter disappointment to me to find this prejudice against the English. It looks discouraging for the after-the-war projects. I cannot explain it any more than it has been explained to me by an Edmonton man who says,

"We just don't like 'em because they know it all. The other immigrants come to better *themselves*. The English come to better *us!*"

And then there are the little things that one might think

of as very unimportant, the little social differences. A Winnipeg man told me of his trials in getting an office clerk among a batch of young English University men whom he tried one after another. They would insist upon calling him "sir" whenever they addressed him, they "wasted time," so he said, in always rising and standing and doing nothing when he went into the room, instead of "holding tight" (to their chairs) and going on with their work, and, worst of all, they insisted on trying to find a non-existent tea-pot to make some afternoon tea for him, and he had never known that business and professional men stopped working in the middle of the afternoon to drink tea! This all may sound "piffling," but it creates trouble, and the farther West one goes, the more trouble.

And here is another example, a more serious one, of the "great divide" between England and Canada. On the Pullman coming from Winnipeg I became acquainted with an English officer who is over here on some war business. At one of the small stations a Canadian officer boarded the train accompanied by a private soldier. These two Canadians chummed up as equals, shared the same table in the dining car, "swopped" stories on the Observation platform. Said the English officer to me, as to one who would perfectly understand, which I did, "That's the kind of thing that I can't stand over here—no discipline!"

"Oh, they're just friends," I said.

"But it's not done in the Army!"

"You mean the British Army," I said. "Of course, there one never sees a Tommy and an officer traveling together, but here I've seen it so often that I'm used to it now— It seems all right."

"It's all wrong," he said. "Some of our undisciplined Colonials may lose the war for us."

Then he went on to tell me a story of one of the first Canadian Contingents to arrive in England. They were to be inspected by a British general and the commanding officer was anxious to make a good impression before his superior, so he said to his men,

"We're going to be inspected by the rajah! Now, boys, stand

straight, don't spit and for God's sake don't let me down!"

The Englishman grinned as he told me the story, but he said quite seriously, "Now what can you expect at the Front from a regiment like that?" But I was laughing so hard that I couldn't answer him for several minutes, when I said, "I'd expect them to go a long way toward winning the war!" But the English officer simply couldn't see it in that light. He told it as a humorous story, but as one with a fearful warning, while I heard it as a humorous story with a high promise in it for the doings of those Canadians. I have been thinking of it since and have analyzed my laughter. The reason I laughed so heartily, and why I still laugh whenever I think of it is because I realize how very serious is this humorous story to those English who hear it! I really wish I could know whether you, Sir John, are laughing and, if so, the exact complexion of your laughter!

.   .   .   .

Victoria, B. C.

Dear Sir John:

This town would warm the cockles of your imperialistic, yes, even your English, heart, for certainly the large majority of the people here are, in your phrase, "loyal to *us*." The pure English language is spoken in that soft low tone which I have so much loved to hear and which I have always known I could not successfully imitate in spite of my years in London and in spite of the assertion of my American and Canadian friends that I have really taken on the "English accent." Roast beef, cauliflower and Brussels sprouts are here served in English fashion, and I am having delightfully thin bread-and-butter for my afternoon tea. Great attention is paid to gardening, the women doing most of it now, for the boys have gone "home" to fight for "the Motherland." They have marched away singing "Land of Hope and Glory," instead of "Canada, my Canada!" or "The Maple Leaf Forever!"

All about in the outlying districts are deserted farms with rusting machinery. Some of the fields are only half ploughed and some are merely growing hay, but numbers of Americans have come here from Washington State and taken over some of the agriculture. Certain of these farms, I am told, belong or belonged to the "English Failures" who could not seem to make things go in this new country. When they heard the call of Mother England, they sold their land and their stock for any mere song that offered. I have cried over some of the stories I have heard.

Here on the Pacific Coast Canadians talk almost as much of the Yellow Peril as of the German Peril. "When this war's over, then we'll have to take it up with the Japs," said a Vancouver man to me yesterday. I asked him why, and he said, "Well, you know, the States are bound to have trouble with them." I asked what that would have to do with Canada, and he said, "Why, of course, if the States went to war with Japan, Canada would help—have to!"

I reminded him of the Anglo-Japanese Alliance, and he said "That wouldn't make a bit of difference to us Canadians. If the Americans have any trouble with the Japs, we'd jump right in with both feet."

Here you see again the likeness of the "language." While I was in Seattle, I heard a group of American men discussing the war. They all agreed that it wasn't their business *unless* Germany attacked Canada.

"Why then?" I asked. "Canada, being a part of the British Empire, would have to take her chance."

"But being our neighbor, we'd have to take *our* chance in helping to drive them out. You'd better believe your Uncle Sam would raise real hell if Germany tried any funny business with Canada!" was the reply I got.

So you see how it is, don't you, Sir John? It is not only geographically that these two nations are very close. Frankly, I believe that Germany has a clearer understanding of this fact than has England. I am convinced that if a German warship should get past the British Fleet and start bombarding any part of the Canadian coast, East or West, it would be of set purpose to bring the United States into the war. Sometimes in my keenness to see my country among the Allies where I feel she belongs, I almost wish that Germany would commit herself in this way. . . .

Hamilton, Ontario

. . . I have finished the special newspaper articles I engaged to do, and now I am on my way to the Middle West of my own country. Hamilton is, as you know (I beg your pardon! You don't know!) not far from Windsor and Windsor is just across the river from Detroit, center of the Ford Motor Industry. For the small price of tuppence ha'penny I shall cross the river, remaining on that side of the Border till my return to England.

I think that if I had not spent these several months in Canada I should probably feel like a foreigner among my one-time "own people" in the Middle West. As it is, I feel that I shall not return so utter a stranger, and yet I shall be stranger enough, in all conscience. . . .

CHAPTER XVI

MY OWN PEOPLE

"YEAH," said the man, putting down the dipper from which he was drinking, and pointing with extended finger to some fine looking buildings across the fields, "that sure is the place you're asking about. 'Experiment Farm' it used to be called."

"It doesn't look like it."

"How's that?" the man caught me up. "I thought you was a stranger hereabouts?"

"My friends in the East, who asked me to hunt it up didn't describe it as being like that," I lied cautiously. "I had a picture in my mind, you see."

"How long since your friends seen it?"

"Twenty five years, I should think," I answered.

"Yeah!" he laughed. "Things do move *and* improve in less time than that! Your friends used to live hereabouts?"

"They used to visit."

The car waited for me in the dusty road. Through the gateway of Canada I had entered the Middle West. For many years I had carried pictures of Experiment Farm, my old home. I had always intended to return to see what it was like, perhaps to reveal my identity to some I had known in my youth, if such persons could be found. Now I felt that wisdom was all against the revelation of my identity. As a stranger I could better get the information I wanted. In the days when I lived there, strangers who, if affluent, drove by in fall-top buggies or democrat waggons and, if tramps, trudged slowly along the rough roads, caused comment always and suspicion at times. I knew that now, in motoring days, this would not be the case. People motor everywhere, stopping for gasoline, stopping for drinks of water, stopping to inquire directions. I was safe to make inquiries about my old home, the home I knew must be very near, but which I could not place.

Instead of getting the driver to inquire, I left him in the car and waded through rather deep grass to the man who hung over the fence with a dipper. He was middle-aged, sunburnt and wrinkled. He wore a straw hat, a gingham shirt and overalls. Behind him lay a fine expanse of land, all under careful cultivation. Set back from the fence over which he leaned were a shiningly-painted house, a barn and other out-buildings. As much as I dared, I examined his features to see if I had ever known him, but, after all the years, recognition was impossible.

He answered my unspoken question. "When they called that place 'Experiment Farm' I didn't live here. I was something of a youngster, as you might say. My folks had their farm five miles East, but when we went to mill, we always had to pass it and my father used to stop and ask, 'Anything new goin' on?' because they was always tryin' new things, which was why they never lifted the mortgage."

"The mortgage?" I repeated. Not to this man would I tell how well I remembered that tragic mortgage!

"Yeah. Old —— Now, what was his name had that farm? Blamed if I ain't losin' my memory! Oh yeah! It was ——" and now he repeated the name of my people. "He was always tryin' things he read about in a paper called 'The Scientific Farmer' and sendin' for seeds to Washington, but things didn't always turn out the way the paper said they would, and so the mortgage stayed on. He was a great reader and so was his wife. I remember they had some shelves over the stove in the kitchen piled full of books and old magazines—I remember as well as if 'twas yesterday. He read in 'The Scientific Farmer' that you could make molasses out of cornstalks, and that was one of his experiments with a special kind of corn."

"Was it good?" I asked. I knew it was good. I used to eat it on my bread, and I wept bitter tears when the supply of the special kind of cornstalks gave out, and molasses from New Orleans took its place.

"I never tasted it as I know of."

"My friends in the East told me that the farmer and his wife are dead, but there was a girl, I understand, an only child. Do you remember her?"

"Gosh! I guess nobody'd ever forget her, little spitfire with red hair. But she wasn't their child. They were old folks and lonesome and they took a niece to raise. Seems as if I remember the boys and girls at school used to call her 'Red-headed Johnnie Bull' because she had such a temper, and we heard her father's folks was English, so she came by it honestly."

"What became of the girl? She's the one my friends want to find out about."

"She went away to college. I remember that well, because my aunt went to a sewing-bee to help get her clothes ready."

"But if they were so poor, with a mortgage and all that, how could they afford to send her to college?"

"Sent herself, so far as I could make out, by what they called 'self-help,' doin' things in the college kitchen. 'Twan't hard, even then, to find things to do to help get an education, and in these times every mother's son and daughter can get to college if so be they've got the grit. But this girl, folks said what was the use her goin' to college because there was one thing she was so dumb about—couldn't do the easiest arithmetic sums at the district school. I used to hear a cousin at the same school tell about it."

"What became of her?"

"There you've got me. After her folks died she never came back. But once I heard something about a piece she wrote for a St. Paul paper—leastwise it was the same name, Lizzie Banks —or no! It was Elizabeth Banks, but maybe she used the long name after she went to college."

Within me I laughed. The joke was on me. Here was fame, news reaching my old home of my having, if perchance I had changed from "Lizzie" to "Elizabeth," written a "piece" for a St. Paul paper!

I saw that the man had told me all he knew, and I changed the subject. "You've been very kind in telling me," I said. "I have some Chicago papers in the car. Would you like to have them to read? The news from the war is in them."

"If you mean that war over in Yurrup, what I got to say is what do they keep it up for? Always fightin' and scrappin' about something! It's that there king business, one king tryin' to get something from another king, an' that Rooshian Czar and all."

"The Russian Czar isn't to blame," I said. "It's the Kaiser trying to get everything—at least that's the way I understand it."

I trailed off in this fashion because I did not want to appear too knowing. I was traveling through the Middle West not to instruct the people but to instruct myself on their point of view.

"Yeah! The Kayser, too! I'm glad we got nothin' to do with it."

I started for the car. "Then you don't care for the newspapers?" I asked.

"Well, if so be they got some good stories and poetry in 'em, my girls would like 'em, and mostly Chicago papers print a good housekeepin' page, an' my wife's a holy terror at wantin' new receipts."

He followed me to the car and thanked me for the papers. "There's a crick runs through the farm you was askin' about," he said.

"Yes, I know," I answered, adding quickly, "My friends mentioned that as one way of tracing it."

On the bank of the creek that still divides a meadow of what was once Experiment Farm, we parked the car and ate our lunch. In the course of conversation I learned that the driver I had hired with the car was a young university law student. I said nothing to him of being from England, but allowed him to believe that I was from New York, hunting up the whereabouts of friends who had lived in the neighborhood many years ago. He was the son of a mechanic in a village not far from Madison. I ventured to mention the war and asked his opinion as to whether the United States should or would get into it.

"Why should we?" he asked surprisedly. "What have we got to do with it? I've studied the matter rather thoroughly. An Austrian archduke gets killed by a Servian—probably good riddance!—And Austria starts war about it, and then there's the devil to pay all over Europe, and old England jumps in— trust old England to get a finger in the pie if she can! And here's poor Canada— I've got a lot of friends there that I met two or three years ago at a Rocky Mountain summer resort where we were all waiters together at a swell restaurant— well, she's got pulled into it because she hasn't any navy of her own, though, of course, ours could look after her all right; but she's not a cad, so she won't take the protection of the British Navy and not help herself, so she sends her boys over yonder to get killed!"

"Oh! Is that the way you look at it?" I asked.

"Sure! But what gets my goat is that the papers say that a lot of snobs and millionaires down East actually think *we* ought to jump in because they want to cross the ocean on British war ships!"

"War ships?" I echoed.

"Well, what are those armored boats that carry munitions over but war ships? Take the Lusitania, for instance."

"You think the Germans were right in sinking the Lusitania?" I asked with as much calmness as I could muster in my horror.

"No! It was a terrible thing, but what I say is that Americans had no right on a British boat."

My heart sank, as it had not sunk when I heard the farmer who leaned over the fence, give his opinion of the Russian Czar. Here was a smart young American, working his way through the University, a student of history, a delightful representative of the young Middle West, expressing himself so ignorantly about the greatest conflict the world has ever known. I saw that he was British in features, except for that subtle something I am now noting which both Canada and the United States engraves upon the faces of their sons. This young man had a British name. I was sure he came of pure British stock. Silently I looked him over.

"What do *you* think about it?" he asked. Before I had a chance to reply he added suddenly, "I intend to go over there some day when the mess is cleared up. I want to travel and see the world. We can't rightly appreciate our own country till we've seen other countries."

"No," I answered convincingly. "No, indeed!"

"Perhaps you've traveled over there before the war?" he said interrogatively.

"Yes, rather a lot."

"You know all these places, Austria, Germany, France, Belgium and the rest?"

"Yes," I said.

"And England, of course?"

"Oh yes, England," I answered, and I think the tears and agony of my heart over England's plight and England's sacrifices and sufferings must have shown in my eyes and in my face, for immediately he said,

"You like England?"

"I love England," I said simply.

"Yes, I'd like to travel in England myself more than any other place. Stratford-on-Avon, the Cathedral cities and all—you know."

Almost I lost my patience. I wanted to take this young American by the shoulders and shake him and cry, "Tourist-love, cupboard-love! That's what you have for England, but my love is different!" I contained myself as never the red-headed, freckle-faced little spitfire who, long years ago had sat by this creek and dangled her bare feet in its shallow water, would have contained herself. I asked him to drive the car slowly along the road and meet me a mile further on. I determined to cross the fields and take a tour of inspection around Experiment Farm.

In the woods I stopped under oak trees which I seemed to recognize as those in whose bark we children used to cut our initials. I came to one which I thought was that where a neighbor boy had cut his own just above mine. He was thirteen. I was twelve. On that day we had vowed we would get married when we were grown up. He would have to be "of age," twenty-one, which would make me twenty—so fearfully old! Supposing our childish romance had matured. I might have lived in the same spot all my life. I might have been the mother of just such a young man as was now driving the motor slowly along the road. How would my husband be feeling about the war? How would I have been acting? Should we have had any clearer comprehension of its great issues than the man up the road who had leaned over the fence, or his wife, who was such a terror at wanting new cookery receipts from the Chicago papers? My son, the son I would, perhaps have had, would he have known more about the war than the smart young fellow in the motor car?

I passed Sam Englewood's place, with its fine house and barn. I looked at the garage where he would be sheltering that wonderful two thousand dollar car of which I had received such a graphic description a few years ago—or perhaps he would have a still finer one now. I fancied the mistress of the yellow painted house with the cupola. There would probably be a "hired girl" to help her in the busy seasons when the haying and the harvesting and the threshing were on. . . . "The best heating furnace now in the whole neighborhood. . . . Their bathroom like those you see in Milwaukee, with the tub setting right out in the middle of the room, so you can get all around it to clean it without breaking your back. . . . He was two years older than you, so tall and gawky, and he used to draw you on his red sled. . . ."

Yes, I remembered it all so well now, as I plodded through meadows and fields, the very ground over which he had drawn me on that radiant sled.

I came upon a haystack at Experiment Farm. From a nicely curved hollow in the side a hen darted forth, cackling, for all the world like Jerusha Jane used to cackle when she had laid an egg for my college fund.

I thought I recognized in the white painted "ell" attached to the large farm house, the whole of the little house in which I had spent my childhood. It had not seemed so little then. Auntie had an ambition to add a sort of shed-like "ell" to it, and now it was an "ell" itself! I remembered our parlor with its ingrain carpet and its cane-seated chairs of which I had felt proud and puffed up. I fancied it was now used as a pantry. In the yard

I looked about for the old pump which so often had to be "primed" to make it bring up the water. It was replaced by a great windmill. A woman came to the door of the "ell," doubtless the mistress of the house. She looked very clean and bright in her chambray frock and white apron.

"Would you give me a drink?" I asked.

"Better have a glass," she said, bringing a tumbler. "Sometimes tramps come along and use the dipper."

The sound of a bell came from the house and the woman rushed away, saying "Excuse me. It's the telephone!"

A telephone at the one-time isolated and lonely Experiment Farm house! I went toward the car and we drove past the district schoolhouse. Was it the same one I attended where my "dumbness" at doing sums had so often been ruthlessly exposed? Yes. There was the date medallion over the center of the peaked front between the two doors, one for girls, one for boys. In my day the teachers had been paid eighteen dollars a month "for settin' round and hearin' the children say their lessons—big money for easy work," as some of the farmers had remarked. . . .

I got out of the car and in the little graveyard I walked among the dead. They lived again and I dwelt with them—my own people.

.   .   .   .

The nearest church was a few miles from Experiment Farm when I was a child. It is there now, the same building of yellow brick, rather low and squat-looking, though once it had been to me an architectural wonder. To-day being Sunday, I had the same driver take me out from the city to attend the morning service. I found that the inside of the church had been remodeled. The pews were more comfortable and there were kneeling stools covered with brussels carpet. I saw a finer, larger organ.

I attracted little attention, though a stranger. Sunday motorists often stop to rest or worship in the country churches they pass. The minister of the church, of course, has a car of his own— Our old minister had only a jolting "sulkey" and a pony. In some of the pews I saw familiar faces. They were the sons and daughters of the boys and girls with whom I used to go to Sunday school.

The choir led and the congregation followed in singing one of the same hymns that had so often puzzled me as a child, meaningless then, meaningless now. The minister prayed to what seemed to be a local god, a sort of male Ceres whose sole concern would be for the weather and the crops and the people of the neighborhood. He informed the Deity of many local happenings, births, marriages, illness, deaths, and asked his blessing on the ice-cream social to be held during the week.

The text was from the thirty-first verse of the first chapter of Genesis: "And God saw everything that he had made, and behold it was very good. And the evening and the morning were the sixth day."

Amazed and bewildered, I sat through a sermon describing the literal creation of the world in six days, the "sinning" of Adam and Eve, the appeasing of the wrath of the Jewish Yahweh by the sacrifice of innocent birds and animals upon the temple altars. I saw no difference between this sermon and the kind of sermons I had heard more than a quarter of a century ago. I tried to remember the number of years that had passed since I had known people who believed these things— I had forgotten that anybody believed them. Once, amusedly, I thought of the long-ago time when I spent a week in prayer for something I did not get. Afterwards I heard a sermon on the subject of prayer in which the preacher assured his hearers they had but to pray for anything they wanted and receive it. Then my childish voice had piped out shrilly in contradiction, " 'Taint so!'"

But now I had not the privilege of outward protest. I must listen in respectful silence or leave the church, and I had no notion of leaving. I was waiting, watching, listening for something I must know, so I would endure to the end. And while I waited, I thought again of how it might have fared with me had I remained here among my own people. I looked over the congregation of men and women as they listened to the preacher's denunciations of other members of his own profession who were declared to be "in league with Satan" because they had dared to question the scientific truth of the verse which he had taken for his text. There were references to Darwin which proved that the preacher had never studied or even read him.

The sermon ended with a jump from the first chapter of Genesis to the last chapter of Revelation:

"If any man shall take away from the words of the prophecy of this book, God shall take away his part out of the Book of Life, and out of the Holy City, and from the things which are written in this book."

The thing I had waited and watched and listened for did not come. I wanted to know if any mention would be made in prayer or sermon of the greatest war the world has ever known. There was nothing. The preacher and his quiet, prosperous farming and village congregation in this section of the Middle West passed the hour of worship as though there were no war in the world.

I drew my motor veil closely about my face and pushed my way through a smiling and chattering throng in the vestibule. Once it occurred to me that I might go up and speak to the minister, make known my identity and ask him if I might tell the people something about the war and how, if Germany succeeded in her designs, the United States must finally suffer. Then I felt that such a proceeding might interfere with a propaganda plan that was revolving in my mind. Besides, I was angry, enraged at these "safe and secure" farmers and villagers who ignored the war. To attempt to speak to them in anger would spoil the effect of any work I might hope to do for them in the future.

I found the car parked not far from the church and my young driver deeply engaged in reading Ernst Haeckel's "Das Weltbilt von Darwin und Lamarck." At sight of the title of the book I gave a start and I think I must have made some exclamation, for he smiled and asked,

"Are you shocked, coming right out from there to this?" and he nodded toward the church.

"No," I answered, in spite of the fact that I *had* received a shock, though not of the sort he meant. My temper cooling as we sped along the road, I thought of the strangeness, the originality, yes, the greatness of this country of mine, this part of the Middle West where dwelt my own people. Where else in the world could such an incident as this have taken place? I stepped from a church where a "doctor of divinity" preached that the world was constructed by Yahweh in six days, into a motor car driven by a mechanic's son who was working his way through a great university, and I found him reading Haeckel! Then I noticed, attached to the side near the driver's seat, a clever contrivance for holding books where were stored another volume of Haeckel, "The Riddle of the Universe," and a work on English jurisprudence.

As we drove on, the landscape smiled about us. Fields and orchards promised plentifully for the later harvest. The cattle were sleek and fat; every farmer had a telephone, a gramophone, a motor car. Further on I passed again the creek that gurgles through the meadow of Experiment Farm. I knew I was due back in England soon, to work in hostels and canteen, to be terrified again of air-raids, to mingle with women who wore deep black and sorrowed always in their hearts, yet worked on, waited on. Here was peace and plenty, a freedom from fear. My country, my land! These people would tell me that I had really nothing to do with that other land, all those other lands of "effete monarchies" as they called them. I was tired. My very quiet and self-repression and final anger had increased my weariness. Suddenly I turned to the driver.

"Are there many ministers and congregations like that in the Middle West these days?" I asked.

"I guess they're mostly the same," he answered. "I was brought up like that."

"Like what?"

"Like whatever he preached about," he said, laughing. "What was it?"

"About the world being made in six days, and everybody being damned who doesn't believe it—and no mention of the war."

"My folks are like that, and everybody else I knew in the town I come from, but I got away— You know a fellow can always get away! If you had been raised as I was raised, you wouldn't be surprised or mad, but only amused a little, or, perhaps just sad. About not mentioning the war, I don't understand what you mean, myself, but, of course, they preach about the war in the big city churches—tell how thankful we ought to be that we're not in it. I agree with the preachers there, anyway."

"You're thankful that we're not in it?"

"Why yes! I'm thankful in the same way that I'm thankful when I read of an earthquake or a volcanic eruption in a foreign land—thankful that it's not here, but sorry for the poor devils who are in it."

"It's not the same!" I retorted. "We couldn't stop the earth from quaking or the volcano from erupting."

"You mean the Americans when you say 'we'?"

"Yes!"

"But we've got nothing to do with it!"

. . . .

Days and weeks have passed. I've "done" the Middle West farming and village parts as far as my dwindling finances will allow me to travel. In Michigan, Wisconsin, Illinois the burden of the cry is the saying of the young university motor car driver, "We've got nothing to do with it!" In the village churches, the people and the services are like unto those in the neighborhood of Experiment Farm. The war is something afar and apart from these people, moderately prosperous, kindly, intelligent. They have no understanding of its causes or its issues and cannot be convinced at present that it will affect them. Nobody seems to have done anything to enlighten their ignorance. In an incidental, accidental sort of way I have tried to draw them out, but the task of informing them is almost like trying to teach a child the higher studies when the ground has not been prepared by drilling in the elementary ones. This does not mean that I find these people uneducated or stupid. A good many of them are college educated, belonging to literary circles, frequenters of the public libraries. The degree of their general intelligence certainly surpasses that of the average English farmers and villagers. I have been meeting wonderful American women who do all their own housework, make their own and their children's clothes in the smartest fashions, provide the most nourishing and tasty meals for their families, belong to musical circles and literary clubs. Now that I have got away from that part of the country where I spent my childhood, I am letting it be known that I am an American who lives much of the time in England. Once in a while I find a man or a woman intensely thrilled and interested, but *only once in a while*. And they all say, "But anyway, in these times you ought to be home because, as an American, you've got nothing to do with the war." They are sympathetic and generous and are buying a good many of my dog stories.

I meet people of German descent. They seem to be good American citizens, certainly as good as those of British, French or Italian descent, and I don't find that those of British descent are any keener to be in the war on that account. Those who left the various European countries when they were quite young, or even in their full maturity, say that when they came over here they left "all that" behind them, "all that" meaning in this case the war.

Chicago

It is different in the large cities out here. They talk quite a good deal about the war, but express surprise that I, an American, should live in the war zone. A great many are outspokenly anti-British, though some are a little pro-French, "because the French helped us to lick the British."

The Germans are pushing their propaganda amazingly, but I cannot find that the British are doing anything whatever that really counts in making their righteous cause known and understood. The first year of the war the Teutons used all their energy in trying to convince the people out here that Germany was right. Next they took up anti-British propaganda, and now they are working the "passion for peace" business. And such cleverness, such subtlety as they are showing! One had not learned to expect it from so phlegmatic a people as the Germans.

Surely the Germans have reason to laugh up their sleeves at their success in getting hundreds of innocent American writers to help them, even those whose sympathies are all with Britain and the Allies. I have only escaped this fate because of a subtlety of my own which makes it easy for me to understand the subtlety of others. I presume this is the result of my many years work in detective journalism. It having become known that I am an American journalist freshly over here from London, I have been approached by editors, literary agents and managers of syndicates with requests for articles about England in war time. I have been asked to describe my personal fear of air-raids, how food is restricted and the English manner of mourning. One man suggested that I write for him to syndicate a "bright article about London in the spring of 1914.

"Great heavens!" I said. "I've forgotten what London was like in the Spring of 1914. The things that have come since have swallowed up such memories."

"The way you say that convinces me that you can do exactly what I want," he replied. "Think hard about this last spring and then think back how it differs from spring in the time of peace. Then you can write the description of, say, April or May, 1914. Don't mention war. Write as if there were no such thing as war in the world. That Adelphi place where you live—I know it—those gardens by the Embankment, the Thames with the excursion boats running to Richmond— What about that statue of Bobbie Burns in those gardens right where you live— What is it underneath it—how does it go?"

Automatically I repeated:

"THE POETIC GENIUS OF MY COUNTRY FOUND ME AT THE PLOUGH AND THREW HER INSPIRING MANTLE OVER ME. SHE BADE ME SING THE LOVES, THE JOYS, THE RURAL SCENES AND RURAL PLEASURES OF MY NATIVE TONGUE. I TUNED MY WILD ARTLESS NOTES AS SHE INSPIRED."

"Great!" he cried. "You can bring in that quote. It's along the very line I want. Doesn't it perfectly describe peace! Then there'll be the tulips and daffodils all around in front— Say, don't the pigeons sometimes get on Bobbie's head? Seems as if I remember seeing one perched there as big as you please!"

Pigeons on Bobbie Burns' head? Yes! And on the head of Robert Raikes, whose statue in knee-breeches is further on in the Gardens. He was the man who started Sunday Schools. I remembered how I laughed when I discovered him standing there within a real stone's throw of my flat, because there immediately came back to me part of a verse of a hymn we used to sing at our Sunday school held in the Wisconsin district school-house:

—"As Robert Raikes went on his way,
He saw some naughty boys at play,
Although it was the Sa-a-bath day!"

It was a Sunday, too, and little London children were playing on the path upon which he now looked down. Wondering if he would be shocked if he saw them, I wandered back and stood before Bobbie Burns with a live cock-pigeon perched on his head and preening his feathers preparatory to wooing a somber little gray lady watching from a branch of an opposite tree.

"Ye high, exalted virtuous dames,
Tied up in godly laces,
Before ye gi'e poor Frailty names,
Suppose a change o' cases—"

had gone flitting through my mind as I watched Bobbie on that spring Sunday in the long-ago days of peace.

I looked up at the Syndicate Man, who was silent, and back again flew memory to the fountain playing, to the large smooth stone basin where the sparrows bathed. I saw the children drinking from the tin cup suspended on a chain at the Fawcett Memorial not far from the bust of Arthur Sullivan, and overlooking it all was beautiful Adelphi Terrace toward which I could point and say, "In those buildings I have my home."

Then I thought of the Gardens now, with some sort of war office huts they were preparing to build, taking in so much of the ground that used to be allotted to rocks and grass and flowers, including the band-stand in the center. I remembered how in the early autumn following the outbreak of the war, the band played so many airs of allied nations, Britain, France, Belgium, Russia—how I used to long to hear the notes of the Star Spangled Banner. I remembered an Italian who used to sit near me on one of the penny chairs and how he had said hopefully,

"Pretty soon—not now, but soon, they will add another, and then I shall stand up very proud when they play for Italy," and just then everyone in the Gardens, far as well as near, was standing for "God Save the King!" Then I had left the Gardens with a bitterness in my heart, for even from the first I had believed, with Roosevelt, that we "belonged."

I thought again of still later times, of the sound of bombs dropping near the Gardens, for, near, too, was Charing Cross Station and Hungerford Bridge, from which so many boys must start for camp or for the Front. The War and the Admiralty offices were in the neighborhood, Whitehall was but around the corner, the District Railway just there, carrying its daily thousands. Here were the Adelphi Arches, solid, deep and "safe," if anything could be safe. Old men and old women were hobbling toward them, some with blankets and camp stools, prepared to spend the night, mothers were carrying babies, while older children hung onto their skirts, white-faced, with the fear of some unknown horror in their eyes.

I looked up from my memories, glad and sad, to see the Man of the Syndicate eyeing me in a pleased sort of way.

He rubbed his hands together. "I've been studying your face and reading your mind," he said. "You *can* do it! You get me!"

I smiled back at him.

"Oh yes," I said, *"I get you!"*

CHAPTER XVII

AT SEA

THIS boat looks like a Joseph's Coat. I had vowed I
would never travel by the American Line so long as it
adhered to the Kaiser's scheme of decoration. Yet here I am.

I engaged passage by a British boat, with a gun in the right
place, and then, three days before sailing date, came the soft
low voice of my shipping friend, J—— over the telephone at
my hotel.

"We'll have to call it off. No passengers this trip. Taking
something more valuable than you!" he said.

"I'm not afraid," I called back. "I'll sit on it!"

"It might go off, and then you'd go up."

"Or down! I'm willing to take the risk. I'd probably get
saved, and then what a story I could write!"

But no! I had to sail this particular week, and there was
nothing for it but a transfer to this boat.

Here I am, without a scrap of dignity left me. Who could
be dignified on a boat with her country's flag daubed in red,
white and blue at bow and stern and "done" in spectacular
electric lights, like an advertisement, along the sides? We
started out with highly-polished reflectors which blazed out
the colors of the flag, the name of the ship, the name of the line
and the name of the nation to which the ship belongs, my nation, the United States of America. We have had some rough
weather, the reflectors are looking dull and the lights are not
working properly. Our boat must truly be a sight for all the
gods and fishes of the sea, and a joke to the mermaids as well.
I sit on deck and write my notes, and frankly feel ashamed.
Shade of Charles Dickens! What was that he wrote on the last
page of his delightful little Child's History of England which
I used to study at school in the Middle West?

"It was in the reign of George Third that England lost North America by persisting in taxing her without consent. That immense country, made independent under Washington, and left to itself, became the United States, one of the greatest nations of the earth. In these times in which I write, it is *honorably remarkable for protecting its citizens wherever they may travel with a dignity and a determination which is a model for England.* Between you and me, England has rather lost ground in this respect since the days of Oliver Cromwell."

Charles Dickens, how dare you intrude into the privacy of my mind just now?

What a voyage that was I had to Canada a few months ago! I remember there were a lot of little Canadian children on board. They had been over with their mothers to see their fathers, who were on leave in London. The poor little kiddies were put to bed every night in life-jackets, some of them protesting because they were uncomfortable to lie on. In the day-time they wore them, too, and I used to play with them, telling the children they were camels with humps, and when one little boy protested that camels didn't have humps *all around* the back and front, I manufactured natural history to meet the situation.

There was a young American doctor on the Canadian boat. He had been in London when war was declared and had joined up with the British, went to France, got wounded and was now trying to return to his native country by way of Canada, hoping somehow to get to his home across the Border. He explained to me that it was bound to be a difficult undertaking, because he was no longer an American citizen, nor was he an Englishman. He was a man without a country. I wonder what has become of him. Did he get across the Border and what can be his status?

All sorts of memories gather round me as the boat wabbles on its way Eastward, taking a round-about zigzag course which, I understand, was suggested by his Imperial Majesty, the Kaiser.

When I was on the Border I was told that twenty-eight

thousand Americans were already known to have crossed and joined up with the Canadians. I seemed always to be meeting them in the various places near the Line. All sorts they were . . . soldiers of fortune who would probably rather fight than do anything else; scapegraces of all ages who were, perhaps, leaving their country for their country's good; young boy idealists, going over to join as in a crusade. Then there were the mature men, many of them between thirty and forty who had to go because they had heard "the call" and dare not refuse to answer. I was somewhat surprised at the ease with which they were taken on by the Canadian recruiting officers until I learned that all that was necessary, besides passing the physical examination, was to do a bit of easy lying about where they were born. Rather beautiful lying, some of it was, but often even that was not necessary. Say a man was born in one of the many large or small towns by the name of "Hamilton" scattered all over throughout the various States. When he gave the true name of the place of his birth, the officer would say "Hamilton, Ont."—"Right you are!" and the thing was done. . . . That Oath of Allegiance—I wonder how many thought out just what it meant. Some, of course, took it carelessly without so much as analyzing the words, but it seems to me that a mature man, intelligent, broad-minded, loving his country and proud of his American citizenship, might rightly be termed "nobleman" when he gave up his birthright for the call he heard to go and fight in France. . . .

There was that Minnesota boy who followed me across into Manitoba, convinced, by something I had said, that he must go over and help. *He* couldn't have been more than twenty, but he understood just what he was doing. I had shown him a "Light," he said, and he must follow it. I've got his name, but little other information about him, except that I know he was rather a well-to-boy at some college—what college he would not tell me. Was he afraid that I might change my mind about what I had agreed must be his duty to Humanity if he had seen the "Light" as he assured me he had? Did he think I might write to his people and get them to interfere with his enlisting? . . . His people—who are they? "Maybe you'll see me in

London on leave one of these days!" he had called out as my train moved on toward Western Canada. . . .

I don't think I ever saw a more beautiful boy. I should think his soul must be like his face. . . . Was I right to encourage him . . . If I were his mother . . . He never told me if his mother were living. . . .

There are numbers of British passengers on board. One of them has just passed and said to me,

"Aren't you glad it's an American boat and you can sit there reading all nice and safe?"

"No, I'm not!" I retorted.

"Not glad it's an American boat, or not glad you're safe?" he laughed.

"Neither!" I called after him.

He stopped in his steady jog-trot round the deck. He is one of those passengers who boast they never "do" less than six miles a day in crossing the ocean.

"Aren't you an American?" he asked surprisedly.

"Yes. That's what makes me so mad to be 'safe'!"

"So you think your country ought to be in? Well, I'm not so sure. How does the song go—'I must love someone, and it might as well be you!' Some one great country ought to be out. Besides there are the munitions. We've got to have them. I've just been over to see about things in that line. I cross often, and always choose an American boat these days as a 'save-your life.' "

"I've been crossing by British boats to spite the Kaiser!"

"What good does that do? Does he know it?"

He laughed, and I laughed, too. "Well, I've done my best to convey the information to him by getting it published in the American papers!"

The man resumed his jog-trot up deck. He is rather a good sort, seemingly, but I wish he were not getting rich through the war. . . . I have been feeling so ashamed that some Americans are doing that.

I have been thinking about those Americans who went down on the Lusitania. Whatever else could be said of them, they were sports. They had their warning from Bernstorff in the newspapers and on the little slips that were handed to them as they walked up the gangway, but they weren't held back by that. . . . Yes, they were sports.

My mind keeps turning back to Chicago and the rest of the Middle West. What can the British be thinking of that they've done nothing to counteract the German propaganda out there? Since the war started a few British speakers have been going over to New York, Boston, Philadelphia and such places, been wined and dined by their admirers of the "blood-is-thicker-than-water" sort, and then made nicely punctuated speeches to the already converted gathered together in smart drawing rooms. These people didn't need any attention. Their sympathies were, from the beginning, with the Allies. Have they not been accustomed to crossing every year? Haven't they friends of their own kind all over England? During my other trip, when I stayed in the East, I came into contact with a good many of them myself. That was how I knew so well that the whole country was impatient to jump into the war but was being held back on leash by President Wilson!

Now that I've gone farther and seen deeper, associating with all kinds of Americans in other parts of the country, I am convinced the other way. At the present time and under present conditions, Wilson could not draw a united country into this war. I believe there would be something like a revolution if he tried to do it, even if he had the constitutional power, which he has not.

The people I've been meeting lately are not cowards nor money-grubbers. They just don't see what they've got to do with it all, and they are inclined to be suspicious of "perfidious Albion." Britain certainly has not been clever or far-seeing in the propaganda line, if she really wants the United States to come in. She seems to have been feeling that, like Truth, "the eternal years of God are hers," that, just because she is right, people are bound to see her rightness, even in the Middle West. My trip out there seems to have given me a keener insight, a more enduring patience, and over and over again I find myself asking the old question, "How shall they believe unless they have heard, and how shall they hear without a preacher?"

A State Department official in Washington said to me lately, "The British have the smartest Secret Service in the world." I reminded him of certain things that did not seem to prove it, and he replied that it was the ignorant and too-cautious British politicians that held the Secret Service back, and cited some instances that seemed to prove his point.

I have been dipping into a book this afternoon which I got from the ship's library, a history of the Franco-Prussian War of 1870. How strictly and cautiously neutral England remained during that conflict. It seems there were good people who did not think she ought to have made money (they called it "blood money") by supplying munitions and other things to both sides, while there were old men and old women and little children besieged in the cellars of Paris, eating stewed rats.

.   .   .   .

I am reading another book that intensely interests me. It gives an account of Henry Ward Beecher's experiences when he went to England in 1863 to explain the position of the North in our Civil War. Quotations are given from the London Times which show sympathy for the South and hostility to Abraham Lincoln, advising him to stop the war, since the North could not possibly win. There are reproductions of posters displayed throughout England when Beecher was there. On one of the posters reference is made to "the suicidal war raging in the States of North America, urged on by the fanatical statesmen and preachers of the North." On another there is an appeal to the Men of Manchester:

"What reception can you give this wretch, Beecher, save unmitigated disgust and contempt? His impudence in coming here is only equaled by his cruelty and impiety. It behooves all right-minded men to render futile his attempt to get up a public demonstration in favor of the North, which is now waging war against the South with a vindictive and a revengeful cruelty unparalleled in the history of any Christian land."

"Attend, and show by your hearts and hands," runs a Liverpool poster, "that the industrious classes in this country are opposed to the bloody war which Abraham Lincoln is now waging against his brother in the South, and the dastardly means he is resorting to in employing such tools as Henry Ward Beecher, a minister of the Gospel!"

The book lies in my lap now, and I sit back in my deck chair thinking of the stories Uncle John, out on Experiment Farm, used to tell me of the slavery days before that Civil War. Uncle John was an elderly man when I was yet a child, and when a young man, he helped on what was called the "Underground Railroad," by which means the slaves escaped from the States to Canada, then a British colony ruled by England. I remember how avidly I read in "Uncle Tom's Cabin," written by this same Henry Ward Beecher's sister, the account of Eliza's escape on the ice and her landing at Amhurstburg, just outside the now beautiful little town of Windsor, which I have so lately visited, across from Detroit. Slaves had to set but one foot in Canada in order to be free, and thither they journeyed, footsore, though joyful, sometimes with the help of Uncle John, singing,

> "I'se on my way to Canada,
>   Where cul-led folks are free!"

As Uncle John would tell of these thrilling adventures in those stirring Abolitionist days, I remember how Auntie would join in and tell some stories of Canada's help, though at that time she and Uncle John had not married or even met. Once, when Uncle John told me never to forget that to the blacks Canada was always the Land of Hope, Auntie took down her beloved volume of Cowper and read reverently:

> "Slaves cannot breathe in England; if their lungs
> Receive our air, that moment they are free,
> They touch our country, and their shackles fall."

Then Uncle John shook his head sorrowfully and said, "Strange, strange, that England should have helped the South when we fought to get rid of this stain on our country!"

Yes. Strange! Strange the inconsistencies and the misunderstandings of nations, as well as of individuals! . . .

. . . .

There was a terrible storm last night. I went out on deck and found that the breakers had so dashed against the flags and the lights that emblazoned them that some of the reflectors had been washed out to sea.

"The flag does not show at all," said a voice in the darkness.

"And we must be in the war zone," another replied.

"Yes, I should think we were," I spoke up.

"And nothing to show we're neutral. They may take us for British, French, Italian, a merchant ship of one of the Belligerents," said a very English voice.

As the wind increased and the storm grew more furious, we felt our way in from the darkness of the wave-washed deck to the dining saloon below. As now in the sudden glare of light I looked about among the passengers, I thought I had seldom seen so cosmopolitan a company. This American ship seemed to be carrying people belonging to almost every land, except Germany and her allies. We gathered round the piano and sang "The Star Spangled Banner" and then, suddenly, the leader of the neutral orchestra waved his baton violently in response to an American voice that shouted out, "Rule Britannia! Everybody sing it! Britannia Rule the Waves! She's ruling them now! Our lights are out. Our flag doesn't show. Rule Britannia!"

It was amazingly inspiring, this request of an American citizen, and everybody sang as though to wake the very depths of the ocean. Stewards and stewardesses came in, cabin boys sprang up around the piano, sailors pressed their faces against the portholes and we could see their lips moving, though their voices could not penetrate through the storm. We sang on, trying to drown the sound of its increasing fury. In all my crossings this was the worst I have ever known. Were we safe? I could see anxious looks on many faces, questions in many eyes. I forgot submarines and war zones and thought only of ships lost in storms at sea. In the midst of the silence that followed the last verse of "Rule Britannia!" another American voice called out:

"I give you all a toast, a neutral toast. Touch glasses! Drink:

"TO HELL WITH THE KAISER!"

We forgot our fear of the storm as we raised our glasses, clinking them so hard together that some of them cracked. We heard the waves dashing against the sides of the ship, and it seemed to me that the whole sea was groaning in torture, that the spirits of the dead from the Lusitania, the Ancona and the Arabic joined us the second time we touched glasses, crying with us, "TO HELL WITH THE KAISER!"

After all, I believe I am glad that I had to come by this neutral boat.

. . . .

This morning before leaving the boat, I saw that the old gentleman who examined passengers' landing papers, was going over mine very carefully, his finger touching every word. Finally, in the tone one would use to a naughty child, he said, "Go to your state-room with the lady!" and pointed to a frightened looking young woman who beckoned me to follow her, saying she must examine my bags. I told her they had all gone off, and asked her if she were a customs official.

"No, I'm a service detective," she said, as she opened my state-room door, then bolted it. Then she spread my paper before me, the paper where I had written on the line demanding my nationality the words, "American (but not a neutral!)"

"What does that mean?" she asked, with attempted sternness, pointing to the confession.

"What it says!" I replied.

"If you are an American, you *must* be a neutral," she insisted.

"Oh no, you're mistaken," I said. "You ought to be pleased that I'm not neutral."

It seemed that she wasn't, so we argued back and forth, I somewhat belligerently, she apologetically, till finally she exclaimed tearfully, "I don't know what they meant for me to do. Have you been in Germany?" "Yes," I answered. "Haven't you?" whereupon she answered proudly, "Never!" I explained that I had been there in 1913 and she demanded to know if I were *sure* I hadn't been there since. Sure! In a trembling voice she asked me if I would object to unfastening my bodice so she could see if I were carrying any papers in my corset. This done, and pronouncing me paperless, though she certainly made no inspection sufficient to guarantee that fact, she asked what hotel I was going to in London. I told her I was not going to a hotel but to the address I had put on my paper. She next asked for the name of "the lady" I was going to visit, and when I explained that I was not going visiting, she insisted that if I patronized neither hotel, lodgings nor boarding houses, I *must* be going to visit. Finally, she looked despairingly at a locket I wore round my neck. "If you are thinking to ask me to open my locket," I said, "I am sorry to tell you I won't!" Then she unbolted the door hastily, saying she hoped she hadn't offended me, but she would have to take me to see another official. I followed her to the library and waited while she spoke to a uniformed officer who examined the paper she handed him. Then he dismissed the unhappy young "detective" and coming over to me, said "Good morning, Enid! How did you like Canada?"

"Very much!" I answered. "Any further investigation into the subject of my 'neutrality'?"

"None!" he answered, trying hard not to smile. "If you hurry, you'll catch your boat-train for London. Good-by!"

I looked back from the gangway and saw him nodding toward me as he talked with another officer. Their khaki-covered shoulders were shaking, so perhaps all England hasn't lost her sense of humor, after all.

To-night, back in my Adelphi flat, in pulling off my stockings, a crumpled bit of paper fell out of one of them. It was the last of the Democrat's daily "steamer letters" which the steward kept in "cold storage" by instructions, handing me one every morning at breakfast. In my hurry this morning I pushed it into my stocking and had entirely forgotten it when the young woman asked if I were carrying any private papers back to England. I laugh until I cry when I think of the international complications that might have followed an official demand for a complete "show-down" of all my clothing before I was allowed to leave the boat, and this, which might have been taken for a spy's code, discovered on my person:

"TELL YOUR BRITISH FRIENDS TO KEEP UP THE FIGHT TILL HELL FREEZES, BY WHICH TIME THE AMERICANS WILL BE READY TO COME OVER AND HELP FINISH IT ON THE ICE!"

CHAPTER XVIII

"DIGNITY BE DAMNED!"

SINCE my return to London, I have been busy getting my notes and "impressions" into some sort of chronological order.

All those which had to do with the present state of opinion— and lack of opinion—in the Middle West, and the need for British propaganda to counteract what the Germans are doing, I have put together in a many-paged schedule letter, which, the day before yesterday, I sent to B——.

At his office, they have plenty of money and plenty of enterprise, and I asked him if he could start my plan going at once. To-day I had a telephone message from him.

"I've sent your letter to Lord Robert Cecil at the Foreign Office," he said. "That's a big scheme for propaganda in the Middle West. It's not for us, but for the government to take it up. Lord Robert wants to know if you'll call at the Foreign Office as soon as possible. He'll appoint someone to see you and talk things over. Write out any more ideas that have occurred to you since you wrote to me."

He rang off, and at once I flew to my typewriter and got off more notes. So many memories come back to me, so many ideas fairly chase one another through my brain. That Syndicate Man, wanting me to write about London in Peace Time, and then to follow with another article telling about London in War Time— The Germans have got hold of all sorts of people over there to help them. Certainly there was no German blood in that man. He was quite as much British-descended as I am. The Huns are hellish, but they are clever.

．　　．　　．　　．　　．　　．　　．

I have been to the Foreign Office. The official with whom I talked seemed to know my newspaper work very well. I handed him my latest notes, which he spread out before him along with the schedule letter which B—— had sent to Lord Robert Cecil.

"Tell me more of what you have in mind," he said, and I talked, referring occasionally to other notes I had in my small note-book.

"But you say the Germans have already done so much," he said discouragedly.

"The British must do better!" I retorted.

"Still, they've got in ahead of us. They struck while the iron was hot."

I seemed to have a Jeremiah to deal with, so I determined to be a Mrs. Wiggs of the Cabbage Patch.

"The iron hasn't cooled off yet, and they haven't won the war yet!" I said. "The only reason my people aren't in the war is because they don't understand what it's about or how it can possibly affect them. It is up to the British to explain it to them in very plain and simple language. I've been associating with what are known as 'the common people,' those people Abraham Lincoln said God must love, or he wouldn't have made so many of them. They are the ones who will have to make up an American Army. They must be educated not only by simple methods, but by quick ones—very, very quick ones!"

He looked at me in such a manner that I guessed his unspoken retort.

"You haven't said it aloud, but still you are saying that it isn't the job of the British to educate my people. But, yes, it is, if it's worth your while. A Washington man asked me a few days before I sailed what you British were thinking of to stand back and merely think your Just Cause would plead its own case. I told him you were thinking of your dignity, and this is what he said: 'You tell them dignity be damned, when their house is afire!' "

He smiled, and I left him, a pleasant, quiet official, fingering my notes in a depressed, dignified way. I could see him just so, as I reported to B—— on what I considered the futile result of his sending my scheme to the Foreign Office.

*   *   *   *   *   *   *   *   *

A letter came from the Foreign Office to-day:

"WE ARE ACTING ON SOME OF YOUR SUGGESTIONS, AND HAVE PASSED ON OTHERS WHERE THEY WILL BE VALUED."

So it seems I've done my bit!

CHAPTER XIX

IN DAYS OF HOPE—AND HORROR

THE first Americans in uniform have marched through London, and I was one of a party in a Trafalgar Square window to see and welcome them. When the first line of these Engineers came into view, I confess I did a lot of staring. Their features rather took me by surprise, but something held me back from commenting aloud. Not so with another member of the party. She has been over here for the past twenty-five years without having once returned to her native land, but she lives and moves and has her being as a representative American woman in England. During these happy first days of the entry of the United States into the War, she constitutes herself a sort of spokeswoman for America.

"Why!" she gasped, holding her far-sight lorgnettes close to her eyes, "They're not Americans! They're foreigners!"

"That's what I was thinking," said an Englishman. "Can't understand it at all."

As line after line passed, I scanned the men's faces. Now I knew what had made me almost jump in my surprise when I had seen the first line. It was that they looked like a new race, difficult, indeed, impossible, to name. In spite of my recent tour in the United States, I had allowed myself to anticipate a British-looking contingent, and there was nothing whatever British-looking about these men. Possibly there had been some remote British ancestors but, if so, they had left no visible means of identification.

"My God!" exclaimed an American expatriate man. "What does it mean? I tell you they're not Americans!"

"Yes, they *are* Americans! I saw a good many like them in the United States last year, also in Canada," I put in.

"Canada, did you say?" interrupted the Englishman. "Canada's a British colony."

"Dominion!" I corrected, smiling. "But anyway, I saw any number of Canadians out West who looked like these men. It's the mixture of many nations."

I noticed that one of the engineers looked very like Theodore Roosevelt must have looked in his early manhood. Then I fell sadly to thinking of Roosevelt, longing to come over, and held back on leash, by Wilson, so it was said. Would he strain hard enough to break the leash? I had a letter from him only the other day. It came in answer to mine, telling him how glad I was that we were finally "in," and asking when he was coming over, and should I see him? Such a characteristic answer, and somewhat pathetic:

". . . That's a mighty nice letter of yours . . . I only wish that it were likely I would be allowed to go abroad with a division. . . ."

.   .   .   .

Yesterday morning when I went to the kitchen I found two pigeons strutting about the floor as if they owned the place, in spite of the fact that I had put a liberal breakfast on the window-sill bird table. They were actually pecking at the linoleum, and as I started to prepare my own breakfast, they both made a swoop for the bread-board, grabbed the first slice from the edge of the knife and fought until they had torn it in two. They devoured it so fast I thought they would choke. Great lumps of it stuck in their gullets. As one of them perched on my hand, I felt of its body. It was as thin as a rail. Then, suddenly, sparrows came flying in right over the bird table. The thing made me feel quite sick. The birds long ago learned the times for their meals and never before had they appeared out of time. I have never believed that they came to me because they were hungry, for Londoners carry a good many paper bags of bread about with them in the Gardens. One of the most beautiful sights in London is the feeding of the pigeons in the fore-court of St. Paul's, at Nelson's Monument, the National Gallery and the British Museum. Some visiting Americans have criticized this custom as making these places dirty, but it is a part of the London and Londoners that I love.

After my experience with the pigeons and sparrows, I went

over to Embankment Gardens to investigate. Not a soul there had a paper bag for the birds. The park keeper told me it is on account of the food restriction. To-day the birds came again right through the open window, and, instead of the usual number, there were dozens. I suspect that my regular "boarders" have chattered abroad among their feathered kind that "over at Number Five they do you well."

.   .   .   .

An old lady has been fined five pounds for feeding bread to birds. She had been seen throwing it from her window into her garden, and someone reported it. The dear soul told the magistrate that she had always given the outside crusts to the birds, that, in any event, she would not eat this part of her loaves, because it was "not quite clean." She said her only son was at the Front and the birds were her only companions now. . . .

I've taken down the bird table from the kitchen sill. For the sake of the birds, I don't want to be reported myself. Of course, Bernard Shaw, the Pennells and John Galsworthy would never tell on me, but there may be people who don't feel quite so friendly, since I've got into the habit of ringing up Bow Street Police Station whenever I see lights shining from uncurtained Adelphi windows.

The sparrows and pigeons come right into the kitchen now twice a day. It seems I can claim a small amount of standard flour every week besides my bread, and I make a very palatable sort of "Johnny cake" of it, which not only helps out with the birds but lets me have something to give my friends' dogs and poor street strays as well. Dog-biscuits are now being made of a material that is suspiciously like ground-up straw. And who would have believed that in England, the land of dog-lovers, people would be writing to the newspapers demanding that all dogs not engaged in "war work," should be killed, and quoting as Christ's dictum "It is not meet to take the children's bread and cast it unto dogs?" Of course the gentle Christ never said it. He would have advised a sharing of the bread. Is the war killing some of the most beautiful of English characteristics? It seems to be bringing out some heretofore unsuspected selfish traits in some people's characters, although it is bringing out some lovely things in others.

Henrietta hasn't time to use up her allowance of flour, so she brings it to me and I make it into nice cakes for Daniel . . .

Those damned Gothas—

   .   .   .   .

As I was saying, those damned Gothas broke into my writing last night, or, rather the housekeeper broke into it by nearly tearing the door down trying to tell me they were here. . . . I was so interested in my work that I never heard a sound till her banging and shouting began. She was surprised that I didn't hear the warning of the barrage. I grabbed my typewriter and went to the lower basement with her, but I couldn't write, of course. My nerves are getting every which way. I should like to be calm and matter-of-fact, like an Englishwoman who joined us down there. She was passing when the warning came, and knowing of the secure depths of the Adelphi basements, rang the bell and asked for shelter. She had a bag of her special treasures on her arm, jewels, money, letters, which, it seems, she always carries on her person, day and night, and down there she sat, talking and knitting for five whole hours, with London being bombed and we not knowing but each second would be our last. . . . I tried to talk with her, but I couldn't for the chattering of my teeth, and I found that my hands had got quite numb from neuritis.

   .   .   .   .

I find that a good many of my newspaper articles on the subject of economy are of much value to the British Food Control Department. Who would have thought, when I stood on a starch-box to reach the kitchen table in the Experiment Farm house, that the things I learned then in the way of cookery would help to conserve the food of Britain and thus help to win the war! This same Standard flour they now use is the sort of thing we called "shorts" in those days, when I was taught to make really nice muffins and griddle-cakes from it. A Canadian boy from the Beaver Hut came in the other day bringing an American "buddie" with him and begged me to make them some crullers "like mother's."

"Not with war-time ingreejunts!" I said, and they looked so disappointed that I made up my mind I'd do it or die. So I went around to various friends and begged bits of frying fats and portions of flour and a lump of sugar here and another there, watered the condensed milk and got some dried eggs. Then I started at cruller-making and to-night I telephoned the boys to come along over. I didn't bargain for their bringing five American Blue-jackets along with them. They've eaten all the crullers, even to the holes. I know they were good, for I had one myself, but I've told them I run a risk from offending "Dora" if it becomes known that I make appetizing things. A baker was fined five pounds because he made light sausage-rolls. It seems that the police sergeant, who arrested him, and the magistrate who tried him, had not, since food restriction began, eaten any but heavy sausage-rolls. Vainly the baker explained to the magistrate that he used the same kind of dark flour and the same amount of shortening that other bakers use in the making of heavy sausage-rolls, but the magistrate said that the object of the Light Pastries Order was to prevent the production of attractive food. If that magistrate knew about my crullers, he would fine me because, according to his war time experience, all cakes should weigh heavily and taste like sawdust moistened with hair-oil.

.   .   .   .

I am feeling rather impatient to be doing something for my own country. My English women friends are nearly all in khaki uniforms of one sort or another, which are vastly becoming to them. One blessing the war has brought to women is the abolition of hobble and long skirts. We are all showing our ankles now, regardless. Brown, of the khaki shade has always been considered "my color," and I do want an American uniform with buttons and the letters "U. S." all bright and shining.

Something will soon be ready for me, though it cannot yet be explained, but this morning the American mail brought a letter counselling patience, and advising me to keep right on "brushing up" my German.

.   .   .   .

There was another raid last night. Henrietta had been here early in the evening and said she'd leave Daniel for the night. I told her this morning that he had awakened me by pulling the blankets off the bed, so that I got down to the cellar shortly after the warning and before the bombing began. She said she would like to leave Daniel for "the next month or two," but I told her I was expecting soon to have a "job" to do which would probably take me away from London. "Oh well, *till* then!" she said, so Daniel's bed-blanket and his comb and brush have been brought around and he's residing here again. He's great company.

It would seem wonderful to have a rest from the fear of raids. Now that they've taken to coming in the daylight, it is difficult to arrange the time of one's baths. I used always to take a warm bath at night just before going to bed, but often the raids start about that time, and as I didn't want to be caught in the tub, I changed around to morning baths. Then when those forty Gothas made their wonderful morning tour through the sky (at first there was a report that they were just a little advance fleet of saluting Americans!) I began to think daylight was also a bad time for baths. However, at Experiment Farm, where we had no proper bath-tub, we all managed to keep clean with stand-up baths, washing ourselves on the instalment plan, and I think I can do it again.

.　　.　　.　　.　　.　　.　　.　　.

No! I shan't be wearing a uniform after all. I am to make myself as inconspicuous as possible. My experience in detective journalistic work during the past many years seems to have been just the very thing to help me now to help my country and the Allies. Mine will be a "secret service" job.

The thought that I can be so much more useful than if I were in uniform, reconciles me to any lack of war-time "style" in the way of clothing! I can afford to laugh at that threatening anonymous letter I found in my letter-box yesterday. It was on paper without any water-mark and was printed in the way children print on their slates at school. It tells me to remember that ever since August, 1914, I have been on the German Black List of "non-neutral 'neutral' journalists" along with Edward

Price Bell and a few other select souls, and that I am listed under *four* names.

Well, just let them wait till I get at them *incog!*

.   .   .   .

The raid started at eleven last night. I hadn't gone to bed yet, but was at my desk writing when Daniel came bounding in from the kitchen where he was having a night-cap of watered condensed milk, which he likes, on account of its being sweetened. He set up such a barking that I thought there was someone in the public hall, but it turned out to be a warning, and we both flew down stairs.

.   .   .   .

I have been reading a yellow water-soaked, mud-bespattered letter. It has given me comfort, which I needed badly. These continuously recurring raids are so affecting my nerves that I get little sleep, day or night. How in the world do the poor boys manage to sleep at all at the Front? It is now more than two years ago that I sat here at my desk trying to think of a subject for my weekly article for the Referee which had to be done that day. There had been a raid the night before and I was so unstrung that I simply couldn't seem to think. In a sort of automatic way, not knowing what I was doing, I began striking letters on the typewriter, trying to get my fingers limber, till suddenly I noticed that I had written the words "Are You Afraid?" Then, I went right on with an article, calling it by that title, and I told the boys at the Front that they shouldn't pay any attention to the fact that they were afraid—that everybody was afraid, bound to be, and nothing to be ashamed of.

The writer of the letter I have received says that on a certain day when we was assigned to "danger duty," he was so afraid that his knees shook and his teeth chattered. He had just made up his mind to confess his fear and ask his commanding officer to give the job to a braver man, when somebody handed him an English paper, thinking he'd be hungry for home news. It happened that the page turned outside had my article on it, and he was confronted with my query "Are You Afraid?" Then, instead of asking to be let off, he went on and accomplished his task—all because I, an American journalist in London, was so afraid myself that I could think of nothing to write about but FEAR. *My* fear, it turned out, was actually the cause of his rising above *his* fear! In the letter there are two or three sentences blacked out by the censor. Perhaps he attempted to tell me what he had done. What strange coincidences, if they *are* coincidences, the war brings about. What is it? I am becoming superstitiously afraid not to follow my idlest impulses, wondering if there is Something outside myself which I must let guide my actions. Was I inspired to write that article? What is Inspiration? Whence comes it?

. . . .

At last the devils have hit the Adelphi. The bombs dropped in almost a straight line from the Embankment, where they knocked large pieces off the Egyptian Obelisk, made holes in the Sphinx and tore up the tramway tracks. Then they skipped right over our building, which makes up the Terrace, and struck the Little Theater, which is used by the Canadian boys as a part of the Beaver Hut— It seems one of the boys came over here to inquire if I'd gone down to the basement. The third bomb hit Charing Cross Hospital. The glaziers are at work putting in windows that were broken all around the neighborhood in houses where no other damage was done, but there is not even a cracked glass in the Terrace.

. . . .

A week of horrors! On Wednesday, Jess —— came in, looking terribly white and defiant, in her "Y" uniform.

"Tom's killed," she said, "and I'm going to have a baby, thank God, though we didn't have time to get married!"

Yesterday, Henrietta came. She stooped and picked up Daniel, then stood stiff and straight in the doorway, looking at me, and never saying a word, but I knew. I went over to her. "Jim?" I whispered. She nodded.

She is driving her car to-day, Henrietta the bravest, most tragic figure among all my friends. "No vote, no baby!" she used to say in the old suffrage days, and now, forever and always, it will be with her, no Jim, no baby.

. . . .

There is a letter from the mother of the American boy who

followed me across the Border and enlisted with the Canadians. After months, she found my name and address among his things, killed only a week before his own country came into the war. I had no way of tracing her, so I could not write to her when I saw his name on the casualty list.

She has written me a sweet letter, without a word of blame. I wonder could I feel the same toward her were the case of motherhood reversed. How can one tell? I am sending her the Memorial notice I wrote when I learned that he was dead:

IN MEMORIAM.*

TO THE AMERICAN SOLDIERS DEAD IN FRANCE

By Elizabeth Banks

I heard a voice from Heaven saying unto me, Write, From henceforth blessed are the dead. . . .

In August, 1914, the agonized cry of Belgium and the appeal of invaded France reached the shores of the United States, and hundreds of thousands said:—

"They suffer greatly over there. Let us collect money and send them food and clothing and hospital supplies."

Then, because of American generosity, millions of dollars came across the water, bringing relief to the sick and homeless, comfort to the aged, and smiles to the faces of little children.

There were other Americans—at first a few hundred and afterwards many thousand who, while hearing the cries of Belgium and France, heard yet more the call of all humanity, of all peoples threatened, of Liberty assailed.

So piercing and so clamorous was this call that it came not only to their ears but to their souls, and, looking up, they saw the VISION. Then a hand beckoned, and, because the hand was so compelling, they followed it.

.   .   .   .

They were not of any one class, those American men who first saw and followed the Vision. Young University men looked up

* Reprinted from the Evening News (London), "America Day", April 20th, 1917.

from their books and saw the light; mechanics lifted up their eyes and saw it too; preachers were enveloped by it in their pulpits; blacksmiths knew it was a different light from that which blazed from their forges; farmers in the harvest fields felt that something more brilliant than the sun was round about them; lawyers, doctors, writers, and painters beheld the light and followed after the beckoning hand.

Some followed directly over to France and others across the border into Canada, and thence through England to the fighting line, and so they formed the first American Overseas Force at the Front, a unit in spirit, although they were not all together, but scattered about among the French and the Canadians.

From among this contingent many have fallen. Most especially wherever Canadians have given their lives, there too, have the Americans damped the earth of France with their blood.

To all these I offer tribute on this, America's Day.

. . . .

How quietly, how unostentatiously, how secretly have they paid the great price, these countrymen of mine. Here in a newspaper, included in a long Roll of Honor, I read a little notice:—

"— Canadians, — —, first reported missing, now officially reported killed."

That is all. Only those who knew the man's history, as I knew it, will be aware of his nationality. Indeed, when he died, he had, technically, no nationality, though he fought and died as a soldier of the King. I remember the break in his voice as he told me of the oath of allegiance he had taken:

. . . do make oath that I will be faithful and bear true allegiance to his Majesty King George the Fifth, his heirs and successors.

"It's all right, of course," he said, with a wistful smile, "but it makes a fellow feel queer to go away and fight under another flag, even the flag of his great-grandfather; but I had to answer the call, didn't I?"

"Yes," I said, "you had to answer the call."

And now, "officially reported killed!"

To-day, the flag of his native land and the flag under which he and his comrades fought, are intertwined. Now, in Old St. Paul's, British and American voices join in singing their requiem:

"He had sounded forth the trumpet that shall never call retreat,
He is sifting out the hearts of men before His Judgment seat;
O be swift my soul to answer Him, be jubilant my feet!
Our God is marching on."

Hark! Now those voices from the graves in France join in, and we know there is no death, but only Life, for those whose souls were so swift to answer, whose feet followed, jubilant, at the beckoning of that hand in the pathway lighted by the Vision.

CHAPTER XX

"FRIGHTFULNESS"—AND HOPE

ALWAYS, since the war started, I have been afraid, but not of what has come.

I did not see the thing I feared as Death. Never have I been afraid of Death. I would not much have minded it, but whether I minded it or not, I felt it was not for me, just yet.

In the pictures which my fears showed me, I saw myself maimed or mutilated in an air-raid, carried to hospital, helpless, perhaps an invalid always, unable to earn my living, and dependent upon the kindness and charity of others.

The "frightfulness" of the Germans has not brought that.

"Come," said they, at the beginning of the war, "we will work out the principle of the Psychology of Fear. We will bomb the civilians of England and teach them that they have no longer a real island! We will rack their nerves, destroy their *morale,* and then they will cry for peace!"

They did not "get" England that way. They never will. But, in a certain way, they have "got" me. My fear has brought me not the thing I most feared, but another calamity.

Through wear and tear on my nerves, I have lost more than half my normal hearing.

I am not incapacitated for certain kinds of work, but I cannot do for my country and its allies what I had wished and planned. Secret service requires ears that can be trusted to make no mistakes. Only a fool or a criminal would attempt the kind of work I intended, who could not *listen* wisely and well.

In this way the Germans have "got" me, but, in other ways, I have "got" them. If I had not often lived in fear, there are things I could not have written, things which, having been read, led to other things which put "the fear" into the Germans.

One thing I am determined upon. I will not practice what Emerson calls "the meanest vice," self-pity. It is not only mean, it is fatal to one's sense of humor, which is but a sense of proportion. I am not at all sure I could properly be termed a "civilian." Certainly I was not a harmless one. I did the Germans all the harm I could. From the 4th of August, 1914, I have been a fierce combatant. Though technically a "neutral," I always resented being thought anything but a belligerent.

So, perhaps from one point of view, I have got what was coming to me. I called my own tune, and now I pay the piper.

.   .   .   .

Woodrow Wilson is in London. Even I can hear, faintly, the cheers that mark his progress along the Strand.

All hearts are turning to him as the Hope of a war-worn world.

THE END OF PART TWO

PART THREE

The American (1926–1927)

CHAPTER XXI

THE RETURN OF THE NATIVE

"I believe in the United States of America as a Government of
the people by the people for the people, whose just powers are de-
rived from the consent of the governed; a democracy in a republic; a sovereign nation of many states; a perfect union, one
and inseparable, established upon those principles of freedom,
equality, justice and humanity, for which American patriots sacrificed their lives and fortunes.

"I love my country and will support its Constitution, obey its
laws, respect its flag, and I will defend it against all enemies."

IN a great auditorium of a Middle West school I stood among
a thousand children and joined them in saluting the flag
and reciting "the Creed." As I looked about, I understood
what the Principal had meant when he told me I should find
large numbers of "new Americans" in the school. Here were
young Americans in the making, assisting in my own remaking. They had not my fortune in having been born in this
country, yet I saw that they were being given all the opportunities that I had enjoyed as a child and a school girl—yes, more
than I had, because, since then, my country had grown greater
and wiser and richer, and had more to offer her children,
whether born of her or adopted.

About me were fair faces from Scandinavia, dark ones from
Spain and Italy, fair ones again from Germany. There were
little Greeks, Austrians, Hungarians, Rumanians, Silesians,
Bulgarians, Bohemians, French, Portuguese. There were faces,
too, showing British descent, like my own, but they were in
the minority.

The children were all cleanly, many of them nicely and even
expensively dressed. I noticed their happy faces, bright eyes,
quick movements. After the gathering in the auditorium, I

217

went with them to the various class rooms, all light, airy, furnished with single desks of beautiful wood grown in American and Canadian forests. The blackboards were of the latest and most convenient type; there were bright pictures, suitable to the ages of the scholars, on the walls. Bubbling drinking fountains were in the corridors, spacious cloak-rooms adjoined the various class rooms. There were wash rooms and water closets of sanitary and improved type in the basement. Each teacher had a telephonic connection with the Principal's office, and on his desk was the main telephone linking up the school with all the outside world. There was a young girl clerk, graduate of a near-by high school, who attended to the necessary stenography and typewriting, for the Principal was a busy man.

There were wireless sets, conservatories and nature-study rooms, swimming pools and shower baths, a lunch room with milk in sealed bottles, stacked in refrigerators. Besides the pianos, there were gramophones, to the music of which the children marched and danced, and in the playground I saw a dozen little girls, without a teacher, enjoying a folk-dance, keeping perfect time to the music and directions of the gramophone in the center. In the auditorium there was kept going a series of educational moving pictures, graded according to the age and advancement of the children. The school building, its equipment, its teachers, were all of the best. Had it been planned by millionaires especially for their own children, I could think of nothing they might have added for its betterment and beauty. It was a free public elementary school, built by American taxpayers for all the children of all the people.

On my way East, I visited other schools, to study their methods and to watch the process of "Americanization," of which I had read and heard so much and had seen so little. Years ago I talked with Izrael Zangwill about his play, "The Melting Pot," and I remember he expressed surprise that I seemed to have so little knowledge of what went into the pot and what came out. I, a free-born citizen of the United States, living much of my life abroad, knew little of what my country was doing in the way of creating a new race with a great destiny. England I knew and the English I knew, up to a certain point, although now I understand how little really I knew them while I lived there and took so many of the pleasant experiences that came to me for granted. In those days, when I thought of America, I thought only of a people descended, like myself, from early Puritans and later British emigrants.

But now, as I traveled from town to town, from village to village and from farm to farm, I was continually being surprised, and the wonders of my own country fascinated me as no foreign country had ever done. My native land became a land of delight and a place of enchantment. So much was new to me, the returned native, that I felt my place was really among the "new Americans," and it was largely in their company that my re-Americanization took place. Now I could understand Zangwill's play, now I appreciated Mary Antin's beautiful and inspiring story of "The Promised Land," as I had not appreciated it when I read it in England during the year 1912.

I came on to New York and spent some time at Ellis Island. I had become accustomed to reading unpleasant things about "the Island," and I went prepared for the worst. Where I had expected to see sad and gloomy faces, I saw happy ones. I saw women from every quarter of the world, detained on account of some technicality, congregated sociably in a large, comfortable room, learning to swing themselves in American rocking chairs, sewing, knitting, studying dictionaries, reading books and papers in their own language, petting their children and suckling their babies. In another room I found men smoking and having games. I visited children in a fine play room, part of which was turned into a school under a teacher who, I could see, had herself come years ago into the country as an immigrant, and was now giving the little ones their first fascinating lessons in English according to the latest and easiest methods. The children had toys of every sort, some of which were quaintly foreign, having been brought from their original countries. Those who had arrived without toys or had broken or lost them, had been provided with American ones by a thoughtful Uncle Sam. He had even given them toy dummy telephones and they were being taught to use them, these little

Europeans who never before had so much as heard of a telephone. They sang for me songs in many languages, then followed the teacher in the singing of the "Hoppitty, hoppitty" bird song. Some of them, I was sure, had never before been clean in all their little lives. Now they had wonderful bath tubs in which they could plunge and spatter and be washed with sponges made up in the shapes of dogs and cats and monkeys and teddy bears.

In every part of the place there was such cleanliness and healthfulness as none of the immigrants could ever have seen before. There were bathrooms such as in England, only the wealthiest people have. They were the very latest things in plumbing with the kind of taps I always wanted in London but never could afford. My English friends used to laugh when I told of my ambition for them and reminded me that they were "not for the likes of us"! At Ellis Island there is never any lack of hot water in tubs and lavatory basins, and separate individual soap is provided for every person—no "family cakes." Common drinking cups are not allowed. Oh, how those detained kiddies drink and drink, and how they are enjoying the shower baths this hot weather! In the winter, corridors, bathrooms and closets are heated, like all the rest of the building.

The bedrooms have comfortable and hygienic mattresses and springs. The bed linen is changed three times a week if the same person is there that long, and, of course, it is changed every day if the occupants stay but one night. Each person, grown-up or child, has two clean towels every day. There is a good library, a newspaper reading room, a cinema and, in the auditorium, lectures and concerts and plays are given.

I ate the food at Ellis Island, this being the menu one day:

BREAKFAST—Boiled rolled oats with milk. Oranges, coffee, bread and butter.

DINNER—Mutton broth with barley. Ragout of beef, carrots, turnips, onions, boiled potatoes, farina pudding, coffee, bread and butter.

SUPPER—Hamburger steak with onion sauce. Peach jelly, tea, bread and butter.

Milk was served at all the meals to the women and children, and, with crackers, it was also given them between regular meals and at bed time.

So it is that I have seen the bogie place provided by Uncle Sam for the first reception of those who leave the Old World behind them. British newspapers have published many heart-rending accounts of America's ill-treatment of her immigrants, with stories of babies snatched from their mothers' breasts on "the one taken and the other left" principle, because the Quota has been exceeded. On the subject of the increasingly popular "tourist third cabin" travel from Europe to this country, I have just read the following in a British paper:

"As matters stand, an Englishwoman, going on a visit to America of a few weeks duration, cannot travel third unless she is willing to put up with more indignities than the majority can stomach. Before she is allowed on board the liner, her head is examined for lice. Before she is allowed off again, she is stripped to the waist in company with all the other women passengers, then sent single file and half naked past an immigration officer (female)—in other words, from one room to another across a landing. Imagine the outcry if the English treated their American visitors—the students, lecturers, doctors and mere wives—in this fashion!"

I have written some articles about Ellis Island as I have found it and tried to get them published on the other side, but even favorite editors have turned them down. One of them tells me that if he published my "glowing description of the American Reception Palace," all the best British workmen will be getting themselves and their families into line for the Quota immediately. He reminds me that, having published something already about the abuses of Ellis Island, he could do with more, which confirms me in my belief that *habit* is altogether *too much of a habit* with the Englishman!

•   •   •   •   •   •   •   •   •

As I am now living in New York's "down town," I spend an

hour every morning in Madison Square among the bootblacks. That is the only proper way to describe it, for they are my chief companions now that the schools are closed for the summer.

At first, I used to clean my shoes before going out to the Automat for breakfast, the place where I push a nickel in the slot and pull out two delicious crullers, and another nickel in another slot for a cup of coffee, including milk and sugar, as good as any I ever drank in the most expensive London restaurant. There are as many paper napkins, extra size, as one wants for the mere taking of them out of a compartment, and thus it is that I breakfast sumptuously every morning for ten cents. My friends laugh at my enthusiasm over the automatic life and tell me I shall soon be getting my own breakfast over "canned heat" in my little apartment. Perhaps so, especially when winter comes, but just now, during the early days of my re-Americanization, all things like this have the greatest fascination for me. They seem to spell Democracy, and I have been thinking much about Democracy lately.

But to return to the bootblacks in Madison Square. When they used to see my shoes all nicely polished as I sat on a bench with my morning paper, they would pass me with a regretful look in their eyes, which I finally couldn't bear any longer, so now every morning I allow my shoes to look just as bad as they possibly can. A fortnight ago a brown-eyed urchin awoke me from a reverie on the well-keptness of the Embankment Gardens in London and the ill-keptness of Madison Square in New York, with a loud "Hi Missus! Ain't they the limit? Shine?" pointing with disdainful rapture at my feet.

"Yes, the *very* limit!" I laughed. "Can you do anything to make them presentable?"

"Watch me!" he retorted.

With his box of paraphernalia he got down beside me. In the midst of so hard a rub that I squealed out, he looked up earnestly and said, "What was that long word, Missus?"

"Presentable?" I asked.

"You want to give these shoes away, make *present* to somebody with them? They are very nice shoes, most fine, when I finish them! You keep them, Missus, and I shine them regular every day!"

When I had explained the variations of the word "presentable," he remarked, "very in-ter-est-ing!"

"Are you an American?" I asked.

"You bet!"

"But you were not born here— Where?"

"Italy, but now an American, sure!"

"Yes, of course," I said. "Do you go to school?"

"You bet! But it is closed now. My little sister, she goes, too, and my big sister goes to a High— She is very smart, my big sister. She came to this country first to live with my aunt. My mother she doesn't know the English much, but I learn her to read it."

"No, you *teach* her. It is this way," I said, pointing my finger at him. "*You* learn, but *I* teach you."

He dropped his brush. "*When?*" he asked.

I laughed, as I saw his mistake, or rather my own. I was fairly caught on a technical point, but I answered quite as a matter of course, as though I had really offered to become his teacher.

"Well, so long as vacation lasts, I'll come here every morning and give you a lesson, while you shine my shoes."

So the bargain was struck and daily we meet now as employer and employed, as teacher and pupil, and—best of all, as friends. I think his public school teacher will find he has progressed wonderfully with his reading and pronunciation during the vacation, as well as having gained some interesting information about birds and plants and flowers, for we are going in for a bit of Nature-study at off times. Yet, the lessons I am learning from Antonio, or Anthony, as he insists upon being called, because it is "the American," are, I believe, far more valuable and soul-saving to me than anything I can ever teach him.

Yesterday when Anthony had gone from me for his further round of clients, I was watching the thirsty multitude at the bubbling fountain in the center of the Square when I heard a familiar voice of old London.

"Fellow Exile!" exclaimed an American whom I had last seen in London where business, as well as inclination, had held him for many years.

He sat down beside me, which I noticed he did with some hesitation, peering carefully at the seat. How it reminded me of the London habit of the "better classes," when they find themselves obliged to sit upon any seat that is not a tuppenny chair in the parks and gardens there!

We talked of how long we had each been back in our native land, and he informed me that he was taking his furniture out of storage in order to ship to England what books and pictures he wanted to keep.

"I'm going back there for good and all— Taking out naturalization papers," he said.

"You would become a British subject!" I exclaimed.

"I expect to. I've been in New York for six months, and I find I'm simply an exile in my native land. I can't get used again to the people here or their ways. This may be the last trip I shall make to England having to pay ten dollars for a *visa* to my passport!" He laughed. "I suppose you feel about the same, don't you—an exile in your own sweet native?"

"No. I shall have to continue paying for the British *visa* when I go over."

"When are you sailing?" he asked.

"I don't know. You see I am a returned exile re-patriating myself."

He stared uncomprehendingly. "You mean you can *stand* this country after all your years of England? What's the appeal?"

"Democracy! I find I am a democrat. I belong here, and not over there."

"But Britain is the greatest democracy in the world! You can't say the United States has more freedom or that its people have more liberty than they have in England!"

"This is a democracy within a republic— Look at this," and I took out my notebook and showed him "the Creed" I had first heard in the Middle West school.

"Piffle!" he exclaimed. "You actually believe that Great Britain is *not* a democracy?"

"It is partly a political democracy, but not a social democracy," I replied.

"Like *that?*" he said, and nodded to a score of people standing in line before the bubbling fountain.

"You've said it! The proof that this is a social democracy has risen to confront you. There's a brick-layer stopped to get a drink on his way to lunch. There's an insurance broker from the Metropolitan building—I know he's fairly coining money at honest hard work. There's a washerwoman carrying her basket of clothes. There's a Broadway lawyer—I've seen him before and I know. There's a typist girl who probably earns over thirty dollars a week in a business office and, bless me! there's Anthony, my own special shoe-shiner 'new American' boy. I don't know personally any others, but you can see for yourself that they represent all kinds of workers, men and women and children. That bubbling fountain is clean, hygienic, and even if the drinkers themselves were not all quite clean, or had some physical ailment, everybody is safe in drinking there, and everybody has an equal right. There is no order of precedence there. Now, what are drinking fountains like in London?"

He laughed. "I'm sure I don't know, never having drank at one, nor ever wanted to."

"You wouldn't," I retorted. "They have a pewter cup, fastened with a chain—even the Henry Fawcett fountain in Embankment Gardens is like that—everybody drinking after everybody else from a common cup, and running all sorts of dangers to their health. Of course, the 'better classes' wouldn't dream of drinking from a common cup, without some drastic necessity, even among themselves, much less with the 'lower classes,' for whom the common cup is *good enough,* in England, but not here!"

He rose to continue his way up Fifth Avenue. "Shall I give old London your love, and tell all our mutual friends that you've been converted to the real genuine article of democracy all on account of a bubbling fountain in Madison Square?" he asked.

"Do!" I laughed, "and tell them I shall never cease to love and visit them."

"A sort of 'my visit still, but never mine abode' affair, I suppose? By the way, I shall send my boy to one of the public schools over there."

"Which one?" I asked. "You know most applicants have to be registered for them at birth—or before."

"I'm not sure of the particular school, but there's bound to be an opening at one or more of them, because since the war there's many a registered boy falls out because of straitened means at home, so some boy's misfortune will be my boy's good luck."

"Don't be so sure who'll have the better luck!" I laughed, as a parting shot.

. . . .

I have made another friend in Madison Square, an English-woman who drops her aitches. She seems to have arrived recently and tells me she is stopping in New York to visit a sister before she goes out West with her children to join her husband who came over first. It was a particularly warm morning when we first met, and it was the bubbling fountain that introduced us. She was looking very clean, very red and very English as I sat down on the seat beside her. Before she said "It's very 'ot, Madam, isn't it?" I knew her nationality. "I wish I 'ad a drink, but I don't know 'ow that thing works. I'm in me best frock and I'm afraid of being spattered."

"It won't spatter," I said. "It's very easy. I'll drink first to show you."

I drank. She drank. Then we sat again on a seat in the shadiest place. She told me of her children, particularly of Annie, aged eleven, "and that bright you'd never think she wouldn't pass it."

"Tell me of Annie and what she wouldn't pass," I said, though knowing England, I already had my suspicion of Annie's trouble.

"Annie's teacher thought she was sure to pass because she was that bright, and she 'ad Annie do 'ome work studyin' for the scholarship. My 'usband bein' anxious as I was that Annie should pass, we never asked 'er to mind the baby, but only to study all the evenings, but when the examination came, we waited an' waited for weeks to 'ear about Annie, but never any word, and that meant she couldn't go to what they call the second'ry school. So me 'usband said 'e'd get under the quoter an' come first an' then send fer us, so's Annie could get educated.

" 'E 'ad a cousin workin' in a place, which reely 'ad a job waitin' fer me 'usband, as you might say, before 'e started, but 'is cousin wrote an' said not to call it *sure* till 'e'd got through the Island, so 'e said 'e 'adn't a job engaged, but 'oped fer one, bein' teetotal an' industrious, lest they wouldn't let 'im through the Island— Wouldn't you think they'd want 'im to 'ave a job, sure, an' not let 'im in lest 'e did 'ave one?"

I laughed at this quaint way of our Immigration officials in the matter of keeping the exact letter of the Contract Labor law.

"So you came to live here because of Annie's education?" I asked.

" 'Er an' the others. We want 'em all to go to school an' 'ave better chances than what we 'ad ourselves. So when that lady wrote about the scholarships bein' wrong and crool and didn't 'alf show 'em up by tellin' 'ow it was about second'ry schools over 'ere, we made up our minds we'd come."

I tried not to look conscious as I sat beside the woman from England. What need to confess that I was "that lady" who didn't " 'alf show 'em up" in the matter of scholarship-winning and losing in the English schools? I merely asked if she came to the Square often, and would she bring Annie one morning so that I might make the little girl's acquaintance.

.   .   .   .

Annie and I are friends now, and she is going to write and tell me about her new home and new school in our Middle West. For a week every morning she and I have sat near the bubbling fountain after Anthony has polished my shoes into mirrors that reflect the trembling leaves of the trees. Annie is one of those beautiful English children whom I used to notice among the so-called "lower orders" who so often have a something about them that gives them an air of what is known as "birth and breeding" equal to, and sometimes surpassing, the children of the oldest families of the land. Besides her beauty, she is as quick and as smart as any of the little Americans she will meet over here. Her voice is soft and typically English, with never a dropped aitch in her speech, thanks, I know to the conscientious work of some teacher in an English elementary school. I think that one day I will go to visit Annie in her Middle West home, and tell her how, all unwittingly, I had the good fortune to be responsible for bringing her away from her native land to mine.

But I will not keep my readers waiting till that time for the story of what sent Annie's father away from England. In the two following chapters I will describe what I feel convinced will, if allowed to continue, send England's best away from her, some to the United States, others to her own Dominions, in search of a broader democracy, depriving her of the power and prestige among the world's nations, which many Americans would regret to see her lose.

CHAPTER XXII

"SOMETHING ROTTEN IN THE STATE OF ENGLAND—"

FOR years during my residence in London, I took the English educational system for granted. It is easy to fall into the habits of thought by which one is surrounded, and when I had for years heard my friends and acquaintances speak of "public schools," I ceased to wonder why they called the most expensive and exclusive schools in the world by such a name.

Many years ago, interviewing the late Mr. Henniker Heaton, I was somewhat astonished when he said to me, "We British like your women better than your men. I suppose what your men lack is due to the absence of public schools in your country."

"Why, we've got thousands of public schools, and all our boys go to them!" I exclaimed, bewildered, whereupon he smiled in a quizzical sort of way which many noted Englishmen had in those days with "the American girl in London," and turned quickly to a discussion of Penny Postage, the subject upon which I had gone to talk with him.

But that was before I had got into the English habits of thought, some of which I now see were bad for my progress in democratic ideals, no matter how comfortable and pleasant they might be at the time. So it gradually came to pass that though I never had English friends and acquaintances who sent their children to any schools but fee-charging ones, I did not wonder why. I took it all as a matter of course, even among those who were too poor to live in what I called comfort. I was not even taken aback when occasionally asked to lend a few pounds "to help pay that tiresome school bill of Tom's," and when I was in funds, I lent them.

My English friends were all among what is there called the

"professional class," and not, by any means, always the most prosperous of that class. I know that some of them went without proper food, and economized in other ways to the very extreme of suffering and sacrifice, in order to send their boys and girls to what they termed "good" schools. I had friends who, though not keeping a sufficient number of servants properly to do the work of their houses, yet kept always a governess, of sorts, for their little girls. I knew men who got the reputation among the "artistic set" of eating always enormous afternoon teas at one studio, flat or house after another in succession during the week, to save the expense of an evening meal, in order to meet the bills of the preparatory or "public" schools which their boys attended. I knew widowed mothers who scrimped and saved in the most pitiful fashion for the same purpose. I knew a gentlewoman of great family who, after the war, entered into an arrangement with another gentlewoman of title to keep an "establishment" for the patronage of gentlemen in their own set, "clients" who were willing to associate in that way only with gentlewomen of good manners and who were "clean and safe," all for the purpose of getting the large sums of money necessary to keep their children in England's great schools.

This case is not an exceptional one. There are numbers of Englishwomen of the "middle" and "upper" classes who live what are called "fast" lives in order to help pay their children's school bills, and sometimes those of younger brothers and sisters. Many an Englishman in business and in the professions has gone bankrupt or become involved in dishonorable transactions for no other cause than an attempt to keep up the family custom and tradition in the matter of sending the boys to "the right schools."

In other families where sufficient means could not be procured to send both the sons and daughters to noted schools, the daughters were given no chance whatever, remaining at home under cheap and inefficient governesses. After the Suffragette agitations for equal opportunities regardless of family means, young Englishwomen put up a noble fight in the matter of the preference shown for their brothers, and now in these

times of more sensible ideas on the sex question, the difficulty
is increased, because it is understood that money must be provided to send both the girls and the boys to the aforesaid "right
schools."

Then I have known other parents who, while not attempting
to send their children to the noted or smart schools, were yet
in a constant state of worry and economy over the subject of
their education. They would pay moderate fees for their boys
to go to small schools kept by retired parsons for "the sons of
gentlemen," men who knew little or nothing about teaching and
less about the way to rear healthy normal boys. The girls would
be sent to boarding schools run by faded and incompetent
spinsters or widows who, knowing of no other means of gaining a livelihood, criminally turned their attention to what they
misnamed the "education" of girls of varying ages, from almost babyhood to young womanhood.

In London itself I knew there were hundreds of fee-charging
day schools for boys and girls who, for some reason or other,
could not be sent away from home, and I noticed that fathers
and mothers of my acquaintance almost invariably apologized
for sending their children to day schools and having them at
home over night and week ends, as though that were a thing
of which to be ashamed.

With hardly an exception, my Englishmen friends and acquaintances have been what are called "public school men." I
remember now an incident that I thought little of at the time.
At an evening reception I introduced a visiting American man
to an English friend. The Englishman had spent four years at
Eton and, in the course of conversation, the American mentioned with great affection his own public school in Minnesota.
"It's a great school, one of the finest in the Middle West,"
boasted the American, who had afterwards graduated at a
Minneapolis high school and taken his degree at the State
university. For at least half an hour these two intellectual men
talked at cross purposes, the American not understanding that
in England a "public" school was not a free school, and the
Englishman taking it for granted that in Minneapolis, at least,
there was a great "public" school patterned after the English

schools. When I finally set the two of them right, they both burst out laughing, the American remarking, "Well, Shakespeare and Milton notwithstanding, it would seem that our two countries don't speak the same language, after all!" a truer observation than he had at the time, any idea of making.

Years went on, and I thought less and less of the two systems of education and the significant difference between them. I was a busy journalist, investigating and "reforming" many wrongs. The memory of my childhood in the district school and my girlhood in the college where I "worked my way" grew dimmer and dimmer, and I forgot—to my shame I say I forgot a great deal about that institution which I now know to be the crowning glory of my native land, its educational system kept up by the people for the children of all the people. I got so I could talk as glibly as any Englishwoman of "the public schools," visualizing, as I talked, Eton, Winchester, Harrow, Rugby and their kind. My women friends had sons and brothers, some as scholars, some as masters, at such schools, whom I met and from whom I would receive invitations for visits. And always in between times, up to the very year when I write this, I have heard of the struggles to get money for the payment of school bills and, incidentally, bitter complaints of the rise in rates and taxes.

In a vague sort of way I knew that there were other schools called "Board schools" and now known as "Council" schools. Where they were and what they were like, I did not know. I knew that people like my friends paid taxes to keep them up and that they cursed while doing so, especially if at the same time the bills for their own children came in. They would say bitterly, "How can we ever be anything but poor, when we have to educate our own children and pay for working class education as well?"

In the streets I often passed children on their way to or from the Board schools which, by the way, were never situated in any neighborhood where I lived, else I might have noticed the buildings and got more interested concerning what went on within them. I would stop and speak to the children whom I saw with school bags. "Going to school?" or "Had a nice day at school?" I would say according to the time of day, and would get a smiling answer of "Yes, miss, thank you, miss." Sometimes I would find a child crying from having fallen in the mud. I was not pharasaic enough to pass by on the other side, but would stop and pick her up, see that she was looked after and buy her some candy, for I have always loved children.

I had charwomen whose children went to these schools, and sometimes they would call at my flat for their mothers at the end of the day's work. I know I was always "kind" to them, but I was a busy woman, investigating and writing. It never occurred to me then that of all the things I investigated, of all the wrongs I tried to set right, these schools were the most important things of all, till I was fairly pushed into the job, first by one of my charwomen, and later by a Canadian friend.

One day, just after the war, I found Mrs. Bruckins, the char, strangely thoughtful of other things than her work, and I asked if she were in trouble.

"Yes, Madam, it's that Sam," she said, "a great big boy, as I tells 'im, an' not parssin' 'is hexarmination! I says to 'im this mornin' 'Wot ye think ye'll be when yer grows hup, hignorant and knowin' nuthin'?' an 'e says 'Mum, them questions is too 'ard an' my 'ead went round when I see 'em!' 'E'll 'ave no learnin', Madam, when 'e leaves school. Everybody says boys is stoopid when they don't parss, though 'is poor father always did say Sam was bright as Sheffield steel."

Sam's father was killed in the war, and his widow added to her small pension by charring for me and two of my friends. I had seen Sam and talked with him.

"Sam's not stupid," I said indignantly. "He's a very bright little boy. I'm sure he'll pass next time. Why, he's not eleven years old yet!"

"There won't be no next time—they never do 'ave no next time, as the 'eadmaster 'isself told me."

Surely this needed investigation and I determined on a visit to Sam's headmaster, but I was ill for a long time after the war and at this time was incapacitated for work. I rebelled against the misfortune that kept me from looking into the matter of Sam's "not parssin'," and I lay in bed studying books that gave descriptions of the gradual rise of "working class education" in England. Meantime, Mrs. Bruckins and Sam went to the Provinces and passed out of my life, though her wail "They never do 'ave no next time!" rang strangely in my ears and in my heart, but I didn't believe it.

It was some time later that a Canadian friend arrived in England to look after some business for his firm, and expecting to remain there for three or four years he began looking about for a furnished house. I gave him some addresses which I thought might suit for himself, wife and two children, whom he was expecting to join him later. One afternoon he astonished me by calling to say good-by, flourishing his steamer ticket in my face by way of emphasizing what he had to say.

"I ask you as an American, speaking the same language," he burst out, "why didn't you write and tell me the truth about schools in this country when I wrote you we were coming over?"

"I don't know what you mean, and you didn't ask my advice about schools or anything else," I defended myself.

"Well, I'm going home, all on account of the schools in this damned caste-bound country, and good riddance to it!" he said, and then he told me his story. His firm had made him an offer of about five thousand dollars a year and expenses. He understood that living was cheaper in England than in Canada and he and his wife believed they could live well on that sum. Never having been abroad, they were delighted at the chance that offered, especially as they had many relations in England whom they had never seen but whose acquaintance they wished to make. The parents of both himself and his wife were British born, but had emigrated before their marriage, so my friend and his wife were Canadian born. When he got the offer, they planned out their expenses, deciding to let furnished their Canadian home while they were away, the wife remaining in Canada till this could be accomplished. In their plans they allowed for a little saving to put by for a rainy day and the children's future. They had taken it for granted that there were schools in England, paid for by the rates and taxes, quite as good as the Canadian public schools which their children attended. Judge of the Canadian's surprise when he learned that he would be expected, aside from other expenses, to spend several hundred dollars a year for his children's education! He could not afford this and, in any event, declared he would not do it, since he objected to what he had heard about the English educational system.

"Why didn't you make inquiries about schools here before you came?" I asked.

"Why should I inquire?" he snapped. "Hadn't I always heard that the English public schools were the best in the world?"

"But 'public' schools here are not free schools," I said.

"So I've found out! They're snob schools for manufacturing what they call 'leaders'! Well, I wouldn't send my kiddies to them if I had a million, nor to any other pay-schools. I don't believe in 'em. When we heard from our relations what we were expected to do, I asked what about the free schools—what is it they call them?"

"Council schools," I said.

"Yes, that's it, Council schools. Well, my wife's aunt and uncle lifted their hands to God, and bowed their heads in prayer, and then threw five fits apiece, when I said I'd send the kids to those schools. They said we'd be disgraced, that no nice English people would visit us, that the kids would be outlawed from decent little friends, never get invited to any parties—and besides, get lice in their heads; that only 'working class' people sent their children to Council schools. I didn't believe it, so I went to the principal of a school I passed one day, which wasn't very near the aunt's, for it seems they don't have those schools in good neighborhoods. Fine man, that principal! I wouldn't ask for a better to be at the head of any public school in Canada, but the school building— My God! It wasn't fit to house cattle, much less to educate little children in. I put the case to him fairly and squarely, told him what my income was, what our English relations said, and asked for the plain unvarnished truth. When he gave it to me, I told him if I were in his place I'd go out and start a revolution, but being in my own place I'd cable my wife to stay where she was, while I packed my grip and made tracks for a decent country. I wouldn't live here and bring up my children here if they gave me the whole island."

I shall never forget this Canadian's parting remark, "Believe me there's something rotten in the state of England, or I wouldn't have to go back to Canada when I wanted to stay here for a while."

Something rotten? My health was now in a condition that allowed me to resume my work, and I determined to see what that "something rotten" was like. Among my friends there were several, who I knew, were interested in what were called "educational matters," but, when I questioned them, I found they knew nothing whatever about Council schools, having never been inside one. I ransacked libraries and studied lists of books about "schools," but they did not mention Council schools. Even the rows upon rows of interesting looking books called "school stories" for boys and girls had been written as if no other schools than boarding schools existed in all England. It seemed that even in the shops where "school clothes" were advertised and displayed for boys and girls, there was no provision for Council school children except in cheap bargain basements. In a spirit of adventure, (or what my friends called "devilment"), I went into one of the large shops and said I was looking for a suit for my little boy to wear at school. I was well dressed and had an air of prosperity about me and the salesman asked most deferentially: "What school, Madam? We have special suits for certain of the schools."

"Oh, just a Council school," I answered innocently, with a strong American accent assumed for the occasion. His look of astonishment could not have been more pronounced if I had said "Reform school" or "Workhouse school."

"You may find what you want in the basement!" he said stiffly.

In the midst of my investigations I remembered that Bernard Shaw was often saying things derogatory to the various school systems. Would he say them to me? His birthday was near, and I spent an afternoon writing him a congratulatory poem, in which I told him, in rhyme, that I was so glad he had been born. I followed this with some leading questions on schools. Alas! I received only this reply on a card:

"It is true I am sixty-seven years old, but why rub it in? When I was seventeen, nobody ever thought about my birthday. Tactless I call it!"

Plainly G. B. S. was not going to be helpful, but there was H. G. Wells, who always had original ideas about education. I wrote and asked him to come in for an interview. It was a week before I had a reply, and it came on a postcard from Spain:

> "Where the skies are mild and blue,
> Far away from interview,
> H. G. sends his love to you!"

A stone, when I had asked for bread! Then I remembered that Kipling had said "He travels the fastest who travels alone," and I went on with my work, in the course of which I made new friends whom I learned to value as among the best I have ever had. Among them are many headmasters, headmistresses and men and women assistant teachers in English Council schools.

When I started my investigations I believed they would take me three months.

It was nearly three years before I finished them.

CHAPTER XXIII

THE TRAIL OF THE SERPENT OF CASTE

IT is not pleasant for one who loves and admires England to write the truth about the English educational system, for the truth is ugly.

Every year there are educational conferences held in the United States and Canada to which the English educational authorities send their delegates, and such conferences are also held in Great Britain, when they are attended by American leaders of education. Speeches are made in which various methods are discussed, schools are visited, the vagaries of children are dwelt upon and opinions given concerning ways and means of progress in education. Yet at every one of these conferences the delegates from the three different countries are always speaking at cross purposes, because the English have never ventured to tell the truth. The Americans and Canadians go home from such conferences with absolutely no understanding of the English system. They have heard the term "public schools" and in many cases they are under the impression that such schools are free schools for the children of the whole people. They have listened to descriptions of what is best in "secondary education" without any suspicion that in England there is absolutely no connection between elementary and secondary schools as there is on our side of the Atlantic.

At such conferences, England is represented by leaders of what is known as "higher" education, in the persons of university professors, men and women who believe the "public" school system to be the foundation of England's greatness, peers of the realm, noted ecclesiastics, and a duchess and a seventh son of a seventh duke. Not one of these will rise on the platform and say:

"In the sense in which you Americans and Canadians understand it, we have not a democratic system of education in England. We, of the governing class, do not believe in such a system. Our system is of the feudal order, dating back for centuries, built upon the foundation of tradition and caste, and it survives to-day as the most surprising anomaly in a country known as a democracy. Before the World War there was but one other country which, educationally speaking, at all approached us in this respect, and that was Russia, with her separate schools for princes and for peasants. Our system is so arranged that all boys and girls of humble parentage shall be kept in their place, i. e., the sphere in which by the will of Almighty God they were born, unless they show signs of extraordinary talent, or, indeed, genius, such as not one child in ten thousand of the 'upper classes' has ever been known to show at a similar age. This, among the working classes, we call exhibiting 'exceptional ability.' In such cases we believe it to be expedient for the State to help them to gain a higher education than that provided in the free Council elementary schools. We have therefore invented a certain Scholarship System, particulars of which I will now explain."

Now, though no such peroration to an explanation of the English Scholarship System has ever been given, explanations which do not explain are constantly being made. So adept have the explainers been in concealing the ugly truth that descriptions have at times sounded absolutely beautiful. I was recently visiting an American public school and was asked by the principal to explain to her the wonderful "intelligence tests" which she understood did so much to preserve the high standard of English secondary schools. She had, she said, attended a conference where they were referred to, and felt the need of full explanation of them. How was it, she asked me, that the English secondary schools could be kept up to such a high standard and have only "picked" scholars in them?

"Why," I said, in astonishment, "some of the dullest boys and girls in England are attending the secondary schools there!"

"But we were assured that they all passed the most wonderful 'intelligence tests'!" she insisted.

Then I understood. She had not comprehended that it was only the *poor* children who were obliged to pass the 'intelligence tests,' and that *they* were the only 'picked' ones. When I had given this American woman the true explanation of what had sounded so ideal from the conference platform, she explained,

"I call it wicked and inhuman! It would seem that the Americans and the English don't speak the same language at all."

And in certain ways they do not!

I began my investigations of English schools early in the year 1922, and had my report ready for publication late in 1924. Since that year I have spent a considerable amount of time in the American and Canadian schools, and have been again in England to make further comparisons. I use the term "English" in this connection rather than "British," for I do not include Scotland, which is far in advance of England in her educational outlook, having her own laws and her own system, although still behind the United States in democratic education. It would be impossible for the English educational system to survive for a day in modern Scotland.

I cannot here give the history of English schools of the various sorts, for that would fill many volumes, but it is well to remember that, in the beginning, all the schools for the poor were charitable institutions, mostly under the Church. In my reading of history I cannot but understand them as having been started with the idea of making the poor more efficient in their services to the ruling classes, more trustworthy and honest. It was believed that this end would be gained if children grew up able to read the Bible and certain pious books which would inculcate feelings of respect for "their betters," and a knowledge of how to "keep their place." With this end in view, the early instruction was largely religious, and it was for such children as these that the Lord John Manners, afterwards Duke of Rutland, and grandfather of Lady Diana Manners, so well known to Americans, wrote in 1845 that classic little prayer for English peasant children to sing at their schools:

> "Bless the Squire and his relations,
> And keep us in our proper stations."

It will be remembered that Lord John also wrote a suitable supplication for his own class, as well:

> "Let wealth and commerce, laws and learning die,
> But leave us still our old nobility!"

Now, in one respect, the "little learning" that the children got in those early days proved to be a "dangerous" thing to those who wished only slightly to educate them for their own purpose, for from those very schools there went forth some who, when they grew older, began to agitate and, like Oliver Twist, "ask for more." The result was that a system of State education was finally started for what were and still are known as "the working classes." Schools were built by public taxation and put under what was called the "School Board," from which came the name of "Board Schools," afterwards changed to Council schools. Some years ago the various County councils took over the control of the Church schools, while leaving them a certain latitude in the matter of religious teaching.

To these schools the children of the "working classes" are sent. This term at the present time includes the children of laborers of all sorts, artisans, policemen, tram and bus conductors, small shopkeepers, such as green-grocers, hucksters, dustmen, draymen, bar-tenders in the public houses, factory workers, street-cleaners, charwomen and "all such," also some children of very poorly-paid office workers in inferior positions, and those whose fathers are "on the dole."

The schools, having been originally intended only for such children, are built and planned accordingly. They are never located in what are called good neighborhoods or nice streets, although they are not, by any means, all in the slums. During my investigations in London I soon learned to "spot" from afar a Council elementary school building because of its ugliness and ogre-like appearance. Nothing whatever has been done to beautify them outwardly. Dark and grim they overlook the stone-paved grounds across which all the children have to make their way, no matter what the inclemencies of the weather, to the outdoor "offices" as the water closets are termed, many of which are so insanitary that it is difficult to imagine an intelligent populace allowing them to exist. During my visits to the infant schools I often helped to carry the small children to these outhouses through black fog and pouring rain, when the children would get drenched to the skin and afterwards sit in their wet clothing on their return to the school building. Even in winter the Council school children play at recess without their wraps, since only one small cloak-room is apportioned to one school, dozens of coats and hats hung one upon the other, and it would take more than the length of the playtime to sort the belongings of many hundreds of children. In all the London schools I found not a solitary hot water tap for washing wounds and hurts that are bound to occur, although many of the buildings are heated by steam and the supply for such taps would be easy and economical. In some of the schools eight hundred children used two towels, toilet paper was not supplied, common drinking cups are always used, and the only means of ventilation I found was by draughts from open windows, so that sneezing and coughing were common among both teachers and pupils. In one of the newer school buildings I discovered one bubbling fountain, but that had been fixed upside down, so that the children had to squat under it and nearly choke and wet their clothes in the effort to get a drink.

In all London I found but one elementary school with anything suitable in the way of water closets. That is a church school, now taken over by the Council, which was founded by a duke for the children of "gentlemen's gentlemen," and is still patronized almost exclusively by the little sons and daughters of upper servants in Mayfair.

Many of these schools have been made cheerful inside by the personal work and expenditure of the teachers. I found one headmistress had papered the walls of her infants' hall to make it cleaner and brighter for the little ones, remembering how little of brightness they had at home. I cannot speak too highly of the men and women teachers I met in these schools. Some of them are now amongst my best friends. Many of the noblest English men and women of the present generation are to be found in the Council schools and, if their work were known, would be regarded as some of the greatest educators in the world. The younger ones have been well trained in training colleges and the older ones have learne'd much from a close application to the study of the best things in the newer methods of education. It must be said to the credit of the London County Council that the teachers are allowed much latitude for showing their own originality and drawing out the individuality of their pupils. There is a prejudice against standardization either in books or methods.

I found in these schools many of the most beautiful children I have ever seen in any country, charming, winsome, delightful little people, whom any mother belonging to any social class might be proud to claim as her own. My very wide experience as a journalist has taken me into every grade of society, and my friends are among all sorts of people, but among the children of none of them have I found more attractive and lovable ones than in the Council schools of London. That these boys and girls are quick and clever in their studies *might* go without saying, but I do not intend to let it!

Several times a year in London, there are functions known as Junior County Scholarship Examinations. All the children in the London County Council Elementary schools who have reached the age of what is called "ten plus" and have passed a certain preliminary examination three months previously, sit for this Scholarship examination which is known as an "intelligence test," so that the authorities may learn whether they are "capable of profiting by a secondary education."

If their answers to the questions are perfect or nearly approaching perfection, they are provided with a paper which entitles them to enter, free of cost to their parents, a good secondary school wholly maintained by the London County Council or which has what is called "grant in aid" from the Council. These institutions are all fee-charging schools, but must reserve a certain percentage of places for scholarship children. Those children who pass the test excellently, though not so perfectly as the others, are given what are called "exhibitions" for Central schools, which, though they rank as elementary schools, provide a higher education than the elementary, some of them being commercial and some trade schools.

According to the theory of Caste, which governs all educational matters in England, these Central schools are not allowed to be put on a par with the regular Secondary schools, which charge a fee. Exhibition boys and girls, leaving them at the age of fifteen or sixteen, no matter how clever they are or how good an education they have there obtained, find great difficulty in getting such positions as they may desire in certain offices. This is because, in filling out their application forms, say for an insurance or a banking house, they must, after the query "Education? ——" put the words "—— Central School." Then would-be employers who have only the prevailing Caste ideas on the subject of education, more or less politely damn them and refuse even to examine them to see if they can fill the requirements.

Therefore, it will be seen how all ambitious little boys and girls of "ten plus" are very anxious indeed to win a Scholarship instead of an Exhibition.

It is because of this injurious effect upon the future chances of their children that the majority of Council teachers send their own children to fee-charging schools, the women teachers continuing to teach after marriage in order to earn the necessary money for this purpose. I know a good many who, realizing the injustice of the Scholarship system, understanding how difficult it is for normal, average children to pass the examinations; how it affects the nerves of little "plus ten" boys and girls in their classes, are unwilling to subject their own children to the test. I was told of one little girl who had sat for this "intelligence test" and after waiting for two months to hear if she had "passed," actually fainted when the headmistress entered the class room and said "Mollie, you have won a scholarship!"

There are schools which go for years without one child passing the "intelligence test," yet, to my knowledge they are full of brilliantly capable children. So great a thing is a Scholarship considered in the Elementary schools that a holiday is always given after the announcement by the educational authorities, of any child or children in that particular school having won the award. A whole school of a thousand or more pupils gets a holiday if one little boy or girl of "ten plus" is considered by the authorities capable of profiting by a secondary education!

I remember on a June day before leaving England having a boat trip along the Thames and, pulling ashore under a spreading tree for my lunch, I found the lovely spot already taken by a small picnic party consisting of a fine, intelligent looking workman who was most conspicuously wearing his best clothes, his wife and three children, one a pale little girl of ten or eleven. They seemed to be having a glorious time and I felt I could not intrude on their family party, so I turned to row further down stream, wondering, the while how it happened that this father could be absent from his work and these children from their school. A little boy of eight or nine shouted out to me "Jennie's got one, missus!" "One what?" I asked, and then the father leaned over, his face and voice together singing a pæan of joy. "Our Jennie's won a scholarship, Ma'am, and as her school 'ad a 'oliday all on account of her, I made up my mind I'd take one myself from work—making up time in the evenings, you know—and bring us all for a boating and picnic. She's a great little girl, my Jennie and she's going to a secondary school!"

Then I hinted hard for an invitation to join the party, adding my own lunch to theirs and, fortunately, having a large brick of ice-cream, which I had intended to give to some friend farther on, I added greatly to the happiness of the children. But that night in my Adelphi flat, I cried over the pathos of that party and of the little pale-faced Jennie.

The London County Council Junior Scholarship Examinations, a late one of which Jennie had passed, include questions in English and arithmetic. During my investigations there came into my possession the papers which were given the London children of "ten plus" in November, 1918. Here are the two questions in English:

"1.—Suppose that Shakespeare and Nelson met to-day in London. Write a conversation between them."

"2.—'I promise you' said the Captain of the ship 'that I will take great care of the child during the voyage.' Make up a story about the voyage."

Now, at that time, the fathers of the children who were asked these extraordinary questions were fighting at the Front to save England. Let us suppose that a boy of ten and a half decided that Nelson would say to Shakespeare "Ahoy! England expects every man this day to do his duty!" but, for the life of him, he could not think of a suitable reply that Shakespeare, who lived two centuries before Nelson, might make to this observation of the great sailor, so he left that part of his paper blank. When he came to the second question, being a logical and reasoning boy, he was puzzled over the situation. Here was a sea captain taking a little child off on a voyage and promising to take great care of him, but how *could* he take that care? The little "ten plus" boy would have been but six years old when war broke out on August 4th, 1914, and during the only years he could clearly remember, the stories he had heard of "voyages" were of a very terrible kind, interrupted by German submarines. "It's a catch!" decided the little boy, after reasoning the whole thing out, so he wrote on his paper the one word "CATCH!" Then, having failed satisfactorily to answer both questions, he could not get a scholarship, so the educational authorities told him to "stand down" and remain in the elementary school "marking time" till he was fourteen.

Let us suppose that a little girl, when an April Junior County Scholarship examination came, was ill in bed and did not recover sufficiently to return to school for three months. In November, being a very smart child, she had become, as her teachers were convinced, ready for the examination that would take place during that month. If she had recovered within *one* month after the April examination, she would have been allowed to have a special examination, but having been ill for *three* months, she may not even *try* in the November examination. But if she remained in school till she was thirteen and a half or fourteen, she might try for a supplementary scholarship or a free place in a Central school. But when the day of the great and difficult test came (far more difficult than the one she would have had at ten and a half), being at an age when most little girls are liable to "nervy" spells and head-aches and when they should have the gentlest consideration, she failed again from sheer nervousness and stage-fright. Then *all* her chances would be over.

About a year ago a "catch" question in arithmetic was given to these little "plus ten" children which was the limit in wickedness and impudence:

"A number of children were invited to a Christmas party. Enough oranges were bought for each invited guest to have two. Some children were absent, so that a quarter of those present had a third orange. What portion of the children who were invited were present?"

At the time this examination took place I was traveling in Canada, and an English teacher friend sent the paper over to me asking what I thought of it as a test concerning a child's capability of profiting by a secondary education. I asked the principal of one of the most noted Collegiate Institutes in Canada to try the problem on his students. At first he refused, saying it was a "catch" and would not be fair to his pupils. Finally, after explaining to them that it would not affect their credit marks in one way or the other, he gave it out to 126 boys in grades nine, ten and eleven, of an average age of fifteen. He allowed them ten minutes, and only ten of the 126 were able to solve the problem of the oranges!

Let it be remembered that these Canadian boys, like American boys in a similar kind of school, were, in many cases, boys from well-to-do families, surrounded by every advantage which could be given them by parents of culture and education; that they had no reason to be nervous, knowing that the test meant nothing in regard to their scholastic standing or future prospects. Remember, too, that they were four and a half years older than the little London boys and girls who lived in very humble homes, if not actually squalid ones, whose parents belonged to what are termed the "working classes," with little education themselves, men and women who dropped their aitches, and lived crowded together in small rooms. Consider that large numbers of these children had mothers who worked out and that in their spare time, instead of doing home work on their studies, they must "mind" their baby brothers and sisters, often bending their young backs to toil for which their years unfitted them, with stooping shoulders, with worry-wrinkles on their childish foreheads and under their eyes— consider all this and ponder, as I have pondered, upon what it means. It can mean nothing but that the trail of the Serpent of Caste is over the whole English educational system, and that the desire of the privileged few is not to draw in, but to keep out of the secondary schools, the children of the masses.

Let us return to the boy or girl of "ten plus" who failed to pass the 1918 examination. Let us suppose that the father of the little boy who could not manage the Shakespeare-Nelson conversation, returned from the war and "struck oil" or had an inheritance, so that he found he was able to pay the school fee charged by a secondary school. That same little boy, whom the authorities adjudged as "not capable of profiting" by a secondary education, would be taken from the elementary school and placed in the very secondary school which refused him the year before because he failed to pass! He would be given an entrance examination, very easy indeed, not one fifth as difficult as the one he failed to pass, an examination which the headmaster deemed *suited to his years*. All the other little boys there whose fathers paid fees would have had similar examinations. Thus would the London County Council temper the examination wind, not to the shorn, but to the woolly lamb. The children who, last year, could not do lightning calculations in the matter of the oranges fractionally distributed at that interesting Christmas party, may this year be received as fee-paying pupils at the Council's secondary schools, with no hint to the effect that they are incapable of profiting by the education they may there receive. Truly the motto of the English educational authorities is "To whom little is given, of them much shall be required!"

It will be seen that the grading in the schools is always according to age and that no provision is made for the higher State education of children who develop late, or the ordinary, average child. According to the latest statistic which I have on hand, sixty thousand children leave the London County Council schools every year. The authorities have announced that ten per cent of these children are of "exceptional ability," as shown by the fact that they have won scholarships and exhibitions. It would seem that this percentage is expected to be stationary, and arrangements are made to "place" this ten per cent in the secondary and central schools. One can only surmise what would happen if fifteen or twenty per cent proved themselves to have this "exceptional ability" demanded for passing the "intelligence tests." Would not something have to be done to reduce the legitimate number of scholarship children to the number of places ready to receive them? Imagine a humane and kindly disposed man, engaged in marking the papers of hundreds of these "ten plus" children, discovering that nearly all of them really showed this "exceptional ability," yet knowing there were not sufficient places for them in the secondary schools, because there were so many less bright children in those schools who ought really to be in the elementary schools, but whose parents were able to pay the fees. I can see nothing for the humane and kindly examiner but to go over the papers a second time and re-mark them according to a still higher standard, the while sadly repeating to himself that grand old Calvinistic verse of pre-destination:

> "We hope too many won't be saved—
> A number *must* be damned;
> We'd better send some more below,
> We can't have Heaven crammed."

The authorities tell us that ten per cent of the children leaving the London elementary schools each year are "dull and backward." These, with the ten per cent that are said to have "exceptional ability," make twenty per cent of the sixty thousand. There would, then, be left eighty per cent of normal, ordinary bright and intelligent children, the sort of children one finds in every family in every class of society in every country, children of "working class," "middle class" and "upper class," children just like those of the educational author-

ities themselves who would not dream of making use of the
State elementary schools for their own families. This eighty
per cent is not recognized by the State as being entitled to a
higher education.

The last statistics I have of the number of all children in
England and Wales, of school age, show that there were six
and a half million, of which five million, eight hundred and
twenty thousand were on the registers of the various elementary Council schools, leaving about six hundred thousand attending fee-charging schools of good, bad and indifferent types,
and studying at home under governesses and tutors. If we take
the percentage given of the London Council children, who are
considered entitled to a higher education, and compute the
number of average children left in England and Wales, the
result is an appalling thing to contemplate, not only in the matter of the happiness and well-being of the children, but the
progress and future *prestige* of Great Britain. How can she
possibly hope to compete in any way with countries which have
a democratic system of education?

It is now twenty-four years since the Mosely Commission
visited the United States to study and report upon the American schools, colleges and universities. I have been reading over
the reports of the various members of this Commission, and
I cannot help being struck with the small amount of influence
their really fine project seems to have had upon those who
have directed English educational matters since 1903, when
their reasonable and reasoning reports were published in book
form. Wrote Mr. Mosely himself:

"Our visit satisfied us that in years to come, in competing with
American commerce, we shall be called upon to face trained men,
with both enterprise and knowledge. We desire to impress upon
the British public the absolute need of immediate preparation on
our part to meet such competition. . . . The absence of class
prejudice in America serves most materially to facilitate the work
of the schools."

Here are quotations from the reports of other members of
the Commission:

"In many cities one half the public expenditure is devoted to education."

"From the first, it was obvious that we were dealing with an entirely different kind of public opinion from that which prevails in England."

"We found that the free public high schools, attended by rich and poor alike, were the strength and glory of the West."

"We noted that the school equipment was lavish and that an immense amount of money was cheerfully spent on education."

"The aim of American education is to make every boy fit for some definite calling in life."

"The Americans have an intense belief in the education of the masses. They feel that if the people are to be raised, it must be done through the medium of education. Not only do they see in it a 'moral policeman,' but they argue also that in the long run it is more economical to educate the people than to support in the prisons and workhouses the unfortunates who, through an inferior education, or none at all, have been left unfitted to earn their livelihood."

And here is something that should be particularly interesting and informative to those who assert that the American boys and girls of recent years have been taught in their schools to hate the British, written in one of these reports nearly a quarter of a century ago:

"I was glad to find that the old history text books, inculcating hatred of England, are being given up, and others substituted which contain nothing to which any sensible Britisher can possibly object."

The members of the Commission, after lunching with President Roosevelt at the White House, visited some of the Washington schools. In an ordinary elementary school, sitting behind a boy whose father worked in a machine shop, they found the son of the President of the United States. A few months ago in that same school, I came across the young son of Vice President Dawes. When I was in Washington at that time I inquired concerning the sons and daughters of prominent and wealthy men who attended the free public schools there, and was given a list of several hundred, taken at random, by Superintendent Frank W. Ballou and Secretary Harry O. Hine. On it I found the names of children of government officials of wealth and standing, great scientists, congressmen, lawyers, doctors, university professors, eminent clergymen, and several members of the diplomatic corps from different countries. That I found none from Great Britain may have been but an accident. I sent some names from this illuminating list to an English friend who is greatly interested in educational matters and received from him a letter in which he said "It is amazing and it is magnificent, most certainly it is democratic, but I am convinced that it would not work in England." I wrote back, "How do you know? Why don't you try?" and I lately had his reply to that: "Because we are an old country, hidebound, tradition-bound, caste-ridden, if you will. God help us!" whereupon I have just returned my answer: "Never think it! *He* won't help you, and as for the Christ whom you Anglicans profess to worship, he was not hide-bound, nor tradition-bound nor caste-ridden. *He was a democrat!*"

While I was making my investigations in London, the wife of a Church of England clergyman said to me, "My dear, I beg you stop! Think! If you give all the children of the working classes a higher education than that which they can get at the elementary schools, you will make them discontented in their natural sphere. We look to those schools to give us our servants and our working men!"

A year ago I watched a number of Council school children learning to swim in the Serpentine at Hyde Park. A friend who would be called a "middle class professional man," a lawyer, sat near me in a tuppenny chair.

"Mean to say," he exclaimed, "that the Council is using the money we pay in rates to teach children to swim?"

"Are not *your* children learning to swim?" I asked.

"I pay for it at a preparatory school," he retorted, "and then, by Jove, I have to pay rates for these children as well! They tell me the teachers even take them to Kew Gardens and tell them to pull flowers to pieces!"

"A little Nature-study!" I laughed. "Your small Nancy does it, too."

"I pay for Nan to learn Botany," he said, "but why should I pay for bricklayers' and other laborers' children to learn it, when they should be learning a bit of cookery that'll make them decent servants or workmen's wives?"

"The Americans pay for the whole lot by one check," I said.

"How do you mean?"

"By sending their children to the same schools and paying taxes."

He touched his forehead significantly. "As I thought! They told me you'd gone 'Bolshie' since the war!" he laughed.

"No, I've only 'gone American'!" I answered.

Theodore Roosevelt, in addressing the Mosely Commission said, "Education is the only security in a democratic state." The English "upper" and "middle" classes would seem to believe that *ignorance* is the only security against real democracy. It is against this spirit that the men and women engaged in teaching in the English State schools have to contend. Is it any wonder that a few of these teachers have taken on what the enemies of free education call an "inferiority complex," while some have gone to the other extreme by becoming bitterly revolutionary in their attitude? The wonder, which should excite the admiration of the world, is that the majority have preserved their equanimity while working steadily for the betterment of their schools, in faith and hope and, sometimes I think, almost too much charity toward those who would like to bring their labor of love to nought.

At the present time, as I write, an appeal is being broadcasted over Great Britain for funds to provide playing fields for over four million school children. It is pathetically stated that these boys and girls have no means of benefitting by field sports, and someone has suggested that the "great public schools," like Harrow, Eton, Rugby, Winchester, might "give generously," remembering how much they have to be thankful for in the matter of their own fine playing fields; but not even a bishop in the land has lifted his voice to demand the return to the poor boys the full value of not only those playing-fields but the "Public" school buildings and all their funds. These great schools are stolen property. Long ago they were founded for "poor and needy boys" and were gradually filched from those for whom they were intended by chicanery and sharp practice. Their ever-growing funds and incomes were long ago diverted to the education of England's "ruling classes," under the Church of England clergy as headmasters and tutors. Only a few remember this now, so long have they been used by the sons of the old aristocracy, the new plutocracy, the sons of kings and an occasional member of our American "climbing" class. It was at Eton, by the way, that the Duke of Wellington, as young Arthur Wellesley, left behind him the reputation of being a "dull boy, but good at fighting." It was a fortunate thing for England, and, perhaps for the world, that he did not attend a school where, because of his dullness, he would have been pronounced "incapable of profiting" by anything but the most meager education. He is said to have said that the Battle of Waterloo was won on the *playing-fields* of Eton, and was never communicative about the Latin he so badly construed in upper or lower school. He evidently needed those stolen playing-fields to practice for his future profession!

I visited the beautiful Harrow school not so very long ago, and in the library I was privileged to read the original will of that good man, John Lyon, who founded the school for poor boys. I wonder do the wealthy successors of those poor boys ever blush, and are they ever ashamed, they or their masters or their fathers who send them there, when they read this inscription on John Lyon's grave-stone.

"Here lyeth the bodye of John Lyon, late of Preston, yeoman, deceased the 11th day of October, in the yeare of our Lord 1592, who hath founded a free grammar schoole in the parish, to have continuance forever, and for maintenance thereof, and for releyffe of the poore, and of some poore scholars in the universytes; repairing of highwayes, and other good and charitable uses, hath made conveyance of lands of good value to a corporation granted for that purpose.

Prayse be to the Author of all Goodnesse who maykes us myndful to follow his good example."

CHAPTER XXIV

AMERICAN PROHIBITION AND THE BRITISH DRINK SCANDAL

IT is impossible for an American to return home after a long or short sojourn abroad without giving a considerable amount of thought to the subject of the saloon that is not here. For myself, I find my mind often engaged in making comparisons between my own country and England in this respect, and I must admit, without prejudice, that my comparisons are always unfavorable to England.

I say "without prejudice," for I think I am quite free from fanaticism or narrow-mindedness in this matter. It is impossible for me to feel any particular shock at seeing a glass of wine on an English dinner table or always to find sin in the sight of a French peasant drinking from a tumbler a pinkish liquid which I know to be three-fourths water and one-fourth his native burgundy. I have felt no thrill of horror at the report of the young American airman who, after having flown the Atlantic on a chicken-wing, asked for a glass of beer in Berlin. I am not sure that, had I been in my own country at the time of the adoption of the Eighteenth Amendment, I should have approved of all the tactics used by the Anti-Saloon League to incorporate it into the Constitution. I might have felt convinced that Local Option by separate States was the more democratic for our particular form of government, although I should have voted for *any* method that would abolish the *saloon* from the whole country. I do not profess to have studied the subject as I should have done had I been in a position to vote upon it at the time. What I have to say is not about methods, but results, and the results I have seen convince me that though in this matter the American nation has

a mote in its eye, Great Britain has a beam in hers. There may
be those who will think it is not my job to expose that beam in
all its bigness and unsightliness. I believe that it is, especially
as I have given a great deal of my time to a study of that beam,
the while Great Britain has constantly been harping upon our
mote. One good turn deserves another and, sometimes, one
bad turn deserves a reprisal!

I have several times returned to the United States by way
of Canada, and the last time I crossed the Border, I had previously been in several Provinces which had recently "gone
wet." But, in spite of this, of course, I saw no saloons in
Canada, and there was no means by which, in passing through
a street in any Canadian city, I could identify a government
liquor store. I saw no advertisements of wine, beer, whiskey or
brandy. It was evident to me that though Canada's plan for
dealing with the drink problem had partly changed, Canadian
boys and girls would certainly grow up without ever having
seen a saloon and knowing nothing of its evil influence.

I visited a good many Canadian friends and enjoyed delicious meals in private homes, hotels and restaurants, but
it so happened that I never saw, while there, any wine, beer
or spirits on the tables. When I was about to cross the Border
from then dry Ontario, I mentioned to a friend that I had a
small flask of brandy, which I always carried, when traveling, in case of accident or sudden illness, and asked if I were
likely to have any trouble about it when I landed at Detroit.
As he assured me that if I took it into Michigan I should be
fined two hundred dollars and, though this seemed ridiculous, if
true, I did not want to be delayed or bothered, so I gave it
to him. I hope he was not too disappointed to find that the flask
had not more than two tablespoonfuls in it.

In the Middle West and on my journey to New York, I saw
and heard nothing of intoxicants or of law-breaking, since I
was not looking for them. What I did see was how pleasant
and wholesome and prosperous were the American cities, what
queues stood outside the savings-banks on Saturday afternoons,
and how safe seemed the American boys and girls as compared with the English boys and girls. I devote much of my

time to studying children and writing about them, so I particularly noted this.

In New York I met an English acquaintance, and the first thing he said to me was,

"This is a great country of yours, with its prohibition laws that don't prohibit. I can get plenty to drink here!"

"Then what are you complaining of?" I asked. "You were looking for a drink, weren't you?"

"Naturally!" he laughed.

"And, naturally, you'd find what you were looking for."

"Which proves what?" he asked quizzically.

"That as you are not a drunkard and only looked out of curiosity and had a lot of trouble and expense gratifying it, you would soon stop bothering about it. In England you would have got your drink easily and cheaply on every corner. I've traveled a couple of thousand miles since I left Canada and there has been nothing to make me think about this subject one way or another. With hundreds of thousands of other people it would be the same way, but in England it cannot be got out of the thoughts because it's always in sight and within reach. Now, honestly, which do you consider is the better place for workmen who want to get on, London or New York?"

Being honest, he replied, "Well, there you have me!"

Just at this time, in New York and New Jersey, I met three or four women who tried to explain to me that until the prohibition law came, they had been teetotalers, but that now they were engaged in "home-brewing" just to spite the Anti-Saloon League and Volstead. "What's that verse about 'Britons never, never shall be slaves?'" asked one. "Well, Americans never, never will be slaves, either, so have a drink!"

She was down in her cellar at the time, stirring and stewing, for all the world like a witch at a cauldron, and offered me something in a cup, which I tasted. It was a nasty mess, and I was not willing to drink it to spite any number of Leagues or Volsteads. It all reminded me of my boarding-school days when, merely because a thing was against the rules, we felt an inclination to do it. I went away and left her to her silly work. Probably the cellar was the best place for her. If she weren't brewing beer she would be brewing some other kind of trouble.

I know men who carry hip flasks. Some do it in the same spirit that this woman brews what she calls "beer," and others do it because of a life-long habit which it is difficult for them to break. I have met a gentlemanly boot-legger. I have been to a dinner party where all the conversation was about drink, cellars full or empty and discussion concerning whether in certain high society sets, the men or the women could the better "hold their liquor." I found such an experience illuminating, but as I am accustomed to the society and conversation of intelligent and interesting people, I should not wish to spend another evening like that, because it bored me.

On the whole, I have found the situation much better than I had expected to find it from the descriptions of "typical American life" as given in the British press. I am convinced that in some way the genius of the American people will solve this great problem and solve it rightly, but it will take time. We should be supermen and superwomen, if it did not. And we must solve it without the assistance of other nations, who, unhappily, seem inclined to hinder rather than to help. I cannot fancy that any other country than our own would so patiently put up with the meddling of French wine merchants and their emissaries who come over to tout for customers, and the underhand as well as the open work of what is so egotistically known as *the* Trade in England. Let us try to imagine the situation reversed, a new law made in England concerning which even a large number of British subjects were complaining and which many of them were breaking, some because they felt it unjust and others "for spite" against some politician or reform League. And then let us imagine a set of Americans, interested only in filling their own pockets by selling American manufactured goods, attempting to do in England what the Trade with its highly-paid propaganda work, is now trying to do in the United States. John Bull would very soon remember that his house was his castle and his Island his own little tight one, and cause the American meddlers to remember it as well.

But the propaganda work which the Trade of Great Brittain does in the United States is, of course, a comparatively small matter to that which it must do in the British Isles to keep up sales. I know of nothing to which it can so well be likened as a giant Octopus stretching out its tentacles in every direction for new "finds" in the way of propaganda schemes that will help in its self-preservation. One of its tentacles is always stretched out press-wise, and it was because of an attempt to draw in my work as a journalist for propaganda purposes that I learned a good deal about the Octopus and its tentacles.

Some time after Prohibition became the law in the whole United States, I was arranging for a trip to Canada and my own country, and, following my usual custom, I called on a number of English editors to inquire what work I could do for them while on the other side. Said the first one I approached,

"Send me three good articles on the effects of Prohibition in your country."

I jotted down this commission and then asked if he would like something about Dry Canada also.

"No, you needn't bring in Canada," said he. "Mind you," he added, as I was leaving his office, "show the thing up in all its weaknesses, and use your sense of humor."

"Show it up?" I repeated, somewhat puzzled.

"Of course! Keep your eyes open, and your nostrils as well. You're sure to see and smell a lot of spirits over there, and what we want are articles showing how this new law makes things worse, how it creates law-breakers, and drives decent men and women to swallowing hair tonics and scents, and leads to drug-taking."

I explained, with some indignation, that I thought it was well known that I never started my journalistic investigations in that way, that I began them with an open mind, and that I had a reputation for thoroughness and fairness as a writer for the press. He took my decision to decline his commission in a friendly enough way and, indeed, even laughed at my anger and asked for some other articles that had nothing to do with Prohibition. I determined to see if I could get other commissions on this subject that would not hamper my pen or cramp my soul. I consulted other editors in person and by letter, suggesting articles on how Prohibition was working in the United States, meanwhile studying the British papers. I found that, with only a few exceptions, they were busily engaged in showing how Prohibition *failed* to work, and I could see that the writers showed a lack of the real spirit of investigation upon which I had built up my own reputation. I offered an article to one editor telling of the effects of Prohibition in an Eastern factory town, and for answer he called his office boy to bring him a file of the periodical.

"Study the advertisements in this paper, and then tell me if you think I'd be allowed to publish such an article as you suggest, even if I wanted to?" he said.

I studied the advertisements carefully. One quarter of them, at least, seemed to be of firms that dealt in beer, whiskies, brandies and wines in some form or another; restaurants and hotels.

"I see!" I said, looking him squarely in the face. "Whereas once I was blind, now I see!"

Later a friend called on me, and I happened to mention that I was hoping to go over to the United States, but was not sure I could afford the trip, what with the higher steamship fares and the hotel bills.

He assured me that there would be no difficulty in my making a good sum over and above all expenses if I would write articles on the failure of Prohibition in the United States, and suggested that I should be able to give ideas for "smart cartoons" on the subject also. He took out his cardcase and pencil preparatory to writing a note of introduction for me, when I burst out laughing and said,

"You British are very funny!"

"Funny?" he repeated.

"Yes," I said. "You think our American politics are corrupt, and it struck me just now how sweet and pure they are!"

I did not return to America just at that time, and having a curious and investigating turn of mind, I spent the next few months in learning things about the 'bossism" of the Trade in

British politics which convinced me that Americans were mere kindergartners in the art of bribery, graft and corruption. As for the cleverness and subtlety with which the Trade works its schemes and uses its various tentacles, I know of nothing to compare with it except the German propaganda business which went on in the United States prior to our entry into the War.

I have said that one editor whom I consulted barred articles describing "dry Canada." I have since learned that there was nothing short of a conspiracy in the ranks of the Trade to conceal from the British working people the fact that this Dominion was almost entirely dry, and the good results of Local Option in New Zealand and Australia were also little noted in the British press. The Trade was determined to keep the inhabitants of the British Isles ignorant of the fact that the self-governing Dominions were more sure-sighted and fore-sighted *and* more prosperous than the Motherland. Now, any one who understands the close connection between the advertising and the literary departments of a great newspaper, will understand at once the influence that the Trade can exert in this direction. But, of course the Trade does not stop there in its literary work. It "runs" various societies in the supposed interests of temperance, freedom, charity, with the names of some of the most noted and aristocratic people in England as patrons. Such societies publish special little papers and leaflets concerning their work, some of which I have discovered to have been written by my own literary friends.

It is the Trade which is loudest in the cry against "robbing the poor working man of his beer." To my knowledge a goodly number of British workmen would most willingly be robbed of beer, if certain comforts, and even luxuries, which our American workers enjoy were offered in its place. The anxiety of the Trade in this respect is frequently shared by members of the aristocracy and even by employers of labor. I have heard some great factory owners say they *preferred* moderate drinkers to total abstainers as workers, because the first thing a man did when he became an abstainer was also to become dissatisfied! As it is, some employers say there is enough discontent among the ex-soldiers who, at the front and on leave became acquainted with too many prosperous Dominion workmen who put wrong notions in the heads of the British boys on the subject of wages and class distinctions, and otherwise contaminated them. Before the war the British workmen and workingwomen were so poorly paid, that they had very few pleasures except beer drinking. It is true that some of them, if bidden in those days to choose between food and beer, chose beer—and no wonder, as for an hour or so, it helped them to forget their sordid, colorless lives. Since the war, wages have risen and the British workingman is demanding more rights for himself and fewer privileges for the classes whom he has been taught are above him. This newer attitude threatens the prosperity of the Trade, which, every year, spends an increasing amount of money on propaganda, especially directed to false descriptions of the American workingman under Prohibition. Any journalist or author with a slight acquaintance with the United States and without a troublesome conscience can, if he or she has a name that is at all known, add greatly to an ordinary income by "coming to terms" with the Trade. A great many, too, are adding to their incomes without knowing that the Trade is really employing them, since the means of securing propaganda writing may be hidden in many twistings and turnings.

Many a clergyman in the Church of England would have a hard time in retaining his "living" or securing a new one if he came out openly in his pulpit and attacked the Trade or preached in favor of total abstinence, for members of the Trade are pillars of the church, while the connections of the Trade with the aristocracy and the House of Lords are very close indeed and the breweries and distilleries provide some of the most prominent party leaders. It can therefore be understood how the Trade actually controls British politics in such a way as could never possibly be done by any boss or party machine in the United States.

The Trade, of course, has its own avowed newspaper organs, one of which is the Morning Advertiser of London. From this paper, under date of June 16th, 1927, I quote the following, which will be somewhat amazing reading to Americans, even those who are not church people:

GOOD SAMARITAN PARABLE WELL ILLUSTRATED

UNMERCIFUL "HALF-CHRISTIANS" AND PROHIBITION

By invitation of the vicar (the Rev. P. Youlden Johnson), a special service at the Church of St. Mary-at-the-Elms, Ipswich, on the afternoon of Trinity Sunday, was attended by officers and members of the Ipswich and Suffolk License-holders' Association and of the Women's Auxiliary. There was a large and representative congregation. The service was a shortened form of Festal Evensong, and the lesson—the Parable of the Good Samaritan—was read by Mr. H. C. Westgate (district agent of the National Trade Defence Association).

Before commencing his sermon on that parable the vicar thanked the congregation for attending, saying that he regarded it as a great privilege to have them there. They came last year, and he was pleased to have them again. Turning to the parable, he said what a great thing it was to have mercy on everybody. Some of the most unmerciful people were those who were half-Christian—neither one thing nor the other—and he hoped they would never judge the Christian Church by the attitude of some who professed to call themselves Christians, who, for instance, would force Prohibition upon them.

The Church Catholic, said the vicar, was absolutely solid against Prohibition. They would never make men good by taking things out of their way. They would never receive any reward for temptations they had never undergone. They only received credit for those things in which they had been sorely tempted. There was no merit in not being tempted. In every parish there were two important houses. One was the house of God and the other was the people's house. He himself was licensed to take charge of the house of God, and those of them who were landlords were also licensed, and before either they or himself were allowed to be licensed to take charge of those houses in the parish their characters had to be investigated.

Influence of Licensees.

If they were not good citizens they would not be allowed to have charge of one of those houses. Their influence was very great. He wanted to bring home to them the great privilege they held, and the great responsibility that rested upon them to use their influence for the good of their neighbors. That parish, in which he labored, had its full share of suffering humanity, and, pointing the moral of the parable, he commended to them the practical compassion shown by a Samaritan, and he trusted that as in the case of the host of the inn under whose charge the robbed and wounded wayfarer was placed, they would find room for those who came to their inns and would "take care of them."

Before I describe the licensing system of England and Wales which the clergyman in the foregoing quotation would seem to represent as coming directly from the Almighty, I must state that just as Scotland has her own educational system of more democratic tendencies, so she has her own licensing laws which are governed by Local Option. Though it is commonly understood that the typical Scot likes his whiskey, he also likes his freedom. Scotland has, under the Thistle, the motto *Nemo me impune lacessit?* ("Wha daur meddle wi' me?") and makes her own local laws accordingly and the Scots are doing certain things in their own cautious way to minimize the evils of drink. It is a fact that to-day a large part of Scottish agricultural labor is devoted to raising such grains as are used in brewing and distilling, when both the labor and the land might be so much more advantageously used for wheat-growing, but there are many who believe that before many years the gradual working of Local Option will make Scotland completely dry. The Scots have a passion for efficiency which is not always so noticeable in England and Wales, and there seems to be little doubt that a dry Scotland would take the position of dominant partner in the United Kingdom.

The organs of the Trade, and those other newspapers which are noted for the great income they draw from liquor advertisements, seem intent upon showing that Local Option in Scotland is a failure, just as Prohibition in the United States, and Government Control in Canada are failures. The fact that the Trade supports the present antiquated licensing system of England and Wales proves, of course, that it is the most successful method of selling liquor and so lining the pockets of the Trade. This licensing system, absolutely opposed to all modern ideas of democracy, dates back to an act of Parliament in the year 1552. It will be seen that the Constitution of the United States, which some British critics have asserted to be too old and out-of-date for the working of modern democracy is but an infant prodigy in comparison.

According to this method of licensing, England and Wales are divided up into what are called "licensing districts" to the number of one thousand, and then certain men of what are termed "position" or "standing," are appointed justices of the peace for the purpose of issuing licenses for the sale of intoxicants. They take the name of "licensing justices" and the one who appoints them is the British Lord Chancellor, who is a member of the cabinet and a member of the party in power. The Lord Chancellor owes his position to his politics, and he goes in and out with his own party government. It is easy to see that a Lord Chancellor is likely to act on party lines in his appointment of men to act as "licensing justices." These men have almost unlimited power in the granting of licenses and it is impossible not to believe that they may have warm feelings toward the Trade and be open at times, to influences not altogether devoted to the interests of the districts and the people over which they have so much power. Nothing can be more undemocratic than this method of deciding how many public houses shall be licensed in any one neighborhood. The residents have no vote or power in the matter.

Against this system the temperance workers of the country are making a brave fight. In favor of it the Trade stands consolidated, declaring that to give the people of England and Wales the power of Local Option by act of Parliament (for in that way only can it come) will be the insertion of the thin edge of the Prohibition wedge and the final destruction of the Trade. Every artifice and every damnable means imaginable is now being used by the Trade to hold its own, and fanaticism in its advertisements and in its "literary" propaganda is rampant. Here is a choice bit:

"What good are teetotalers? What good did a teetotaler ever do the nation? In the first place he does not pay his fair share of taxation. Before the war he was a little Navyite; during the war he was a conscientious objector. . . . He consumed more than his fair share of food during the war. Seldom can he be persuaded to loosen his purse strings. Charity is not one of his virtues."

Such hysterical outbursts as this are bad for the Trade, even among many Britons who do not believe in Prohibition, but they are exceedingly good for, and should be productive of hopefulness among the very brave band of British temperance reformers. Against such odds as American temperance workers never knew, these British men and women are remaining level-headed, and their freedom from fanaticism is marvelous. Having frequently noticed this in my intercourse with British temperance workers, I have felt some surprise on reading a speech by the Bishop of Durham, when what is known as the Oxford Bill, recently came up for discussion in the House of Lords. This is a proposed measure for a very reasonable form of Local Option, first introduced by the late Bishop of Oxford, and now re-introduced by the Bishop of Liverpool. Speaking against this, and in favor of the present corrupt and antiquated licensing system, the Bishop of Durham said:

While making allowance for the fretful impatience of reforming zeal, in the interval that has elapsed . . . we have further evidence of the failure of Prohibition in America, and this bill undoubtedly enshrines Prohibition. . . . The liquor trade is a legitimate, honorable and, within due limits, a beneficent industry. There will be an end of its organized defence when there is an end of organized and unscrupulous attacks."

To this amazing defence of Britain's greatest social and political scandal, it is encouraging to know that the Bishop of London so lately returned from the United States to England, immediately retorted:

"The position of industry in America has *improved* since Prohibition was introduced. I am surprised that this country continues to try to compete with a dry country."

I have mentioned the great waste of land and labor in Great Britain because of the voracious appetite of the Trade. During the war, after my visit to Canada, when the measures for food restriction threatened to become more stringent, I attempted to call attention to this matter in the British press, but though I found many columns at my disposal when I had suggestions for other economies that would help to win the war, I was assured that "over-crowded" space prevented discussion of this subject.

In Canada I heard complaints to the effect that Canadians were rationing themselves in the matter of bacon in order that they might ship quantities to England where it was said there was not sufficient food for hogs. "That" said my Canadian friends, "is because they turn good grain into drink for human swine, when they might better be feeding decent pigs with it."

I remember particularly a Canadian woman who told me that one of her sons had been killed and the other returned to Canada wounded and a drunkard. I will admit that she was nearly distraught when she talked with me, but, under similar circumstances, what mother would not have been?

"We raise corn and other grains for them to turn into meal, and they turn it into drink. We send our sons over to fight, and they ruin them with the drink they have made from our grain. My boy never was in a saloon, never tasted a drop of drink till he went to England. I tell you I hate England and I wish we were free of her!"

In order to get a proper conception of the amount of good material that goes into malting and distilling, it is well to know the total paid in money alone. Great Britain's drink bill is six million pounds a week, or three hundred and twelve million pounds a year, which, in American money is one thousand, five hundred and sixty million dollars! The entire amount of money spent there for education in all its forms is less than half this sum!

No American or Canadian of my acquaintance, visiting England, has failed to comment upon what to me is the saddest sight in all the land, the little children lined up in front of every public house, waiting for their parents. They are of all ages, ranging from babies of less than a month old, left in their perambulators in charge of older brothers and sisters or in charge of any other chance child of older years. Some of the most lovely children I have ever seen I have found pressed hard against glass swinging doors of public houses, sometimes knocked down as people come out. I have found children fast asleep leaning against the outside walls, standing straightly on their little legs but with heads bobbing back and forth, sometimes even with their mouths open and snoring. They are not all badly dressed or dirty by any means, especially on Sundays when the hours for public house openings on the North side of the Thames in London are from 12–30 to 2–30 in the afternoon and from 7 to 10 in the evening. On week days the hours are from 11–30 to 3 in the day and from 5–30 to 11 at night. Many a night I have stood on the curbs in front of public houses with the children, partly to see that they did not fall in their sleep and injure themselves, and partly to learn what I could about the children of school age when I was making my school investigations. It was easy to inquire what schools the various children attended and then to visit the schools and get the teachers' description of how such children fared at school the next day after their late night watches outside the public houses. Those whom I found waiting for their parents at nine, ten and eleven o'clock were described to me as being "always sleepy" in school. I made the acquaintance of one little boy who, his teacher assured me, failed to win a scholarship on this account. She pointed him out to me. At three in the afternoon the child's head was on his desk and his heavy breathing showed that he was sleeping soundly. His mother was a respectable woman who never drank, but his father, taking advantage of the cordial invitation of the Trade to "make the public house his club," spent his evenings in first one public house, then another, the boy following him and waiting outside till the closing hour of eleven. This child was described to me as being exceptionally quick at learning if only he could keep awake in school hours.

Throughout Great Britain the children suffer in this way, drink and education being diametrically opposed to one another. The Trade has never been known to advocate free higher education, and it cannot be doubted that it is the influence of the

Trade in politics that keeps the subject of alcohol as a poison from being made an obligatory study in the Council schools. Many members of the newer British aristocracy with a large representation in the House of Lords and the House of Commons derive their income from the manufacture and sale of beer and spirits, have, indeed, secured titles because of their "large gifts to charity" and to party funds. It is to the disadvantage of both the Trade and the aristocracy, whether combined or separate, that the children of the "working classes" should be taught to think and ask questions on various subjects, and particularly about the effect of alcohol on the human system. That the matter of the compulsory teaching of its evils in the State schools, the ill-effects upon the health and moral well-being of children standing outside public houses has not been taken up by the National Society for the Prevention of Cruelty to Children, is a surprising thing to many persons working for child-welfare. Children of the tenderest years (even months!) are being "joined up" by their parents to a lately formed beer drinking society for the promotion of "charity" to children and the so-called "anthem" of this society is being sung by thousands of school children who know only that it is a song calling people together to drink beer. Some of the schools are so surrounded by public houses that, as one humorist put it, "A school forms a dry island." The figures of John Bull and Britannia are used as advertisements for beer and spirits. One beer advertisement is in the form of a large Union Jack with the words "The Strength of Britain" (Beer) engraved on it.

A special point is made by breweries of having their drays drawn by beautiful and gigantic horses, magnificently harnessed to attract attention in the street. Children particularly clap their hands when they see them, and when they stop at the public houses to unload their casks, while the waiting babies look on, there are lusty crows and cries of "Beauty gee-gee!" from the occupants of the prams.

There was a day when one of the noblest and most gifted of Englishmen paused and looked at a dray so equipped and drawn, then shook his head sorrowfully and walked on. He was John Galsworthy, who thus describes one of the sad and significant sights in the streets of London to-day. I quote from his novel, "Fraternity":

"Down the center of the street Thyme saw a brewer's dray creeping its way due South under the sun. Three horses drew it, with braided tails and beribboned manes, the brass glittering on their harness. High up, like a god, sat the drayman, his little slits of eyes above huge red cheeks, fixed immovably on his horses' crests. Behind him, with slow unceasing crunch, the dray rolled, piled up with hogsheads whereon the drayman's mate lay sleeping.

"Like the slumbrous image of some mighty unrelenting power, it passed, proud that its monstrous bulk contained all the joy and blessing those shadows on the pavement had ever known."

CHAPTER XXV

THE BRITISH POT AND THE AMERICAN KETTLE

G REAT BRITAIN needs a native-born Sinclair Lewis, to take her people, their customs, habits of thought and traditions, strip them naked, not only to the skin, but to the very marrow of their bones, and discover her to herself, even though that involves the embarrassing necessity of discovering her also to the world.

This is what our own Sinclair Lewis has done for the American nation, most wholesomely and healthfully, though certainly not pleasantly. He is our nasty medicine, against which our stomachs may rebel in the taking, but good for the things that ail us. In the language of that greatest anachronism which has somehow survived past the first quarter of the Twentieth Century, the Church of England marriage service, he has, like Matrimony, been ordained as a "remedy against sin."

Lewis is a great favorite in England. I think that there is more real tender affection for him, personally, there than here. Very greatly do our British friends enjoy seeing him smite us. Other nations also are attracted by the spectacle, and are having many a good laugh, via Lewis, at our expense. With those other nations, however, I have nothing to do at the present. The question which, for a time, bothered me when I saw how Britain was "taking to" Lewis, was this:

"Now, why do these British people like Sinclair Lewis, and, indeed, how can they understand him, seeing that so very few of them have ever been in the United States or know anything really about Americans and their lives, except such as they have met touring England's Cathedral towns, and the Lake District, and sight-seeing in London? Why, why? How, how?"

And then I jumped to a conclusion, a solution of my own problem, which I believe is right. Since the War, no nation loves us, and we are nobody's darling. It seems to be an unfortunate fact that those who do not love one are inclined to glory in one's weaknesses, and laugh at one's foibles. Sinclair Lewis, in so far as the majority of British readers were concerned, was post war. He made us look as ugly as even our worst enemies could desire, and though I do not think that the British are our worst enemies, or even our enemies at all, they are in a state of mind better fitted to consider our weaknesses than our goodnesses. I know an Englishman who has read "Main Street" five times and "Elmer Gantry" three times, and when I asked why, he told me he was studying them as biological and psychical current histories of the United States; that they had the merit of being *both* true and interesting, which was more than you could say for most histories.

As he had never been in the United States, I asked him how he could know that, and he placed his hand dramatically upon his chest and said "Something here tells me so!"

I have before me a letter from an Englishwoman friend. "You must have had a most interesting time," she writes, "in all those 'Main Streets' of the Middle West, and tell me, dear, how can you stand those funny Fundamentalists?"

Yes, I did have an interesting time among the many "Main Streets," and as I settled down to live in some of them for a few days or a few weeks at a time, I thought particularly of two things, the one being that, before I ever went to England, I had lived and had a part of my education in a "Main Street," though, alas! I had gone away and forgotten the good and remembered the evil of the Street. The other thing I remembered was that, since those days, I had spent a considerable length of time, off and on, living in the High Streets of various Provincial English towns, as well as in certain Cathedral cities, so pleasant to visit *entour,* so deadly and damning to the progress of the souls of those who spend their lives within their thick high walls. I found a little more in the way of polished manner in High Street, but not more culture of the mind or the heart or the soul than I found in Main Street. There was better conversation in Main Street, a saner outlook, greater chances of advancement along Life's broadway than in High Street. I met Babbitts in the Middle West towns, but I had also met their counterparts in Birmingham, Manchester, Leeds, Liverpool, when I had been in those towns on my journalistic missions. Given the differences which each country was bound to accentuate, and taking into account the comparative sizes of the two countries, I found the Babbitts very much a matter of fifty-fifty.

And now, in regard to the "funny Fundamentalists," which my English friend doubts my ability to "stand." I made the acquaintance of a good many of them, and my experience reminded me of my trip over the same region during the war, when I visited the old farm home of my youth. I think the people whom I found then gathered in the old church, listening to a discourse on the creation of the world, were, perhaps, not then officially known as "Fundamentalists." At any rate, the term was unknown to me, as I sat there listening to things I had forgotten had ever been taught to me as a child or that anybody believed in the enlightened era of the Twentieth Century. I am no nearer to having anything in common with the Fundamentalists than I was on that Sunday when I rushed out to my young University driver and, to my relieved amazement, found him reading Haeckel. But at that time there were two things that I did not take into consideration, which would have helped me very much in my understanding of what to me was a novel situation. The one was the fact that I had long ago cut myself off from all set creeds of all churches, and the other was that, in England, all the churchpeople I knew gathered themselves together every Sunday—and some oftener— solemnly to avow their adherence to the doctrines set forth in their prayer-book, but which so astonished and horrified me when put in the plain language of a Western Methodist preacher. I forgot, also, that the children of these English friends (especially the more fashionable ones) were always confirmed at a very tender age by a bishop, who, when he asked them if they were convinced of the truth of the Thirty-Nine Articles, answered with all the earnestness of childhood "Yes, verily!"

But in these days when I think of the Fundamentalists of my native land, I have also to think of the Fundamentalists of England's Established church, and, except for the fact that the American Methodist and Baptist really do seem to believe in doctrines which, to me are unbelievable, and the Anglican Fundamentalists so often declare that they do *not* believe the things they *say* they believe, it seems to be another case of fifty-fifty.

A British Sinclair Lewis could, without long search, find a number of Anglican vicars addicted to drink and adultery. He could make the acquaintance of young men, without either piety or brains, who go into the church merely for the "living" it offers them—sometimes a very fat one, if they happen to be connected with ducal or other titled patrons. He might, perhaps, find even a few bishops living in palaces over well-stocked wine cellars, surrounded by acres of beautifully kept lawn, never trodden down by the feet of Council school children who cry out for sports-grounds whereon to swing a bat or throw a ball. He might attempt to explain to one such prelate the real benefits of Prohibition in America, and then describe in print in the American Lewis' own terse way, the bishop folding his hands across his apron and asking solicitously, "But what do your church people do about wine for Holy Communion?"

And then the British Lewis might put on clerical dress and join a party of prosperous clerics, prosperous because they have sold themselves and become procurers to the Trade.

I will admit that all these British proto-types are generally, in outward appearance, "nicer" and more refined to look upon, with speech more pleasant to the ear, than the American types. They make more acceptable callers at the afternoon tea hour, but I find it difficult to think of them as being more presentable at the Throne of Grace.

A common trait among Britons and Americans is the tendency to argue from the particular to the general, especially

if the particular suits one's purpose in an attempt to make a
point, either pleasant or unpleasant, about the general. Not so
very long ago in the Middle West (Yes, it *was* in one of those
modern Main Street houses!) I asked permission of an American woman to bring an Englishman friend to call.

"Don't talk to me about Englishmen," she snapped. "It was
an Englishman that seduced my poor cousin!"

"Well, as to that," I retorted, "it was an American who
ran away with this Englishman's wife!"

A prominent Englishman has recently summed up the whole
American nation in the following general way: "The United
States has produced a well clothed, well fed, contented people,
although one lacking in any sense of proportion." Now, how
any one who has ever known a half dozen Americans could
speak of them as "contented," is a strange thing, for if there
is any vice from which, as a nation, we do not suffer, it is
certainly the vice of contentment. Were we contented, I should
be tempted to give us up in despair. Contentment is death to
the soul, for it is the antithesis of progress, and the soul,
whether of an individual or a nation, which does not progress,
must surely die. The American nation cannot afford to die.
It has too much to do, too many weaknesses to correct, too
many sins for which to atone, too many vital experiments to
try out. Other countries, older, more careful, more cautious,
too afraid of a plunge into the unknown, too afraid of losing
prestige, or money, or both, on "wild ventures," hold back while
we do this trying out, and watch to see if it succeeds *and pays.*
Meantime they comment, they criticize, they smile, prophesying failure, even asserting failure before we've properly done
the trying out, as in the case of the experiment of Prohibition.
No contented people would have risked so much for a moral
experiment, and before either we ourselves or other nations
have the right to cry "Quit! It's a failure!" the American generation that is now in its cradle or even, perhaps, in its mother's
womb, must have grown to manhood and womanhood.

Meantime, having named this chapter "The British Pot and
the American Kettle," let us examine into some of the things
that are being cooked in the British pot, with the dark coating

on its outside, and the things concerning which it accuses the American kettle of being black. If the bubbling, steaming kettle does some hot rétorting, may it not all be taken as a legitimate part of the game?

Within the past few years, quite a long time after the war, but before the present general condition of bickering began, some well known Englishmen made a tour of the United States and were treated most hospitably. One of them declared himself an admirer of our country and asked to be shown everything possible concerning its great industries. When he returned to England from his tour of several weeks, he told in the press and on the platform the following story:

He had, he said visited a great industrial center, and was shown over one of the most wonderful factories in the world, admiring and commenting favorably the while. When he came out of the factory, he was taken up on a hill to get a comprehensive view of the surroundings and, as he himself put it, noticed hundreds upon hundreds of "little black specks" down in the valley.

"What are those black things down there?" he asked one of the guides who was showing him around.

"Oh, those are the workmen's automobiles, parked there in readiness to take them home at night," answered the American, in a matter-of-course sort of way. Suddenly the Englishman threw back his head and roared with laughter, while the Americans stared and wondered what he had seen that was funny. "What is it?" they asked. "Let us into the joke!"

"Why *workmen* going to and fro in motor cars!" said the Englishman, "Ha, ha, ha!" and his shoulders fairly shook. In England, when he told the story, large numbers of the audience and many readers joined in the laugh, but a staunch British workman I know, who has since emigrated from the land of his birth, remarked, "What the 'ell is there funny about it? It sounds to me like a little bit of all right!"

An English educationalist, while here, took a special interest in our schools, and, in the American way, was driven about in the official automobiles from school to school, besides being entertained by many American men who had, of course, attended those same public schools, or others like them, when they were boys. On the Englishman's return to his own country, he was asked for his impression of our educational institutions. The particular thing he had to say was that, on account of the majority of our teachers being women, our men had grown up "soft" without the special manliness which distinguished Englishmen who were taught by men teachers.

Among many other stories told about us, some complimentary, others the reverse, these two stories came back to America and were made much of. They did not tend to create pleasant feelings. In the columns of one of the English papers an American challenged the educationalist to a wordy combat in a debate, to have for its subject: "Resolved, that the American doughboys and their officers who were all educated at American free schools under the tuition of women, proved themselves to be 'soft' and incapable of punching German heads!"

But though Great Britain, as a nation, is cautious in the matter of trying out things and making experiments, many Britons are very quick to follow American lead when new ideas have been proven to be either beneficial or profitable. If they would follow only our beneficial tryings-out and leave our unsalutary *though* profitable experiments alone, it would be better for their souls' salvation. I will mention but one case in point, which happens to be in the line of my own profession of journalism.

One day, not so many years ago, an editor for whom I have done a considerable amount of work of a pleasant and profitable kind, called at my Adelphi flat to arrange for a series of articles which he had merely mentioned to me on the telephone. To my surprise, he began at once to tell me how much my work was liked by a certain great English lady renowned on both sides of the Atlantic, but as it suddenly occurred to me that she might have money invested in his paper, I thought I had better not object to her admiration.

"She wants to write, herself," said the editor. "Actually mad on the subject of being a journalist."

"Then, why doesn't she write?" I asked.

"She can't!"

Then he unfolded his plans concerning the series he wished me to contribute, mentioning subjects to which I agreed and terms of payment which were not only just, but really generous.

"Do them in the 'Mary Mortimer Maxwell' style," said he, "It's 'Mary's' style that she admires so much. She, of course, you understand, will *sign* them!"

"Will she? Why, how good of her!" I laughed. "But don't you think people will notice the similarity between the articles *she* signs and those over 'Mary's' own signature, and accuse one or the other of plagiarism, or very palpable imitation?"

"I'd thought of that, so perhaps *you* had better not use that signature any more. In so far as the name is concerned, let it drop."

"Murder poor 'Mary,' after all these years that she's been so good to me! Why, there's been many a time when, except for 'her,' I couldn't have paid the rent or had a morsel to eat!"

He took my jesting in a jesting way. "It will pay you, for besides journalism, you might even write a book for her and *she'll* pay you for the book. You know this kind of thing has been going on in your country for years. Only lately we've begun to take it up here!"

"Sorry you're copying bad American ways like that," I replied, "but just tell *her* that much as I appreciate her admiration, it's a case of

> 'Lady Clara Vere de Vere,
> Of *me* you shall not win renown!' "

To those who may be curious enough to ask of whom did the lady win renown, I can only answer in the language of Echo, "WHOM?"

This is not a solitary example, even in my own experience. One day a little man with a big name climbed the stairs to my flat and reminded me that, some years before, I had written a series called "The All-British Woman" which was published in the London Daily Express. I had tried to wake up the British people to the fact that they were not only unpatriotic but financially short-sighted in buying so many textiles abroad when they were capable of producing the most wonderful and beautiful fabrics in their own factories. Indeed, I proved to them that they *were* producing them. For instance, they were making thousands of miles of *tulle*, sending it to France to be stamped as French-made, then getting it back again to England and selling it to their women-folk at an enhanced price, though not so enhanced as to make up for the loss caused by so ridiculous a performance.

Said the little man with the big name: "I want to wake up my country to her own possibilities, before it's too late!"

"So did I," I sighed, "and I did wake her up for a little while, but she went to sleep again. If you can wake her up industrially, commercially *and* spiritually, I for one, will godspeed you."

And then he made his proposition. I was to write articles to speed up industrial Britain, giving them a *strong masculine touch* and he would pay me well for the articles, putting his own name over them, and arranging for their publication. People would think he wrote them—so he said, but I doubted that in so far as those who knew him were concerned! I refused his offer, although I suggested that I would interview him under my own name and give his views in his own language. But no! He wanted to give his views in *my* language, and give *some of my views* in my language as being his own!

However, his suggestion that I should write with a "strong masculine touch" appealed to me to the extent of deciding me to send out some work under a masculine nom-de-plume, but though it was as good as any I could have written under *his* name, I got nothing like the price he offered me.

There was a time when Americans were willing to concede to British journalism a higher tone than that taken by their own, but that time has gone by. Indeed, British newspapers have copied more bad than good things from American newspapers, and I do not refer entirely to "yellowness." After doing even this, they do not pause, but go on farther—and "then some." But let it never be forgotten what Britain has done in the way of journalists and journalism of the highest order. I know that W. T. Stead was looked upon as "yellow" when he did his big work in the old Pall Mall Gazette. That was some time before I went to London and had the honor of counting him as one of my best and most helpful friends. I look upon him as the greatest journalist who ever lived, and I believe that he will so be recorded in history. Let us hope the fact that Britain produced Stead and some of his great contemporaries will be remembered when later panderings to journalistic sensationalism for the mere sake of sensation and big sales, have been forgotten, or, at least, forgiven.

All British visitors to the United States criticize what they term American "standardization" of industry and life. Our highly-paid workmen stand all day and watch machines, and strike the British observer as having no individuality! Automatically, without process of mind or initiative, so we are told, they turn out motor cars, farm implements and Grand Rapids, Michigan, furniture! Granted that during the time of work a gifted man may be happier while following the ways of Chippendale, Hepplewhite, Sheraton and Adam, than just standing and watching wheels go round. But how many people could afford to buy such works of art? And think of the time and the means the American workman has for the use of his mind in other ways, though I do not accept the suggestion that it does not require a mind to watch a machine. What British employers make a point of encouraging initiative in their workmen? Every year, many who have initiative are leaving England, because it is not encouraged there. Nearly all British life is standardized in one way or another. What more standardized than the "public" schools there, turning out so many boys "according to plan," who all look alike, dress alike, talk alike, act alike and, when approached with a new idea, all alike respond with the traditional slogan of such schools, "It's not done!" Only when life has given these boys some of her hard, knock-down blows, are they able to break away from their standardization and compete with modern men from modern schools. And what more standardized than the English church? Not content with its present standardized ritual, its bishops are to-day gathered together in conclave, planning out a new standardized way of praying to a Christ who was never standardized.

The scandals of American politics, our party "bossism," the iniquities of the Chicago and New York police forces, shock the British people, who declare that they will never have their country "Tammanyized," but will keep their politics pure and undefiled. Yet, for every scandal in American politics I could point out a corresponding one in British politics, but it would make this chapter a three volume book. The reason the average person (not only British, but, in many cases, American) believes in the moral superiority of the British politician over the American politician, is that the Americans cry their scandals aloud by calling Heaven to witness that they are cleaning them up, while the British keep as quiet as possible about theirs.

"Speak up! Turn on all the lights!" shout the American people.

"Hush! Hush! Keep it dark!" murmur the British politicians. "Don't let the people know! John Bull is a family man and we mustn't let him wash his dirty linen in public!"

Uncle Sam's idea is to attend to his laundry in a public washhouse and hang the linen out on a line stretched in a public yard where the wind will swish it back and forth and give it a thorough airing. While all this is going on, ordinary every day life is not so pleasant in our country as is that in Britain under the "hush-hush" system, but the after-atmosphere is healthier.

As I write, a most interesting and illuminating piece of political sharp practice is being attempted in England, which could certainly give our most daring and unscrupulous politicians points in the art of "wangling." An attempt is being made by the Conservatives, now in power by a large majority at the last General Election, to make the House of Lords, (almost entirely a Conservative and reactionary body) an hereditary chamber in perpetuity. The plan is to accomplish this before another General Election, which may overturn the Conservative majority in the House of Commons and so deliver the House of Lords over to the non-tender mercies of the Labor Party. In order to make the country safe for Aristocracy, the Conservative leaders propose now, by a quick act of Parliament, to give back to the Lords the Veto power, which was taken from them in 1911, a proceeding which, at the time, was called the Castration of the Lords. The Lords are now declaring that there was no castration about it, and that, while passing the Parliament Act of 1911 under a sort of Third Degree pressure, they made a mental reservation to the effect that it should be merely a voluntary birth-control affair for such period of time as was necessary to stave off Mr. Asquith's threat to force them to abolish themselves. This was to have been done by the creation, over-night, of four or five hundred brand new Liberal peers, pledged to vote as they were told and, Samson like, to pull down the temple on their own newly-made coronets and extinguish the wearers of the old ones. In those days, Lloyd George was Chancellor of the Exchequer, and, being "death on dukes," his first budget was an attack on all the great landlords, in the form of a new taxation on land and land values. This was really a very personal thing to the Lords, since they owned most of the land, nine-tenths of which belonged to one-tenth of the population. Had this been more clearly understood by the old-time stone-cutter when he carved the quaint motto over the London Royal Exchange, he would probably have moved the apostrophe two spaces on, making it read,

"The earth is the Lords', and the fullness thereof."

Had it not been for the War, the Peers would have pointed out to the Commons long ago that they were weary in well-doing, or rather in nought-doing. Again and again have their thoughts turned back to the flesh-pots of Egypt in the days when they held up money-bills and were the particular terror of Liberal chancellors of the exchequer. Now, they have made their voices heard by the Conservative government, and the situation is as I have described it above. Given back their old powers, the result may mean a revolution, for, led by the Labor Party, the *masses* are keeping a keener watch over the *classes* than was formerly the case. Yet, if the Peers are denied, in some measure, at least, their demand for a return of real power in politics, the delicate situation that will result must split the Conservative Party. Among the seven hundred and fifty members of the House of Lords (double the number of the Commons) there are many who belong to the Trade, this wealthy and influential clique being known as the Beerage and Distillerage. The Trade also has many representatives in the Commons who will make cause with their noble brothers in the other house. Already the Trade *almost* holds British politics in the hollow of its hand, and if the Lords are given back the Veto power, the control of two active houses of Parliament will pass over to the liquor interests. Let it never be forgotten that, in British politics, MONEY talks. The scandal of the "sale of honors" has in no wise diminished since the War. A Canadian friend of mine, desirous to inform himself about the customs of his Motherland, asked an Englishman to explain to him how, and why peerages were created. The Englishman mentioned an aspirant's "donations to party funds" as an acceptable method of securing the ermine, with "remainder" to the "heirs male of his body."

"Oh, I see!" laughed the Canadian. "Over in Canada and the States, we send such fellows to jail when we catch 'em, but you send them to the House of Lords!"

As Money talks in British politics, so it talks in British Society. I have cut out this advertisement from an American paper which circulates among our smart set:

English Lady who has lived at Court for some years and also at British Embassies, is in a position to arrange introductions in best circles of English society, presentation at Court, etc. Personal friends include leading hostesses in London and owners of famous country houses at whose outdoor and social functions American girls may meet those in English society who compare with their own status in this country.

Arrangements can be made with me direct, or in any other suitable way you indicate.

Address. . . .

I feel that, as a fellow countrywoman, I should do the fair thing by the members of our American Snobocracy, who have answered this appeal of a member of the British Aristocracy, by referring them to the tragic tale of Mrs. de Plays Bingham. The advertiser *cannot* present them at Court unless they first take out naturalization papers or marry a British subject. (See Chapter III.)

There are a good many weaknesses and vices which the British and the American people share in common. One is a particular kind of hypocrisy in their professed attitude on the subject of sex-relationship. Only very slowly, and, at that, but recently, have our two countries yielded to a clean, decent, logical and human view of the equal need of man for woman and woman for man, in the physical, as well as in the mental and spiritual sense. Then, going still further, and taking up the matter of what is known as the "breaking of the moral law," it seems a still more difficult, if not a hopeless thing, to induce the people, and especially the men, of the two nations, to be honest in public profession of what they know to be true. I can best illustrate this hypocrisy and dishonesty by a reference to Nelson and Lady Hamilton.

Every year, on October 21st, England celebrates Trafalgar Day by the laying of many wreaths, anchors and other set pieces of flowers, with remembrance mottoes, at the foot of the Nelson column, flanked by the lions in Trafalgar Square. During the past quarter of a century, every year, with but a few exceptions, on this day, too, a bunch of violets has been found on Nelson's tomb in the crypt of St. Paul's Cathedral, and, on a card, attached to the violets by a ribbon, is always this inscription in the same hand-writing:

"In memory of Emma Hamilton, Best Beloved of Nelson, helper in what he did for England, sharing his triumphs and weaknesses, companion in his joys and sorrows, partner in his sins—willed by him to his country, yet shamefully neglected and left to starve by an ungrateful and hypocritical nation."

From year to year many people have seen the violets and read the inscription—and been horrified by what they have declared to be "desecration" of the old Cathedral. No one knew who put them there till a very recent Trafalgar Day, when a London newspaper man, standing in shadow, saw a woman deposit them. Quickly reading the inscription, he hurried after her and, raising his hat, said, "Madam, don't you think you are a little hard on us? Are we as hypocritical as all that?"

"Sir," she replied, speaking, as the reporter afterwards declared, with a slight American accent, "there is only one country in the world that would have been as ungrateful as yours, and would have treated Emma Hamilton worse—and that is *my* country!"

.   .   .   .

The fire blazes up, showing, in ugly relief, the smoke begrimed Pot and the soot-hung Kettle.

"Black!" roars the Pot.

"Black!" shrieks the Kettle.

The Pot seethes.

The Kettle dances—and now boils over!

CHAPTER XXVI

WHY I AM AN AMERICAN

I WAS born in the United States, but that is not the reason I am an American.

For many years I made my home in a land which I could not believe was a foreign one. It was the land of all my ancestors, and it exercised a peculiar fascination over me. I went there first to stay a little while, and I remained for long. My work of journalism took me back and forth across the ocean every two or three years, so I did not entirely lose connection with my native country, as is the case with many other Americans who reside abroad.

I never became naturalized, indeed, I never even seriously thought of doing so, although there were other people who thought of it for me. And what wonder? If one lives in another land than one's own, identifying one's self with its people and its customs; if one takes up other than American ways of doing things and saying things, falling into habits of thought that were, at first, foreign to one, but, later, become almost second nature, one ceases to be a real American. The accident of birth and the retaining of one's citizenship by a technical formality does not count for much. An adopted country may become like an adopted parent. Birth gives certain advantages or disadvantages at the start, but it is what one does with them, that tells in after life.

At the beginning of the war, I carried from England to a man in the United States this message from his sister: "Tell my brother that his place is here in England where he was born; that his country needs him to fight." Back to England I took the brother's message: "Tell my sister that my place is here, where they took me in when I was a poor boy who would have had no chance in England. Tell her that when this, my country,

286

adopted me and made me heir to all her opportunities, I promised to fight for *her* if she should ever need me for that. I have an American wife, have begotten American children, and I am an American. I owe no duty to England, where I just *happened* to be born."

The man's sister was horrified when I delivered his message. "But he is English!" she cried out, in her anger. "No!" I said. "He is American!"

During the two years preceding the outbreak of the war in 1914, I used sometimes to catch myself thinking hard. In a vague sort of way I began to realize that I was becoming a woman without a country. I was not truly American, I was not really English. Unlike many of my compatriots who live abroad, I was not rich, and I had no axe to grind in a social way. Like them, I found England a "green and pleasant land" in which to live, but what I enjoyed I paid for by honest hard work. Through my profession I made the acquaintance, and often the friendship, of great men and great women. There was many a time when I "scooped" all the other London journalists, merely because those to whom I applied for information or interviews found that I was an American.

I remember being one day in the library of Queen Anne's Lodge, the home of Mr. James Knowles while the editor of the Nineteenth Century talked over with me subjects for my contributions to that great monthly, which he founded. He told me I was standing on the spot, before the fireplace, where Thackeray first met the original Becky Sharp. He pushed forward a chair for me and said it had belonged to his friend, Lord Tennyson. He showed me a poem, saying he was sure I would like to see an original manuscript in Swinburne's own hand-writing. I told him how my aunt and uncle, in the days when I was too young to understand, had discussed whether Swinburne or Tennyson were the greater poet. I happened to mention—I forget just how it came about—that the discussion took place in the Middle West farm house, which was mortgaged, and I spoke of the little district schoolhouse which I attended before I went away to college. I saw a puzzled expression on the kind man's face, and he suggested that it must have been very hard for my people to pay for my education when they were poor.

"Not very," I answered. "I worked my way."

He seemed more puzzled than ever, as he queried, "Worked your way?"

"I washed dishes in the college kitchen, I filled the lamps with kerosene and cleaned the chimneys, I dusted the recitation rooms, I set the tables—*you* know!" I answered.

"No! I don't know— Tell me!" he laughed.

So I told him, and he said, "Wonderful! You will write an article about it for me, will you not?" and I wrote the article on Self-Help in American Colleges. On another day when Mr. and Mrs. Knowles had invited me to their table and to their garden parties where I met many great people, I sat again in Tennyson's chair and asked him, somewhat naïvely, as I can now see, how it was that English people invited me into their homes, knowing so little about me and "without asking who were my ancestors, as I always heard they were so particular about that."

"We all know you are an American and we like you, so what more should we wish to know?" was his answer.

"Then, if I were not American, but were just the same, only English, you would wish to know more?" I asked.

"Perhaps—but you would not be 'just the same' if you were 'only English,' " he smiled.

I did not understand then, as I do now, the full significance of that reply. Whatever I was then, in those early days of my career, whatever I could do then that was worth while, was all because I was an American and had taken advantage of the opportunities my country had given me. It is true that, in later years, when I was more firmly established, my nationality did not cut so much of a figure with either my friends or the public, but that was because my American opportunities had enabled me to establish myself. Those were the days when I used to think and say that England had been very good to me, and so she had; but alas! I forgot how good my own country had been to me first.

So the years passed, and I drifted on. I enjoyed the freedom of England and thought of the country as a great democracy.

What mattered it that, instead of a President, there was a King, instead of a Senate, a House of Lords? I would go to the House of Commons and sit behind the *grille* in the "ladies' cage," listening to great statesmen and sometimes having tea on the terrace. I met members of both houses and would compare some of these smooth gentlemen with many of the rough-and-ready men whom I had interviewed in the State capitols and in Washington. I did not stop to consider that many of those smooth Englishmen had nothing else to do in their boyhood and young manhood but to polish themselves."

As a journalist, I went much among the "working classes" and into the slums among the very poorest and dirtiest of British subjects as though I were one of them, and there were many readers who said of me "What she writes is true, because she goes among the poor as one of themselves. She digs deep." But now I know that till after the war was over, I never dug deeply enough to get at the truth which lay at the bottom of the well. Then, because of my interest in my school investigations and because of my love for England's children of the poor, I dug down till my bare hands were grimy with the mire I found of caste and class distinction, which influenced everything. It showed in the homes, in the streets, in the shops and all other businesses, the houses of Parliament, the schools and, saddest of all in the Church. One day I visited a church school where the vicar was leading the opening exercises. I could see he was a good, kindly man, and that the children loved him. He asked the children to sing for me, and they chose the hymn "All Things Bright and Beautiful." On they sang, filling the badly-lighted, ill-furnished, draughty room with all the brightness and beauty it could boast—that of their childish faces and youthful melody. They came to the verse,

> "The rich man in his castle,
> The poor man at his gate—
> God made them high, or lowly,
> And ordered their estate."

the vicar leading them, and singing softly, so as not to drown their voices. Then I went away from the school exceedingly sorrowful for England that such a lie should be taught to the children of a boasted Great Democracy by a vicar of the State Church, who himself would not send his own children to the school connected with the parish church over which he had charge.

I walked through a street where I saw decorations being put up, where poorly clad women were scrubbing and whitening their doorsteps, washing their windows, and putting pots of bright flowers along the ledges. I asked a passerby for what the people were preparing.

"Why," said he, "the Queen is driving through these parts to-morrow! It seems she told the mayor and alderman that always she had been shown the highways of London, but now she wanted to see the byways. It is expected she will even get out of her carriage and knock at doors and ask if she may come in, so, as nobody knows who will receive a royal visit, everybody's cleaning up!"

Then the Queen of England, her visit proclaimed in advance, drove through the streets of the worst parts of London. She knocked at certain doors and smiled and asked if she might come in and, as afterwards reported, she found the most exquisite cleanliness in the kitchens. They were often rooms in which a family of several people, of both sexes, lived and slept, but that the Queen did not know. She saw children with faces well scrubbed and shining. Tables were spread with clean plates and cups, and, in some cases, with specially bought little round cakes, and carefully-cut thin bread-and-butter, for who knew but the Queen might not say, "They look so nice— May I have one?"

So it was that Queen Mary saw the Byways of London, and carried back to the palace a picture, false and made to order for her inspection. The next day I followed in her wake, going as a poor woman looking for lodgings, and I saw those streets in all their hideous, naked poverty, stripped of their garnishings. In a room, that the day before had been made clean and pretty for the Queen, I was told I could have a share with three other women at a low price, and I could have a part of a bed if I did not mind sleeping crosswise.

Royal tours are made over the Empire. They are long-heralded in advance, prepared for, all the rough places made smooth. The Prince of Wales visits Canada and lives a while upon his ranch. People like him, but how can they know him and how can he know them? A royal personage goes to Paris and the papers announce "So-and-so is stopping in cog as——at the —— Hotel."

"A really fine fellow!" said a young English officer to me concerning a royal prince with whom he had come into contact in France during the war. "But I'm sorry for him—so deadly lonely to be a prince—couldn't chum up with us, though we could see he wanted to and we wanted him to—but there you are—with royalty it can't be done!"

This, it seems to me, is the answer to the assertion that a democracy can exist within a monarchy. It is not because there is a monarch, but because where there is a monarch there is the curtsey, and Caste and the Curtsey go together. Round about the monarch there is the Court and there are the courtiers, then the relations of the monarch to be pensioned and supported by the people. I can see that even a social democracy might exist under a king, either hereditary or elected for life, if all the usual appurtenances to monarchy were abolished, but how can there be democracy where there is a distinct caste which is held to be above criticism and even, in certain ways, above the common law of the land?

I once asked an Englishman what was meant by the saying, "The King can do no wrong." He replied that, in England, it was easily explained, because the King, of himself, could do nothing, but acted only on the advice of his ministers, and therefore did no "wrong."

"Supposing he struck and said he would not take their advice?" I asked.

"There was once a king, and his name was Charles—" he said.

This was at the time when the Black-and-Tans and the Republicans were killing one another in Ireland. An American paper published an interview with a noted English publicist in which the King was stated to have said to someone, "I can't have my people shooting one another down like this!" The government then in power became absolutely black in the face with anger and the British papers grew hysterical, declaring that the King could *not* have said such a thing—he, a constitutional monarch! One might have thought that all that was gained by *Magna Charta* itself had been threatened. So high ran feeling that, finally, on the "advice" of his ministers, the King was forced to make a public proclamation declaring that he never said he would not have his people shooting one another down! Nevertheless, there are many people who like to think he said it and who believe he did say it— Large wonder if he didn't! But incidents like this detract from the dignity of monarchy, turning it into something ridiculous, as though proving that a king may not also be a man.

The King, then, has absolutely no political power. He must speak, act, if not even think, only on the "advice" of ministers, who may or may not be his intellectual superiors. If he has any political preferences, he must never mention them. He and his sons have places in the House of Lords as peers of the realm, but they must not vote or take any part in discussions of the most important questions affecting the fate of the Empire. Recently the Royal Society for the Prevention of Cruelty to Animals supported a humane bill which was before Parliament, having for its object the exclusion of dogs from vivisection. A few weeks ago, suddenly the Council of this Society withdrew its support of the bill on the ground that the Prince of Wales, its President, had declared that he could not continue to hold that position if the Society supported a *controversial measure* in Parliament.

Now, all societies existing for the purpose of preventing or reforming any evil, must necessarily take up controversial matters, so it follows that royal patronage, instead of being a help, must be a hindrance, and for this reason certain societies refuse to accept royal patronage.

During the first year of the war I had my eyes opened widely to the little real influence the royal family had upon the people at large. I was a guest at a large dinner party where the talk was, of course, concerning the progress of the war and ways to help win it. When wine was passed, I declined it, whereupon my neighbor asked if I were a teetotaler. "Not strictly," I replied, "but 'for the duration,' I follow the King," referring to the well known fact that King George had banished all wines from the royal table, hoping to influence his subjects to do likewise.

"*I* don't!" laughed my neighbor, draining his glass. At the end of the dinner our host stood to call a toast.

"Ladies and gentlemen, the King!" he said, almost reverently, and I, an American citizen, was the only member of the company who drank the health of the King of England in soda water!

Such incidents as I have given have caused me to ponder seriously upon the subject of the real place and the usefulness of even the most limited monarchy in Twentieth Century democracy. Not only has royalty no political or real social power in a constitutional monarchy, but one has only to read the daily papers to realize how cut off a British sovereign can be from the most ordinary affairs of ordinary people. Take, for example, the following paragraph from a London paper in September, 1927:

THE KING AND THE TREASURY NOTES.

The King's rôle of salesman at a charity fête at Balmoral has a homely touch about it, and is another instance of the way the Royal Family can do novel and democratic things without loss of dignity.

A curiously interesting incident is the fact, if the report be correct, that his Majesty, on being handed some Treasury notes, seemed for the moment to regard them as unfamiliar and to be unaware of the difference between the ten-shilling and the one-pound note. There is, of course, no need for his Majesty to carry cash at any time, and, of course, the Royal knowledge of philately does not come from any necessity to buy or affix postage stamps.

It is perfectly true that at the close of her reign Queen Victoria was shown a railway ticket for the first time. Her majesty declared that she had no notion that such things existed, and that she considered them an excellent idea.

Many Americans are under the impression that although Britain may not be wholly a democracy socially, it is certainly one politically. "A great thing that judges are appointed for life by the King," they say, "with no haunting fear of future elections to bias them in their judgments!" Such Americans, too, refer to what they call the "more democratic way" of ordering elections, since, as they understand it, a government (administration) can be turned out of office overnight, if it displeases the people. It is certainly true that British governments have been turned out overnight, but not always because they have displeased the people. They are turned out because of a split in the party which put them in office.

It is not true that politics have nothing to do with the appointment of judges, and it is but a pleasing fiction that the King appoints them. The selection of judges is entirely in the hands of the Lord Chancellor, who "advises" the King to confirm the appointments, which the King always does. It would be "unconstitutional" if he did not! The Lord Chancellor is a member of the cabinet, owing his position to his politics, and he can, if he wishes, fill every vacant judgeship with members of his own party.

In the selection of the Cabinet, there is often an entire lack of democracy, for the Prime Minister can hand over the whole foreign policy of the nation to a peer who was never chosen by the people, but was simply "born so." When critics of the American system mention the fact that members of the President's cabinet do not sit in the House of Representatives or the Senate, suggesting that it would be better to follow the British practice, they seem to have forgotten this matter of peers. To be sure, the peer sits in the House of Lords, with which the electors have nothing to do. All things connected with the House of Lords are the very antithesis of democracy. This is why the lately suggested measure for the Preservation of Peers in Perpetuity, is so dangerous to the freedom of the British people. Even the House of Lords in its present subordinate state can retard all legislation, except that referring to "money bills," for two years. Although a small minority of the Lords believe in progress, even to their own abolition, the majority are conservative in the narrowest sense. In the naïvely frank words of one of their recent spokesmen, they are convinced that "to deny the principle of heredity is to deny the origin of the species, which is founded on the undemocratic method of the *selection of the fittest,* heredity being the one streak of science in the casual amalgam of the British constitution!"

In this conservative House of Lords, there is always a *bloc* of ultra conservatism generally standing solidly together when questions of great importance to the real progress of the people are before Parliament. This *bloc* is composed of twenty-six "lords spiritual" (twenty-four bishops and two archbishops), who sit for life as representatives of the State Church. For years they prevented the Deceased Wife's Sister bill from becoming law, and after having finally failed in their efforts against it, they stood out against the Deceased Husband's Brother bill, which, to the ordinary reasoning mind was merely a case of fifty-fifty. They have opposed reforms in the marriage laws and exert all their vast influence against a clean and logical divorce law, which would do away with Divorce by Collusion, the only accurate description of the present law. It was this *bloc,* too, which vigorously and successfully opposed any alteration in the just-passed Legitimacy Act, which, under certain conditions, gives legitimation to children born out of wedlock, by the subsequent remarriage of the parents. In this act there is the following proviso, which is bitterly opposed by many good and broad-minded persons:

"Nothing in this act shall operate to legitimate a person whose father or mother was married to a third person when the illegitimate person was born."

Those in favor of this proviso (and they were the winning party) declared that without it, the sacred institution of the British Home stood in danger. Suppose, said they, a wife is barren or declines to have children, and her husband has a child by another woman. Wishing to marry that other woman, and so legitimate his child, the husband approaches his wife in this manner: "As you know, we do not love one another as married persons should love. The desire of my heart for paternity has been fulfilled by another woman whom I love and who loves me. Divorce me for adultery, in a quiet, decent way, let me provide for your financial needs, and marry the mother of my child and make him legitimate."

The proviso prevents that, even though the wife should wish to free her husband. She may divorce him and he may marry the mother of his child, but the law says that by such marriage he may not legitimate it.

Slowly, very slowly indeed, only by piecemeal, bit by bit, does Britain progress toward democracy. There is not yet equality of suffrage between the rich and the poor, even among men, although it is no longer true, as it was up to 1918, that a wealthy man, owning twenty different residences in twenty different constituencies, may cast twenty votes at an election. But the owner of a great factory may vote in the constituency of the factory and also in the constituency of his residence, while the factory worker can only vote in the constituency where he lives. Women over thirty have the vote, but only under certain conditions. Two women may share a house, halving the rent and taxes and all expenses, but if one does not own a part of the furniture, she cannot vote. A woman of thirty, sleeping in the house where she works as a domestic servant, has no vote. An ignorant boy of twenty-one has a vote, but his brilliant sister of twenty-nine and a half, with several university degrees, who may be a barrister, doctor or member of some other learned profession, has no vote.

Before American women agitated against the law that forces a wife to take her husband's nationality, British women were nobly working against the absurdity which denies a married woman any individuality of her own. This showed up glaringly during the war, when loyal Englishwomen, married to foreigners, found themselves, legally, enemy aliens in their own country. The short agitation of American women brought a quick change in the American law, but the British law still persists. An American man whose business will keep him in England for the next two years has married an Englishwoman, who has now lost her British nationality. If she wishes to travel she cannot get a passport, for she has no nationality at all. The American law cannot naturalize her unless she comes over and remains the length of time required for naturalization. Although she would willingly do this, she cannot leave her husband, and he cannot leave his work. Logic is on the side of the American law, as all thinking women declare, but the old English law remains. Eventually it will be changed, as will other backward laws—but not yet.

Is Britain a political democracy?

I am an American, not because I was born in the United States, but because, having tried conscientiously to reason out certain things that have troubled me, I have discovered what I believe to be the truth. That truth is that the land where I was born, though yet far off from the ideal of democracy, is further on the way than is Great Britain. I am a democrat, and because I am a democrat, I am an American by choice.

I have no illusions about my country. I know her problems and I see her faults, some of them grave and appalling. Like other nations she has stoned her prophets, and one of them she crucified—Woodrow Wilson. Yet, after Crucifixion comes Resurrection, and up from his tomb there sounds again his ringing voice of warning. Let us hear it:

"THIS IS NOT A DAY OF TRIUMPH; IT IS A DAY OF DEDICATION. HERE MUSTER, NOT THE FORCES OF PARTY, BUT THE FORCES OF HUMANITY. MEN'S HEARTS WAIT UPON US; MEN'S LIVES HANG IN THE BALANCE; MEN'S HOPES CALL UPON US TO SAY WHAT WE WILL DO. WHO SHALL LIVE UP TO THE GREAT TRUST? WHO DARES FAIL TO TRY?"